Vik Muniz

on Photography, Mind, and Matter

**Introduction
by Lucas Blalock**

aperture

Table of Contents

Introduction

By Lucas Blalock

I met Vik Muniz twenty-something years ago when he was a visiting professor at Bard College. At the time, I was a photography student and avid film fan who was trying to figure out how to make pictures that related to the stylized worlds I loved in cinema. I was not alone in this pursuit— it was the turn of the century and artists like Jeff Wall and Cindy Sherman and Gregory Crewdson were all the rage. For class, I made a double self-portrait of me popping out of a trash can with a camera to photograph another me in a wig and a dress by splicing together pairs of prints and then gluing them to a board. The images were cartoonish, and I remember Vik seeing them and telling me, "You're funny." From him, this felt like high praise. He also added a piece of advice that stuck with me: "Look at painting. Painters can take all the time they want to create precise compositions. There's a lot to learn from them."

I was curious, but honestly, I felt intimidated by paintings. I was a teenager from the mountains of North Carolina, and the culture around painting felt totally outside my experience. Movies, novels, and music were more my terrain. Picking up on my sheepishness, Vik suggested that I should go to the library and look through as many art books as I could get my hands on. It didn't matter which ones, from which periods, he noted; I shouldn't worry about art history, rather I should find pictures that I felt connected to and then try to learn from them.

That was some really good advice. But more importantly, this conversation gave me permission to become an amateur lover of painting and to get to know something that had felt out of reach, serious, and grand—to enter a world that wasn't mine. He was encouraging me to explore art the same way I had gotten into the Pixies, the Clash, and the Wu Tang Clan, or *Alien, Alphaville, A Clockwork Orange*. This was crucial for me, and it is something I have watched Vik do for other people over and over again in subsequent years. The short of it is that my pictures got better.

Some months later, I and some other students from Bard took the Metro North down to New York City for the opening of Vik's show *Pictures of Ink* at Brent Sikkema's gallery (now Sikkema Malloy Jenkins). At the afterparty, Vik came over to chat. He asked me how things were going, and I excitedly started talking about some idea I had for a picture or a project. Clapping me on the back, he smiled and said, "Lucas, you think too much. You have to trust your intuition. Take more pictures with your gut." I laughed, but a bell had been rung somewhere deep in my psyche. Again, my pictures got better.

With time, I found the crux of my own working method under the unlikely twin signs of Buster Keaton (whom Vik had gotten me to appreciate back in school) and Bertolt Brecht, the German theater practitioner, playwright, and poet, whom I'd gotten into while digging through the influences of Jean-Luc Godard. But even Brecht, whose Marxist Epic Theatre and "alienation effect" might at first appear too haute and austere for Vik's taste, brought me right back to a story about him seeing an electrician perform Hamlet at a community theater in Chicago. I vividly remember Vik, a champion storyteller, recounting that it was truly great because he had seen two simultaneous productions. On the surface, he was watching *Hamlet*, the story of a raving royal seeking revenge for his father's murder. But underneath, he was also watching the drama of these nonprofessional actors plucked from their working-class lives laboring to inhabit roles as Renaissance royals. This double register that Vik described—the dual experience of the world of the production and that of its staging—almost perfectly illustrates Brecht's idea of alienation. I am quite sure that Vik was aware of this, but his ability to disguise a complex idea as a story or a joke is a form of real generosity. The same could clearly be said of his art. When Vik draws in chocolate syrup or in wire or uses cut-up magazines, the familiarity of the materials both lowers the bar for entry and spins a complex web of allusions, slyly folding together the pantheon of art and the objects of everyday.

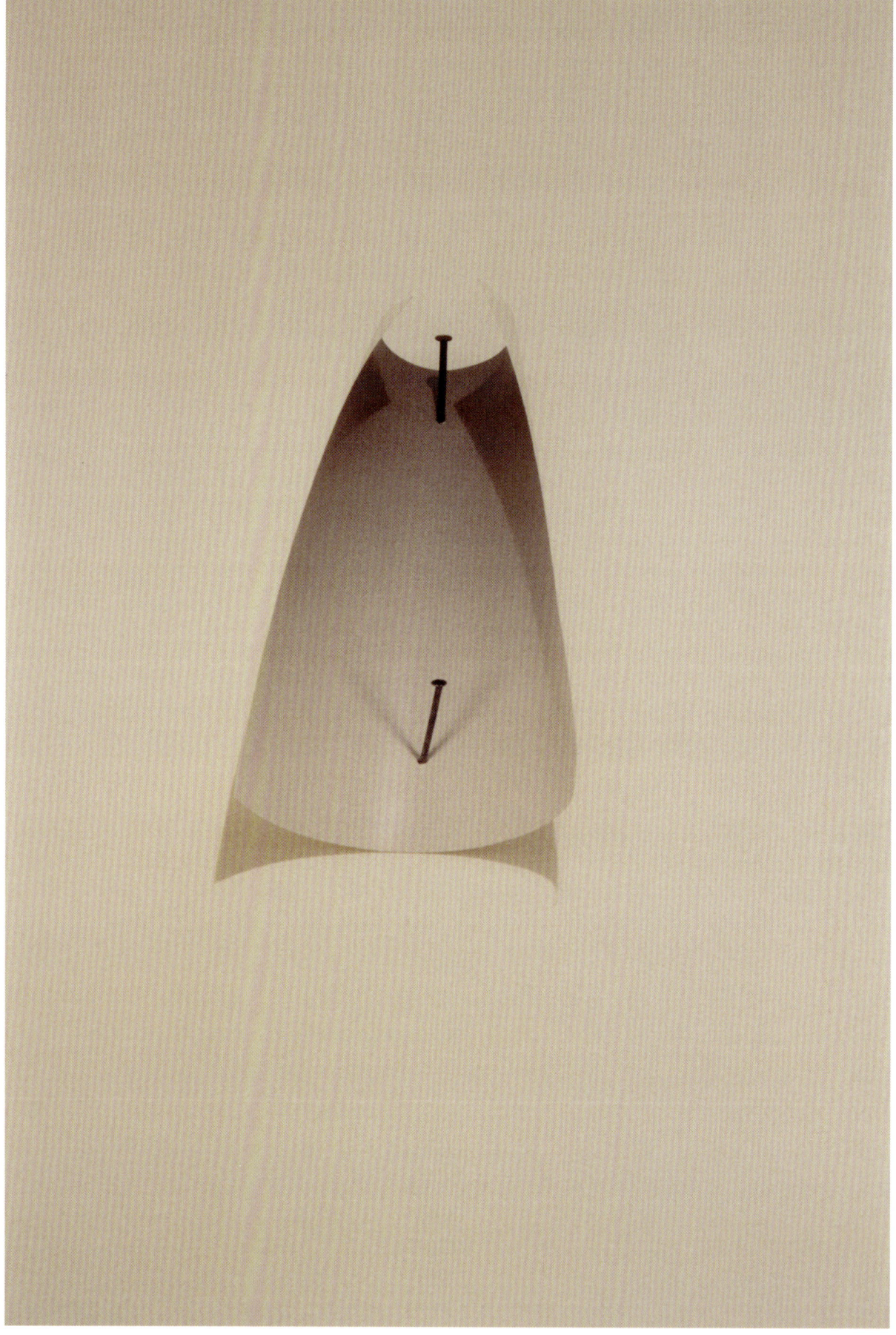

Photography and Inner Life

My maternal grandmother, the wise old woman who raised me, once told me that there were two worlds, one inside of us and another comprised of everything that existed outside, and that these two worlds had to be precisely the same size. She also told me that our existence happened exclusively in this tight, infinitesimal gap between perception and cognition, and that every human achievement has depended on successfully linking these two worlds. Intelligence is what has enabled organisms, no matter how simple or small, to connect with the world beyond themselves. As a matter of fact, the very definition of intelligence is based on an organism's ability to feel and react to the surrounding environment. Based on this definition, everything alive today possesses some kind of intelligence, because otherwise it would be extinct. What makes humans different from other species is that we are capable of not only knowing but also believing. Believing involves feeling and reacting to things outside the range of our immediate senses, through media technologies that often run counter to our instincts, requiring a suspension of our disbelief.

Art-making, at least for me, has been the continuous practice of understanding, challenging, and ultimately re-signifying our relationship to media that extend our senses. I've been asked many times what art is. It has taken me thirty-some years to come up with a short answer that I don't have to explain too much: *Art is the development of the interface between mind and matter, between consciousness and phenomenon.* Anything that can be understood, that can have meaning, relies on a little bit of illusion. I always work with illusion while thinking about reality, because they are counterparts. It was through illusion, through being fooled temporarily, that we got to where we are now.

Imagine it's thirty or forty thousand years ago. A guy walks into a cave and sees, in the cracks on the wall, a shape similar to something he's seen before. It's not just any shape. It's the shape of an animal. Not just any animal, a bison. Not just any bison, the one his tribe killed the winter before, when they were very hungry. Looking at that shape, he thinks of the feast, how people danced around the meat, how happy they were. Then he looks again and sees only cracks on a wall. Not happy with this, he picks up a blunt rock and completes the form, adding a tail and horns. And suddenly all those memories come back.

Representation is perhaps the most important human invention, after the control of fire. That person was the first artist, and when he brought his tribe to look at his drawing, they could see the same animal and they could all partake in the memory of those shared experiences. Through this image, they could even pass those experiences to future generations, beyond their lifetimes. Because of this invention, we have history. It is the foundation of all the other pillars of our civilization, including politics, economics, and religion.

When I define art as this continuous evolution of the interface between mind and matter, I'm describing something that has to do with belief.

We have managed to take this thick layer, the layer separating what we think and feel from what's outside us, and polish it down to a very thin membrane called a photograph. A photograph is almost as thin and ephemeral as an idea, yet it can convey any kind of experience you can imagine: love, time, even death. Photography was the last material interface between mind and matter. Since digital technology has burst that membrane, we no longer have something material dividing what we think and feel from what's outside us. The image, once this powerful tool connecting us to the world, has become an autonomous entity, disconnected from reality and no longer bound to its original purpose. This will have severe implications in how we understand and organize our history and how we perceive the world around us, both personally and collectively.

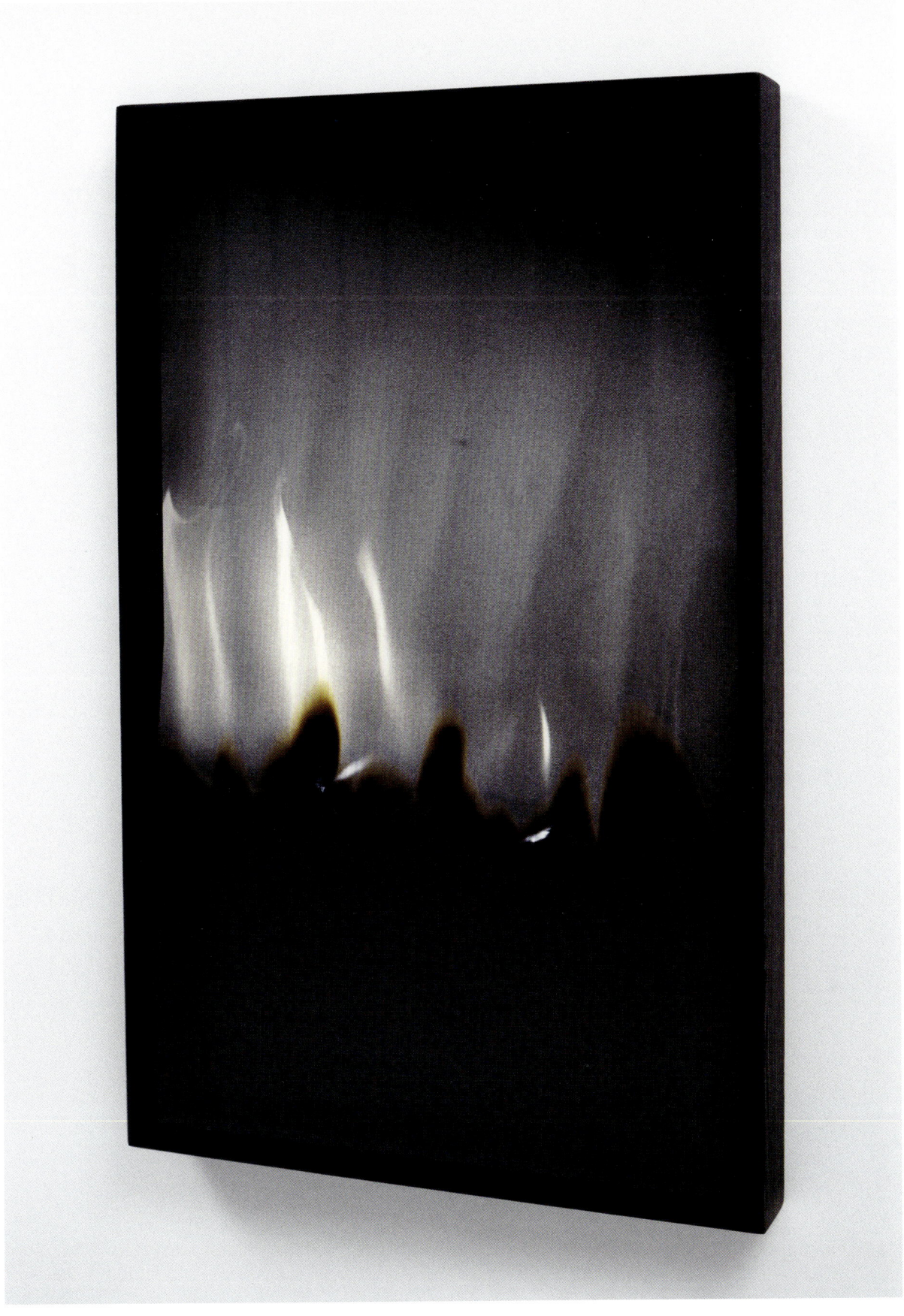

Vik Muniz
Dead Houdini, 1997

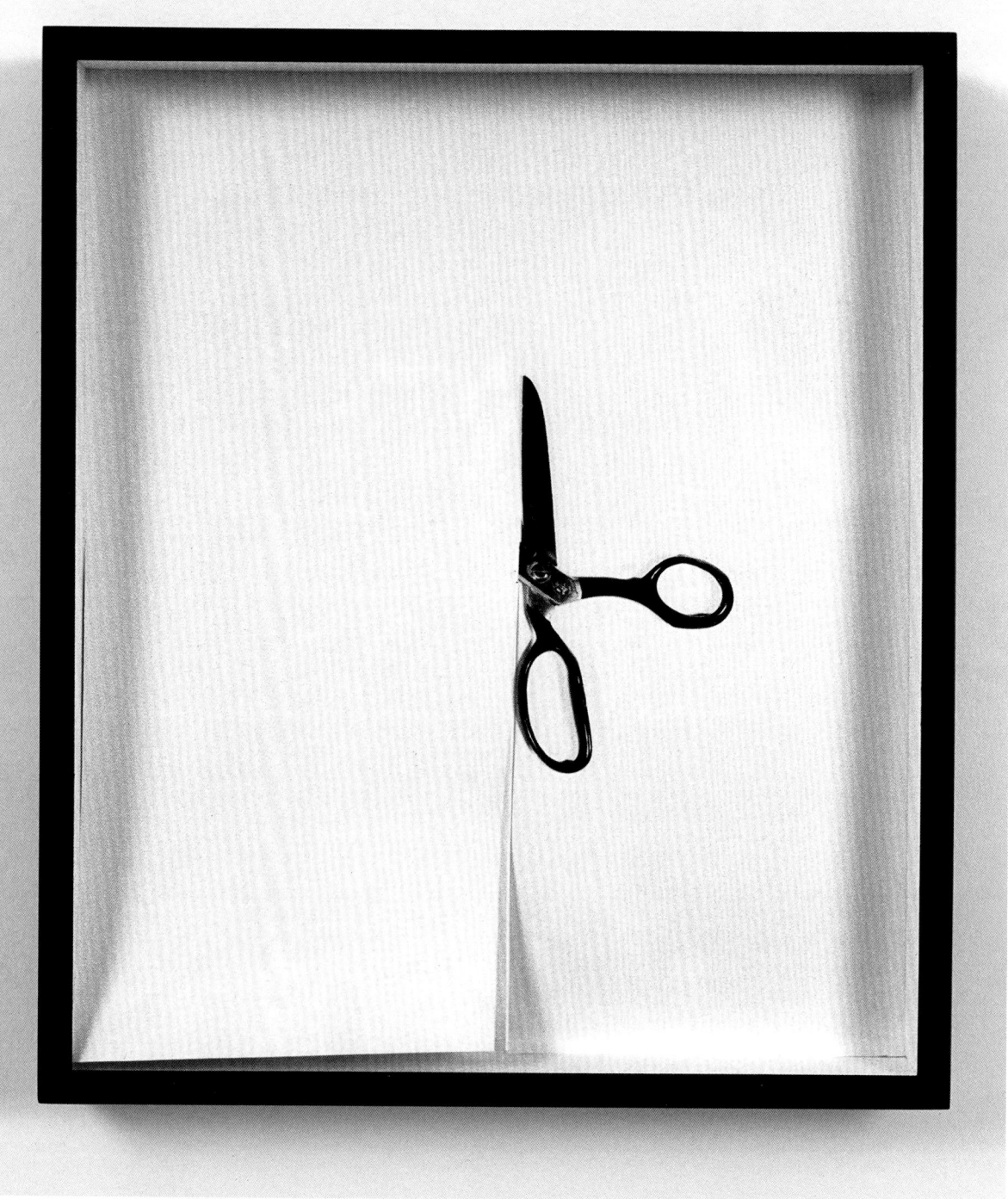

Vik Muniz
Future Diptych, 1990

The Process of Remembering

The first book I bought in the United States was *The Best of Life* (1973), a collection of Pulitzer Prize–winning and iconic photographs from five decades of *Life* magazine. I had just moved to Chicago and didn't know anybody, and I got the book at a garage sale because I felt I could go around and ask perfect strangers, "Ah, do you remember that?" The person would probably say yes, and that would connect us. It was like a photo-album of the human family.

I lost the book when I moved to New York, so I decided to make drawings of the pictures the way I remembered them—memory renderings. I had already drawn some of the photos from the book before I'd lost it, but the whole project still took me two years. Like someone who does the *New York Times* crossword, I would work on them during the weekend, just pick one up when I recalled a detail to add. I was trying to understand how we remember. What do the pictures inside your head look like when you're missing the original reference? How do they develop? (It turns out that facial expressions are very hard to remember.)

My gallerist at the time wanted to show the drawings, but I had grown attached to them, even though they looked kind of bad, with lots of erasures and Wite-Out. So I had a good idea: I photographed them so that I could sell the photographs and keep the drawings. I shot them slightly out of focus and printed them with a halftone-dot pattern, just like the book in which I'd first seen the pictures—an idea going full circle.

I was never sued by *Life* or the Associated Press or any of the photographers, because my pictures looked completely different. To meet the memory of the person looking at the picture, I had gone only halfway. The artist makes 50 percent of the work, and the other 50 percent is the viewer. There is no art experience without the viewer, so you have to consider the visual baggage a viewer brings to the encounter. That's why most of my work is based on icons and archetypes. I never do anything that shocks, because that would raise people's defenses. I work with the utterly familiar, in both imagery and materials.

14

Vik Muniz
Memory Rendering of Man on the Moon, from *The Best of Life*, 1990

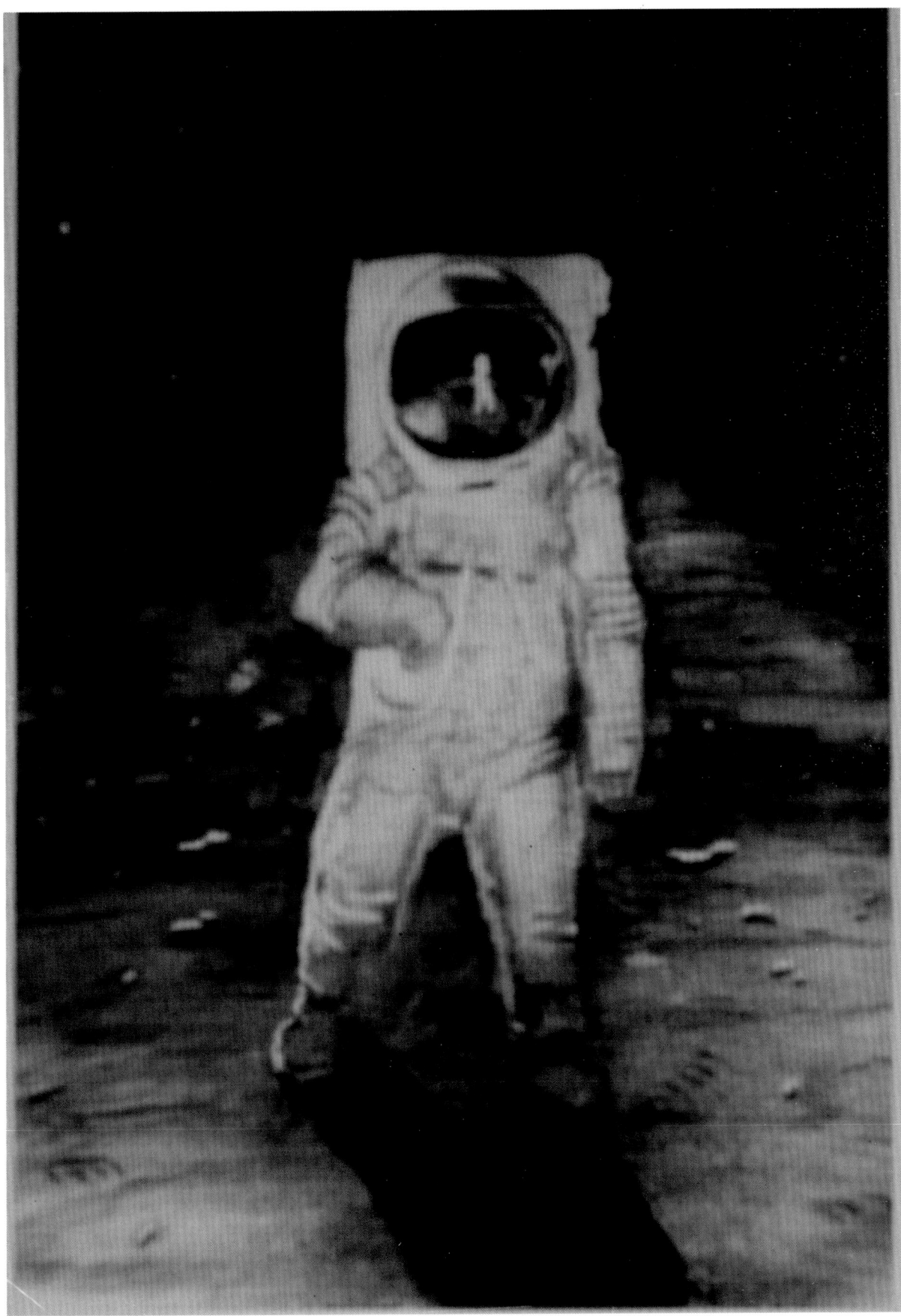

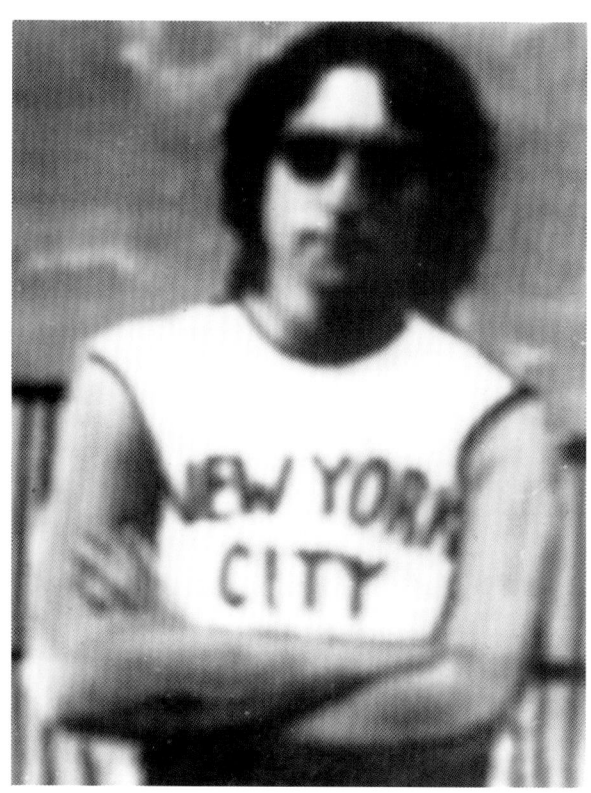

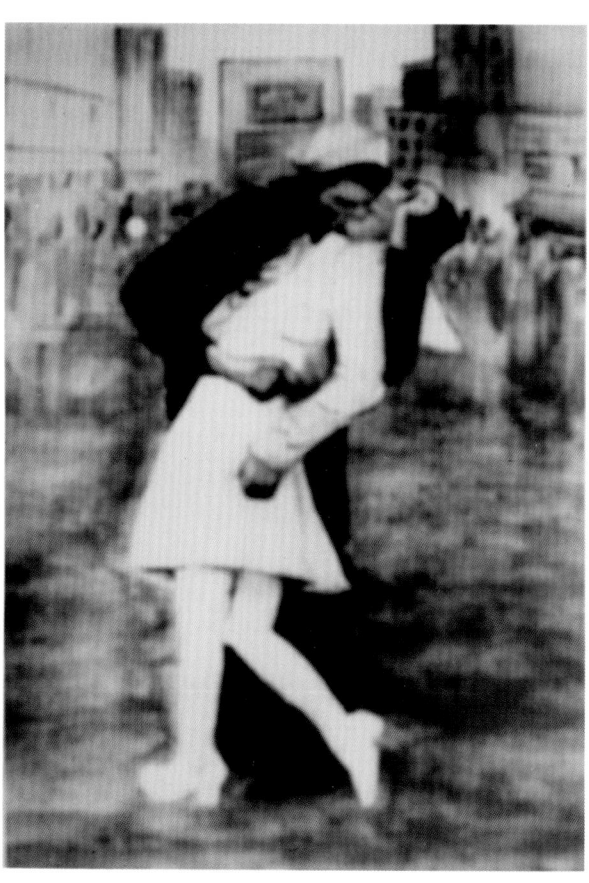

Top
Vik Muniz
*Memory Rendering of John
Lennon in Manhattan,*
from *The Best of Life,* 1988

Bottom
Vik Muniz
*Memory Rendering of Kiss
at Times Square,*
from *The Best of Life,* 1990

16

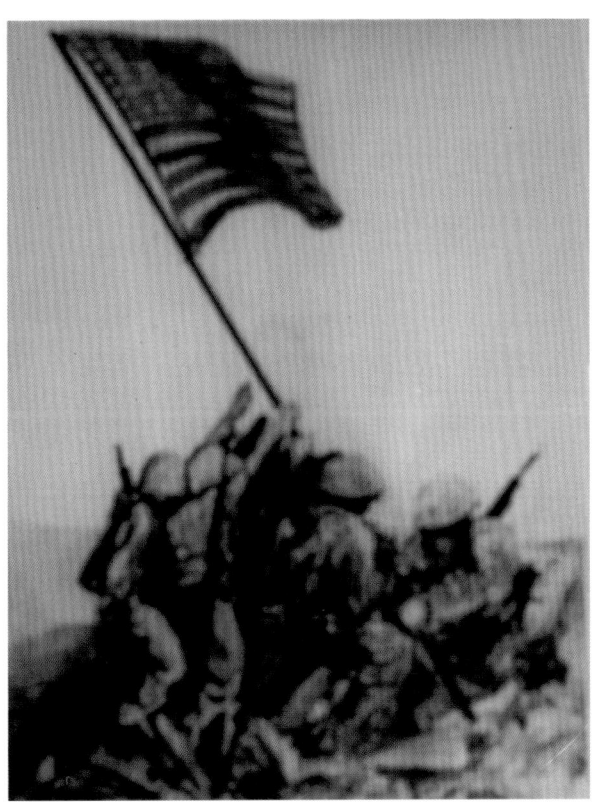

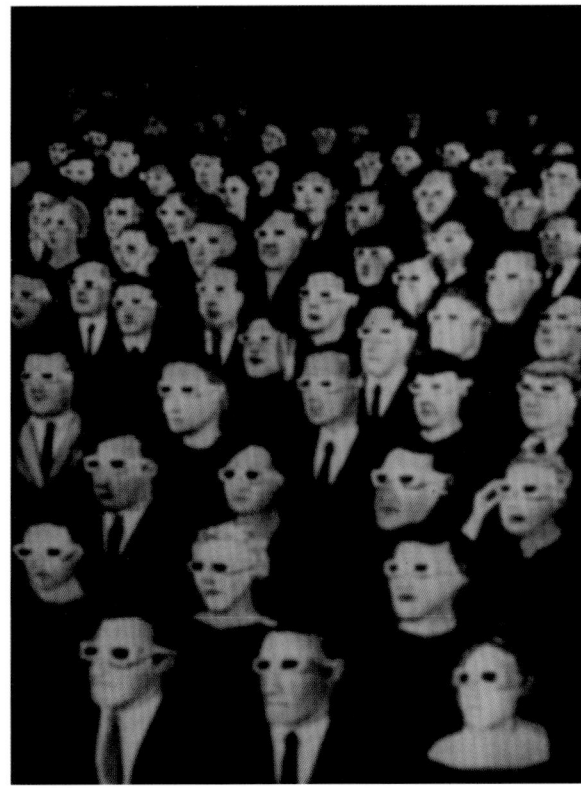

Top
Vik Muniz
*Memory Rendering of Flag
Raising at Mount Suribachi,
Iwo Jima,* from *The Best
of Life,* 1990

Bottom
Vik Muniz
*Memory Rendering of 3-D
Screening,* from *The Best
of Life,* 1990

Drawing and Perception

I was born into a working-class family in Brazil in 1961. My father was a waiter, my mother a switchboard operator. I stayed home with my grandmother—my first memory is of sitting in her lap while she taught me to read. I must have been four years old. The only book in the house was the *Encyclopedia Britannica*, which my father had won in a pool game, and she taught me the same way she had taught herself: by memorizing the shape of each word.

By the time I entered school a few years later, I was reading chapter books, translations of *Treasure Island, Gulliver's Travels*, and *The Merry Adventures of Robin Hood* in Portuguese. But I could only read books set in the same font as the *Encyclopedia Britannica*. It took me three years to learn how to write, because I didn't understand that words could be broken into letters or syllables. I was dyslexic. I had learned to read visually, by looking at the shapes of words instead of organizing them into systems. My copy books looked like the Egyptian section of the Metropolitan Museum of Art. They were filled with hieroglyphs, little drawings in place of all the words I didn't know.

From there, my drawing kept improving. I was the guy who drew caricatures of the teachers for the other kids to pass around the back of the class. When I was fourteen, I won a contest organized by all the public schools in the state of São Paulo, and my prize was two years of classes in academic drawing.

There's a curve with learning how to draw. You learn a lot, you improve a lot, and then at some point you start to reach your limit. I was always curious about why we could see three dimensions in a two-dimensional space, so I began researching perspective and other ideas about how we see pictures. I became obsessed with the phenomenology of vision. I learned that there's no such a thing as a still image. A frog won't eat a dead fly—not because it doesn't like the taste, but because it can't see the fly. Our eyes are not designed to see *things*, only events. We depend on movement to recognize and understand the world. Our eyes make all kinds of different tiny movements, and with them we animate the whole universe.

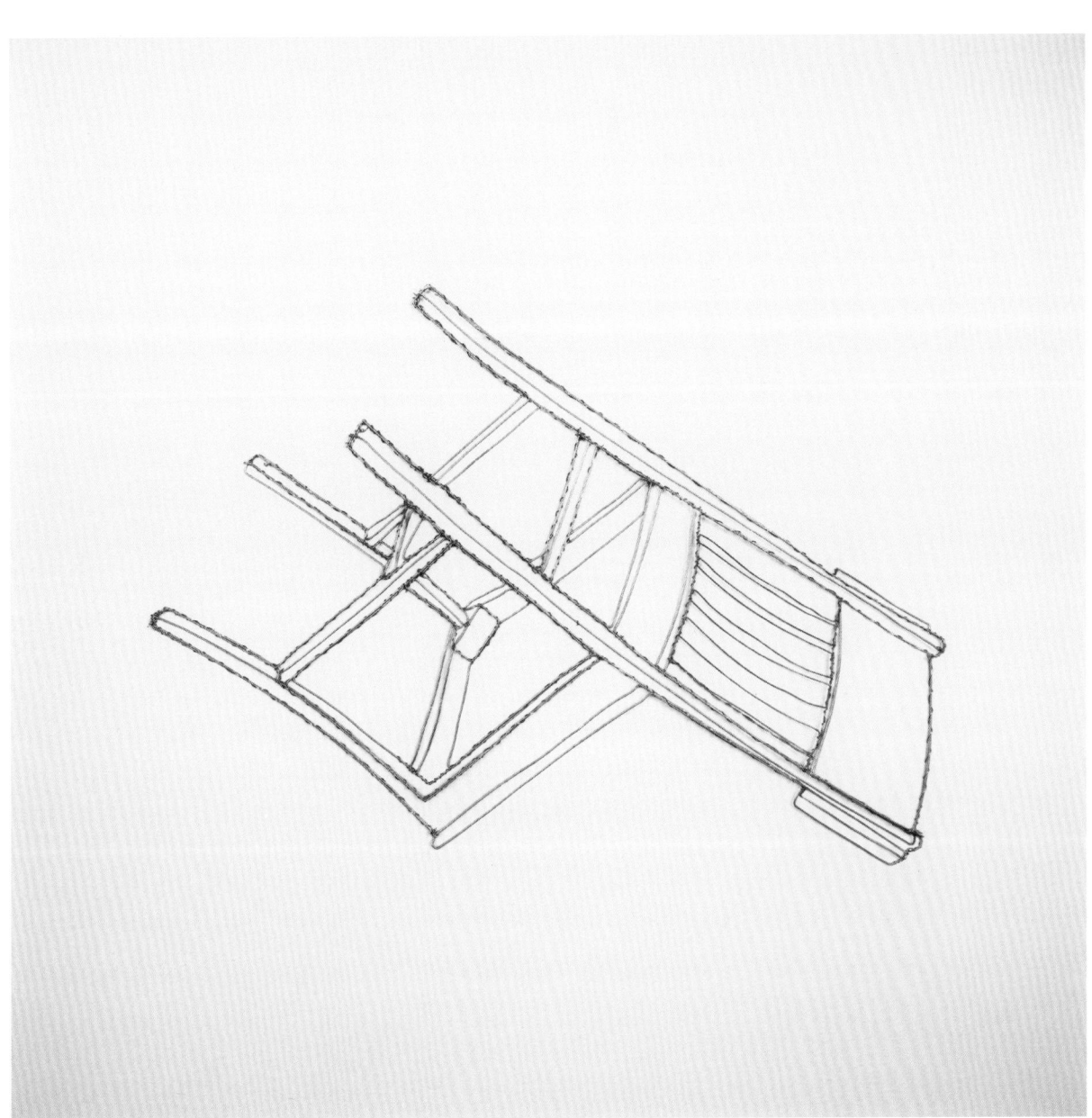

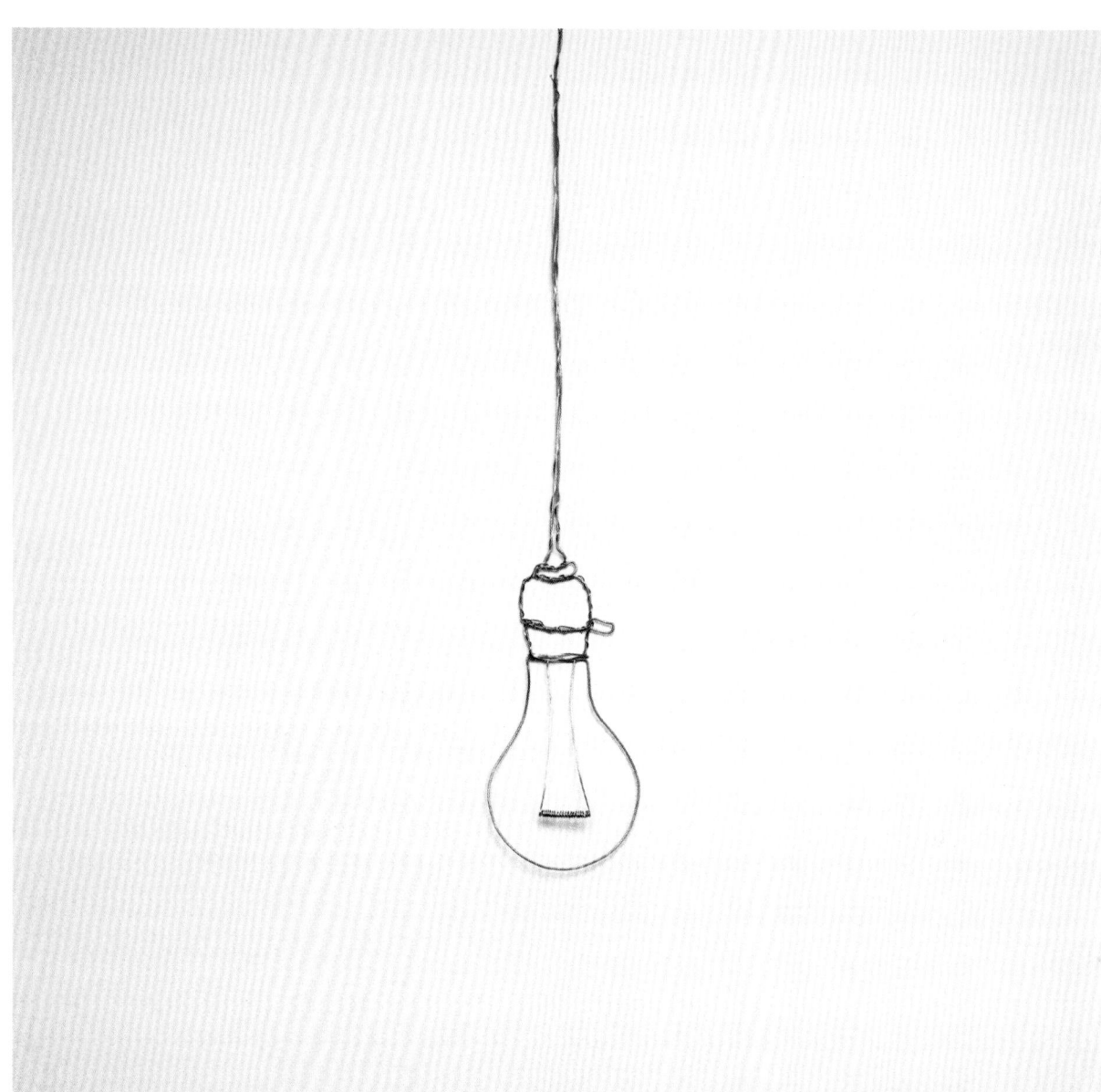

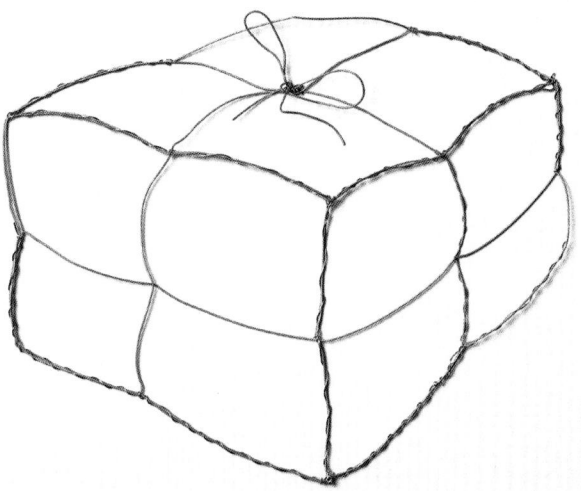

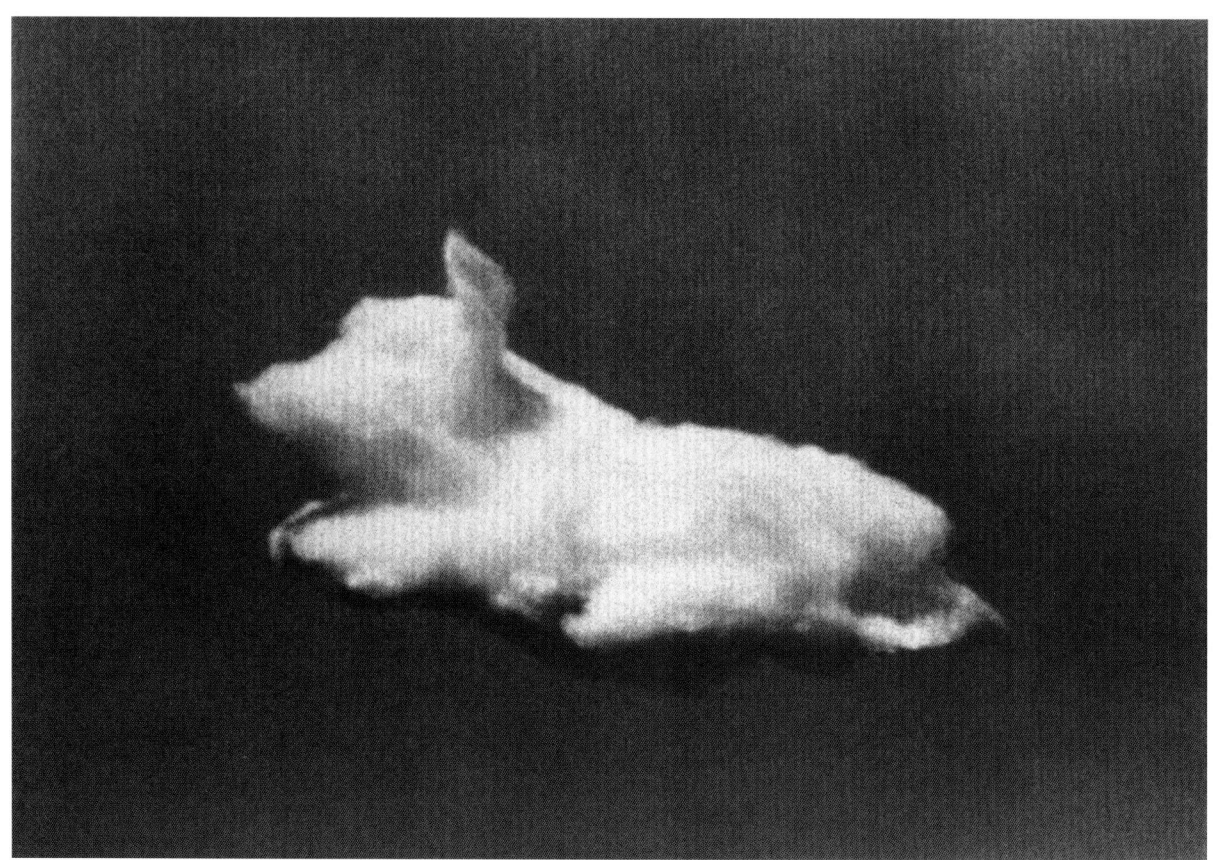

An Image and Its Meanings

We have a handicap called *attention* that only allows one meaning to pass through at a time. But we can control it.

That's why we have cool visual illusions that can be seen different ways, like the Necker cube or the Rubin vase with two faces. These are called multistable images, and by working with them an artist can empower our vision, allowing us to control what we see in the image. If you orchestrate a narrative of these multistable images, you're actually creating an interactive experience, even if you're creating it with a still image.

Gazing at clouds is an example of this kind of vision. When I made my *Equivalents* series out of cotton, I worried that it was slightly too obvious. In one of them you might see a guy paddling a kayak, then a lump of cotton, then a cloud. When you see the guy, you lose the lump of cotton and the cloud. When you see the cotton, you lose the guy and the cloud.

It's interesting to go back to certain principles of representation to understand how we see now. If I do a pencil drawing of you, you'll judge it by how much it looks like you, by its verisimilitude. But in doing so, you're missing the whole point: that it's an illusion, a magic trick. Virtual-reality headsets don't actually fool us, but if I draw a circle with lines radiating from it, everyone sees a sun. The sun is a huge ball of fire located eight light minutes away, but I can bring it *here* with a single gesture. And that is magic.

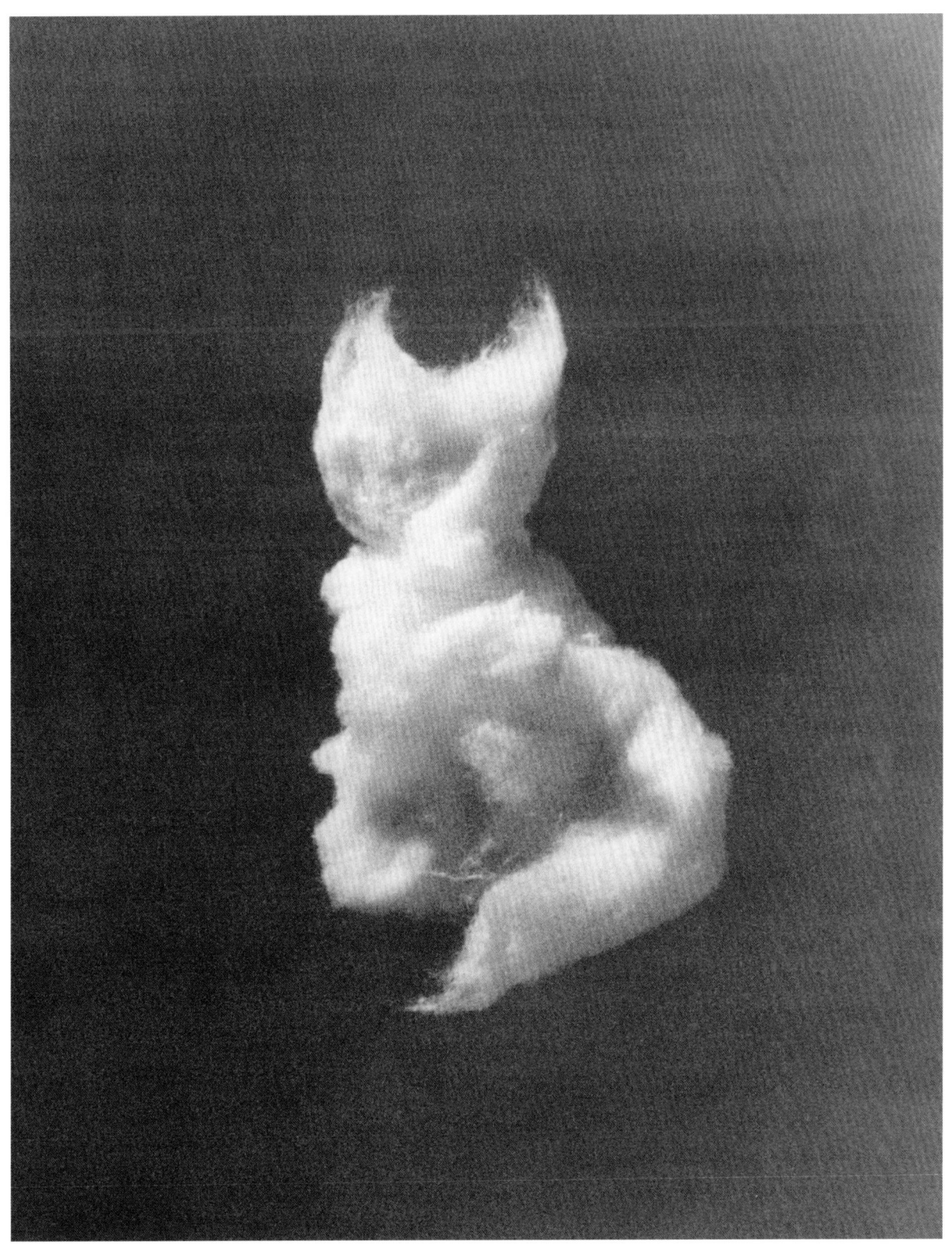

Left
Vik Muniz
Piglet, from *Equivalents*, 1993

Top
Vik Muniz
Kitty, from *Equivalents*, 1993

23

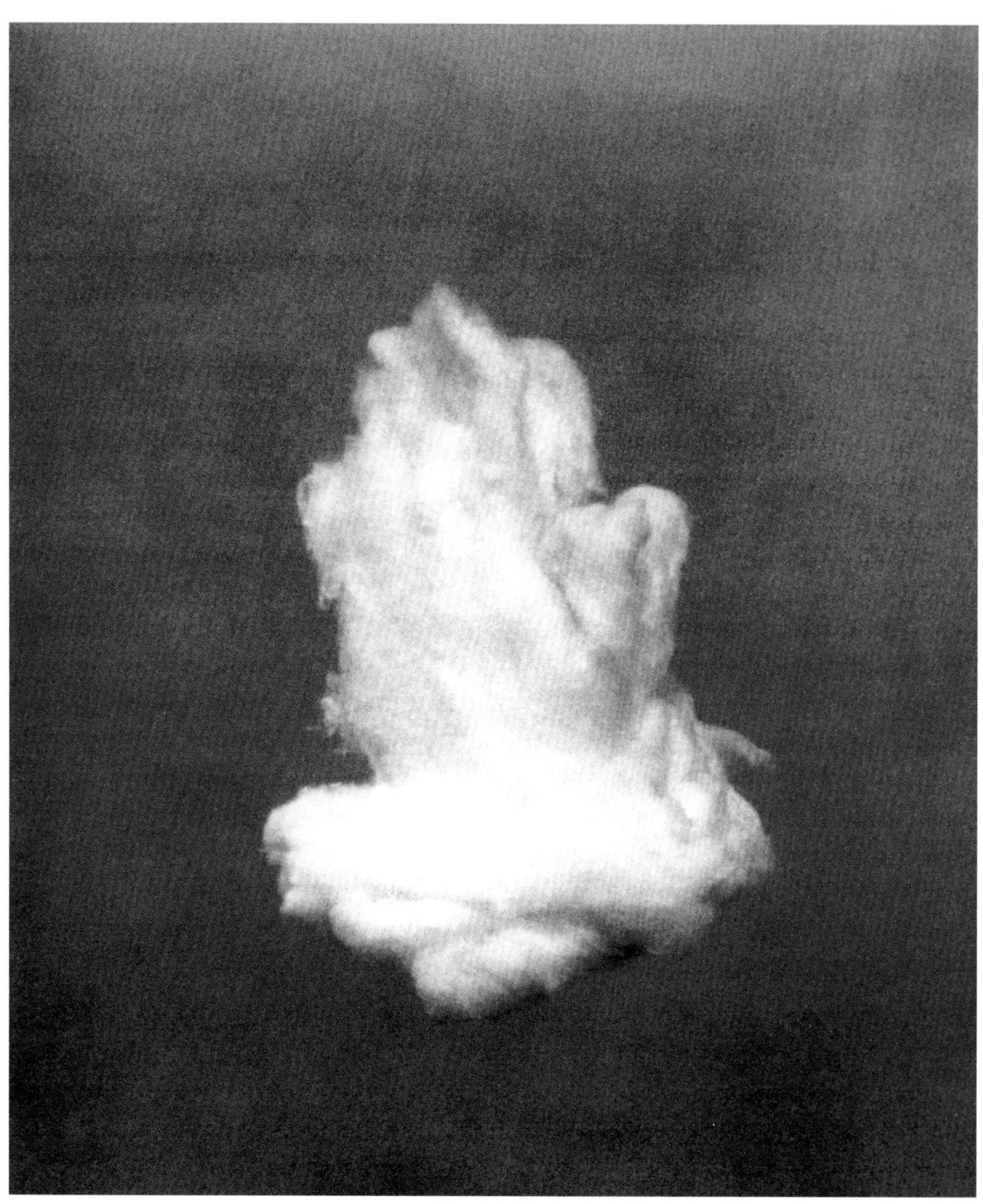

Vik Muniz
Praying Hands, after Dürer,
from *Equivalents*, 1993

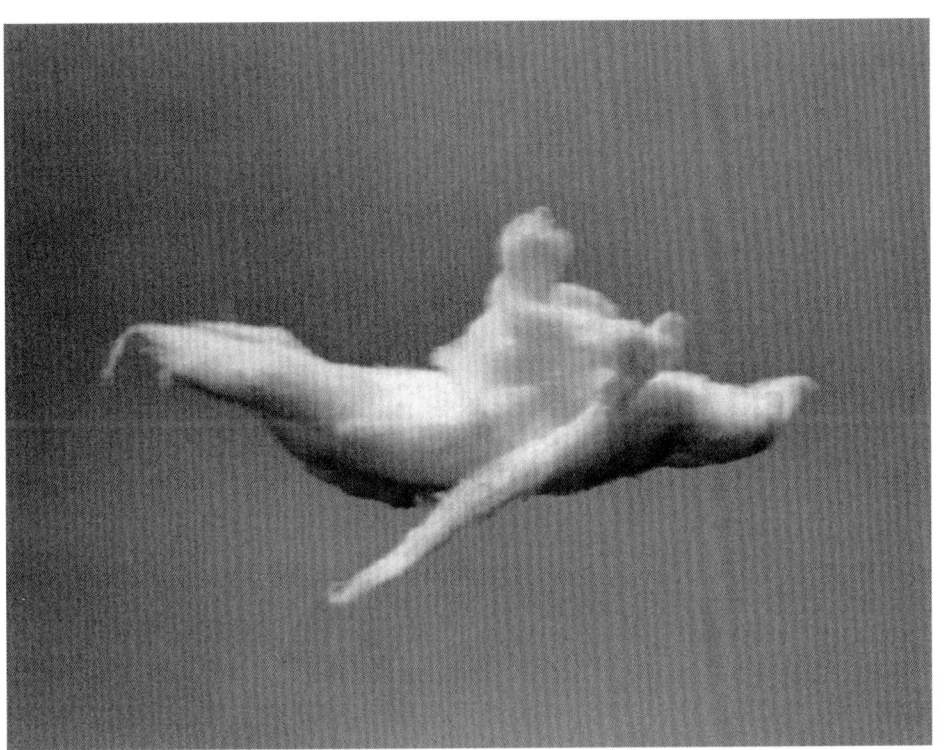

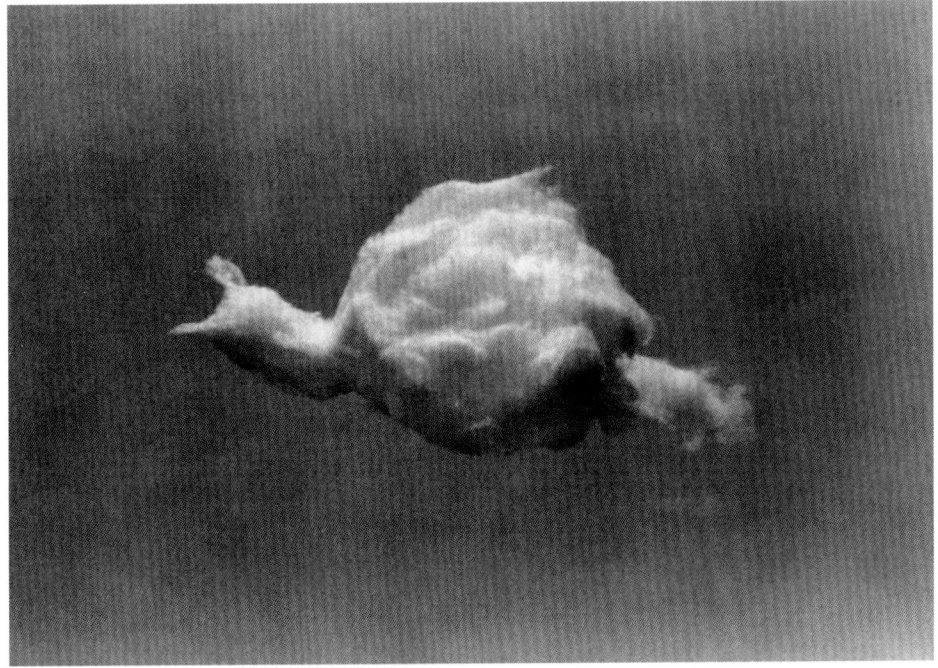

Top
Vik Muniz
The Rower, from *Equivalents*, 1993

Bottom
Vik Muniz
Snail, from *Equivalents*, 1993

25

The Threshold between Material and Idea

Compressed pigment, also known as pastel, is the only technique that shows color precisely as the artist intended. In an oil painting, the artist paints with a color that looks different when it dries. With photography, you end up with a different color when the picture is developed. But the color you see in a pastel by Odilon Redon is the exact color he put there.

One of my pigment pictures can take four months to make. You have to be extremely careful with pure pigment. If you exhale, you ruin the piece—it becomes a cloud of brown nothing. If you inhale, you might die, because a lot of these pigments are extremely toxic, like cadmium, antimony, or lead. I wear gloves, masks, and goggles, because I work so closely with the material.

The finished piece is a very large photograph, and it's quite tactile if you look at it up close. When you encounter it in a museum, the picture changes meanings as you walk toward it to discover what it is and how it was made.

I am convinced that I am a wall artist—nothing I make seems to work as perfectly on a page or a screen. I imagine my ideal viewer waking up one morning and deciding to visit the museum, taking a shower, riding the bus, arriving, finding my picture there. It's a ceremony, one that runs contrary to the flood of images coming at you all the time. You're doing something different—you're going *toward* a picture and placing yourself inside the medium as an actor. You're participating in its creation. Museums and galleries are places where one has the opportunity to ritualize a visual experience.

When I'm at a museum, I spend a lot of time watching people look at pictures. Sometimes I don't even look at the pictures, just the people. They walk toward a picture and then they stop—always on the same spot, as if it were marked by a piece of tape on the floor. Why? Because people stop at the distance where a picture comfortably fills the approximately 100-degree frame of their visual field, where it exists on its own, as a beautiful painted landscape. Then they step back, and all of a sudden they're back in the museum. They're safe and in control. Then they step forward again. Why do they keep doing this? It's simple. When they first see the landscape, they see something that was an idea, something that came from the mind of somebody else. As they get closer to it, they see material, paint or pastel, something that was dug from the earth or extracted from plants or animals. Then they step back again, and they see the idea. They go closer, they see material. The polarity between material and idea is not important; what's important is crossing the boundary, the point at which these seemingly mundane materials become an idea, and vice versa. It's as if a ball has left the hands of a basketball player but hasn't yet reached the rim. There's a moment of change, a moment of truth and transformation. That's the sublime in art: the moment when we connect with something inside and outside of ourselves simultaneously.

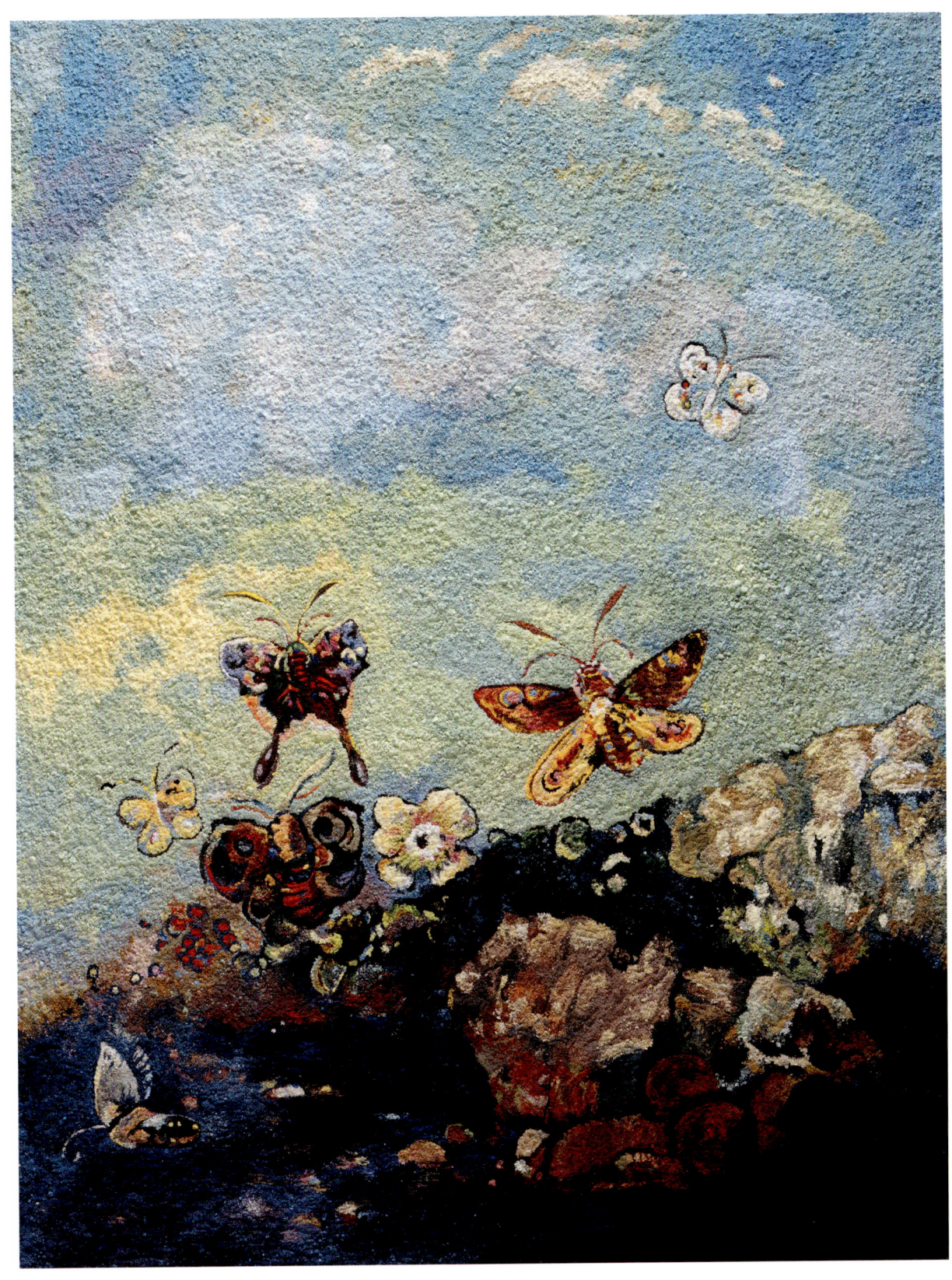

Vik Muniz
Butterflies, after Redon,
from *Pictures of Pigment,* 2006

27

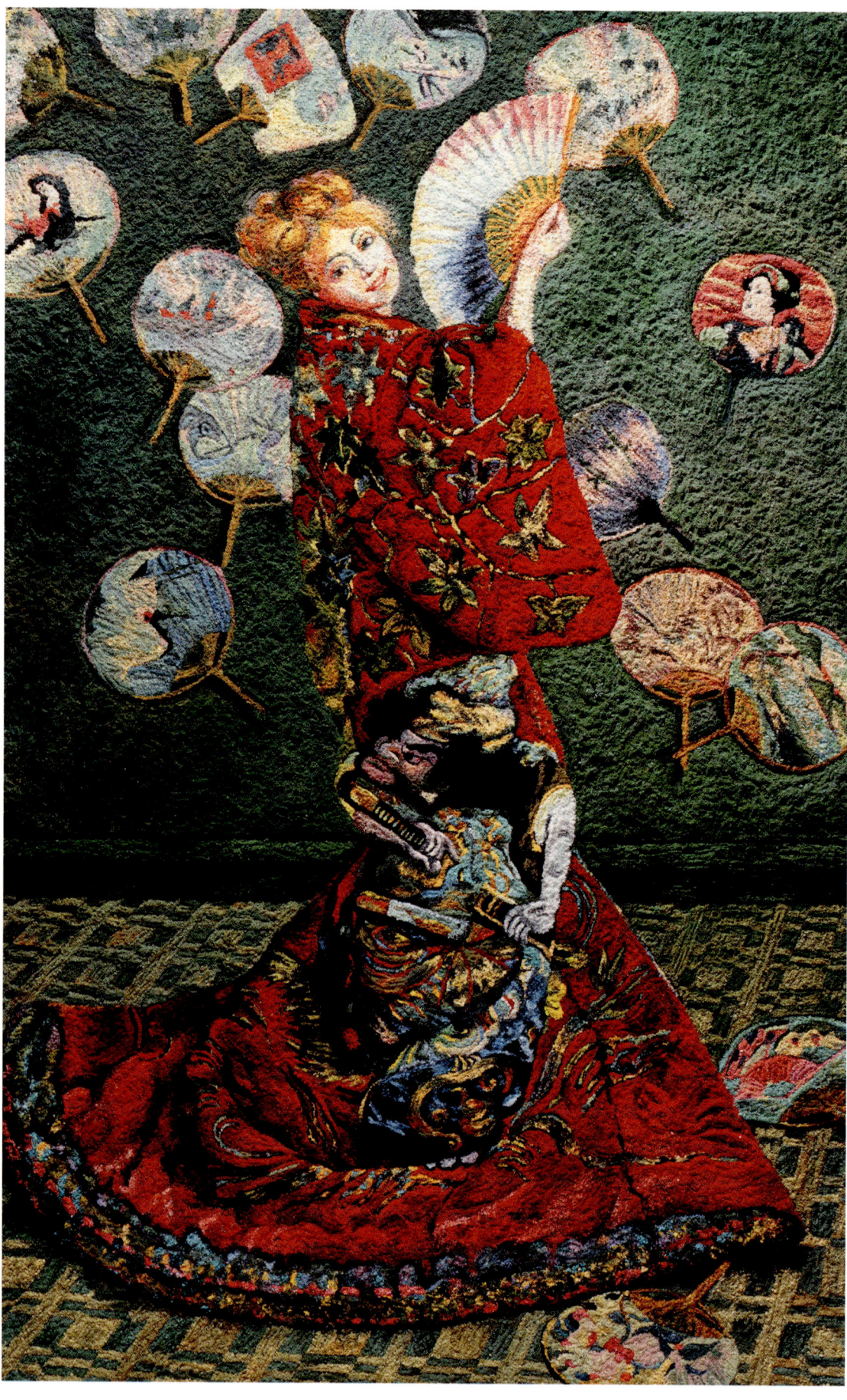

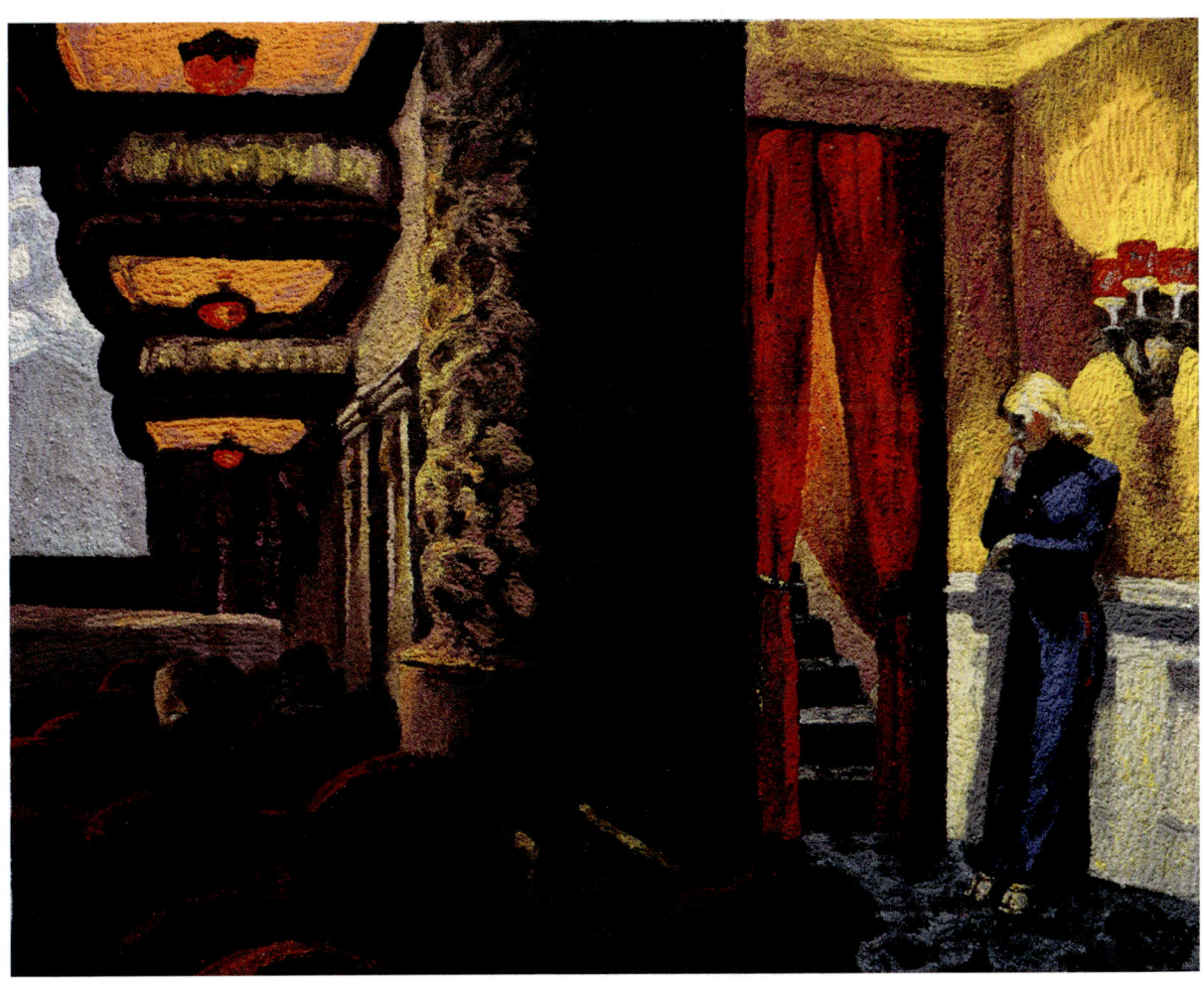

Left
Vik Muniz
La Japonaise, after Claude Monet,
from *Pictures of Pigment*, 2006

Top
Vik Muniz
*New York Movie, after Edward
Hopper,* from *Pictures of Pigment*,
2006

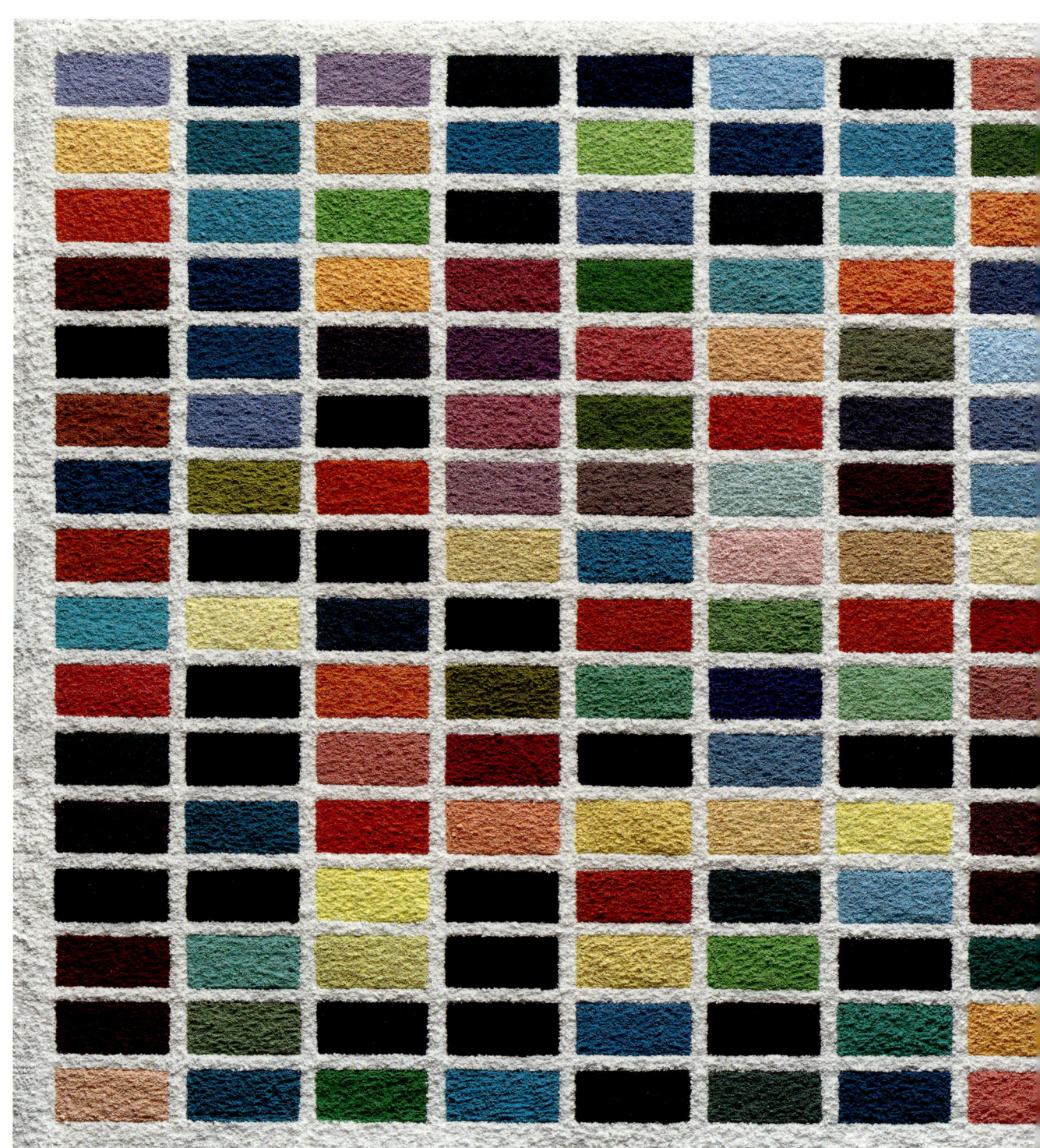

Vik Muniz
256 Colors, after Gerhard Richter,
from *Pictures of Pigment*, 2015

30

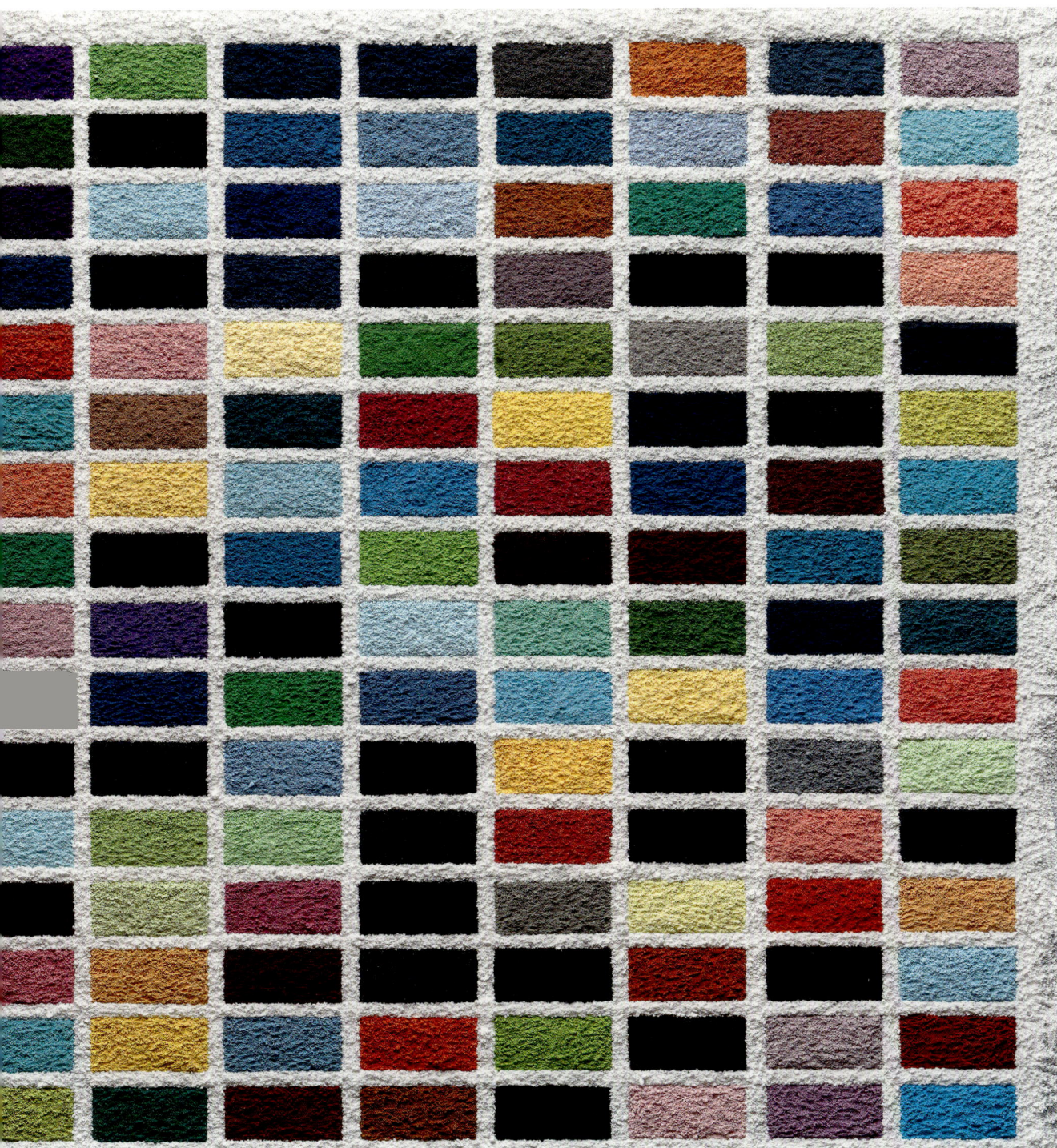

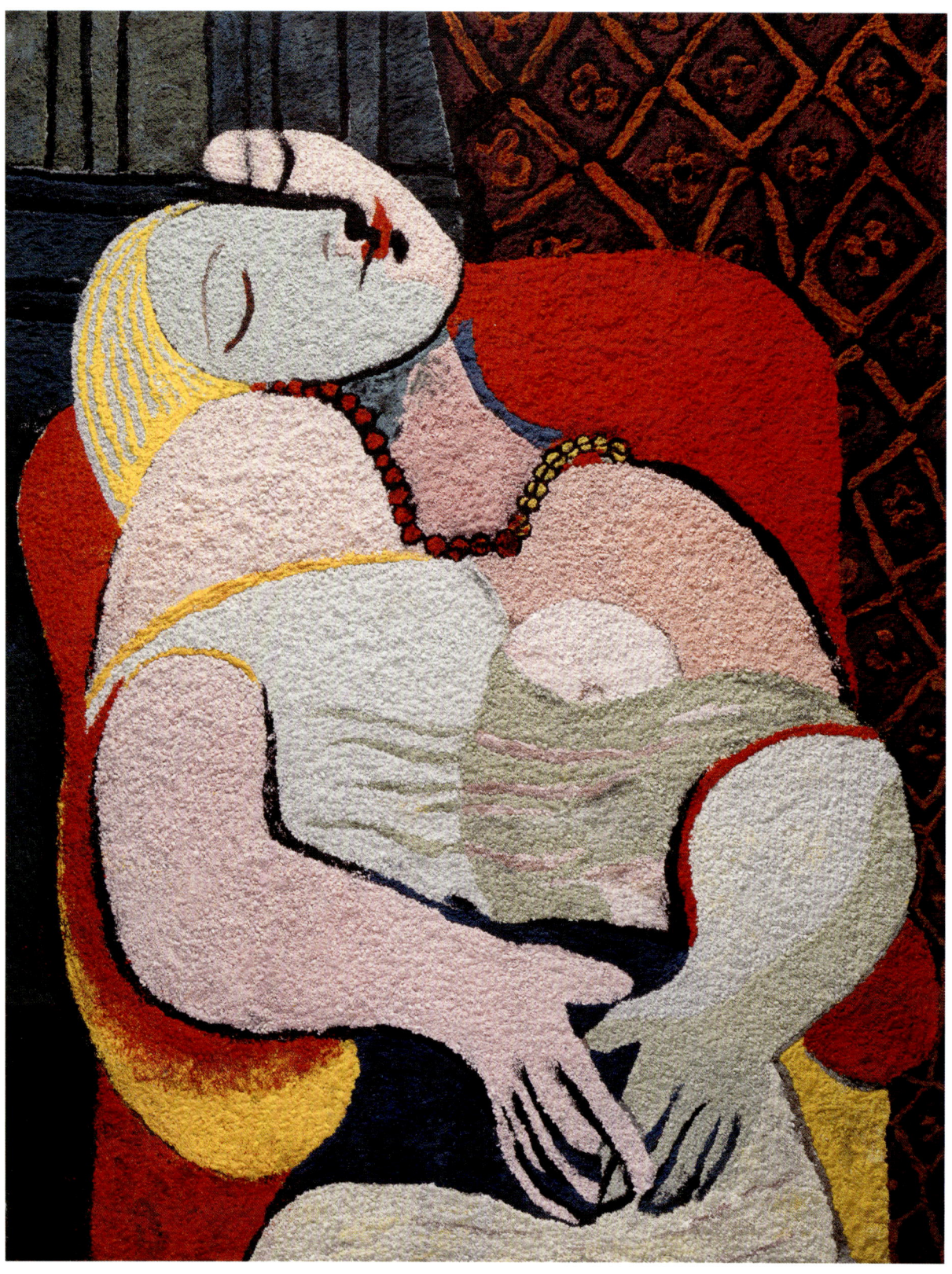

Vik Muniz
The Dream, after Picasso,
from *Pictures of Pigment*, 2006

32

Working in Series

Working in series allows me to take what I've learned from one piece and use it in the next. There's an arc to the process.

Initially, I'm very excited, but the results aren't very good—I'm still trying to learn how to do whatever it is. Then I get to a point where I'm doing it well. The works at the end of a series look very nice. But that's when my interest starts dipping. I'm doing it so well, it starts to feel like work.

When you first see one of my *Pictures of Wire*, it appears to be drawn in pencil. But once you do a double take, you notice that the image is made with wire. You might start to wonder how big the object was, how long it took me to make, how I decided when it was done. Photography creates a layer of ambiguity that makes you think about the way you look at pictures instead of simply identifying a subject and assigning meaning.

I tried to explore this idea a little further by using wire to make landscapes. But it was very hard, and they were not attractive. That's when I decided to use thread. Layering thread on a flat surface generates two different perspectives: a topographic view of the thread itself and a landscape that inspires the viewer to see a much deeper space.

I often use titles that diminish the material. For *Pictures of Thread*, the title begins with the number of yards of thread I used to make them, followed by the title of the original work and the artist. For instance, one is called *16,200 Yards (Le Songeur, after J.B.C. Corot)*. Another is *4,000 Yards (Apple Trees, after Gerhard Richter)*. Collectors tend to buy the ones that are not as good but have more thread in them, which I find interesting.

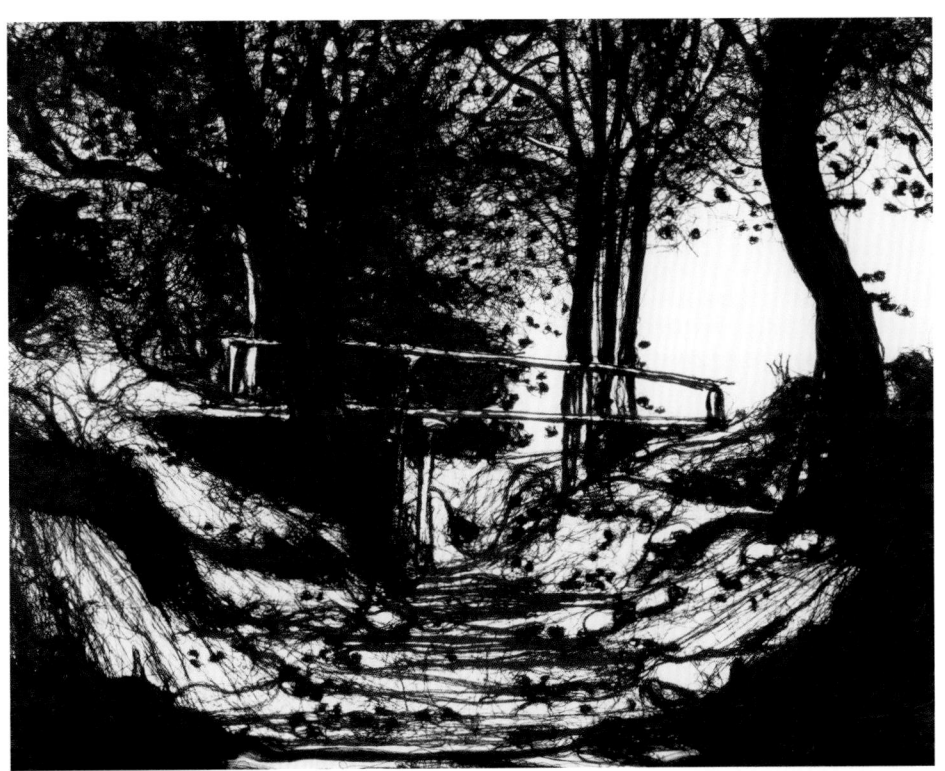

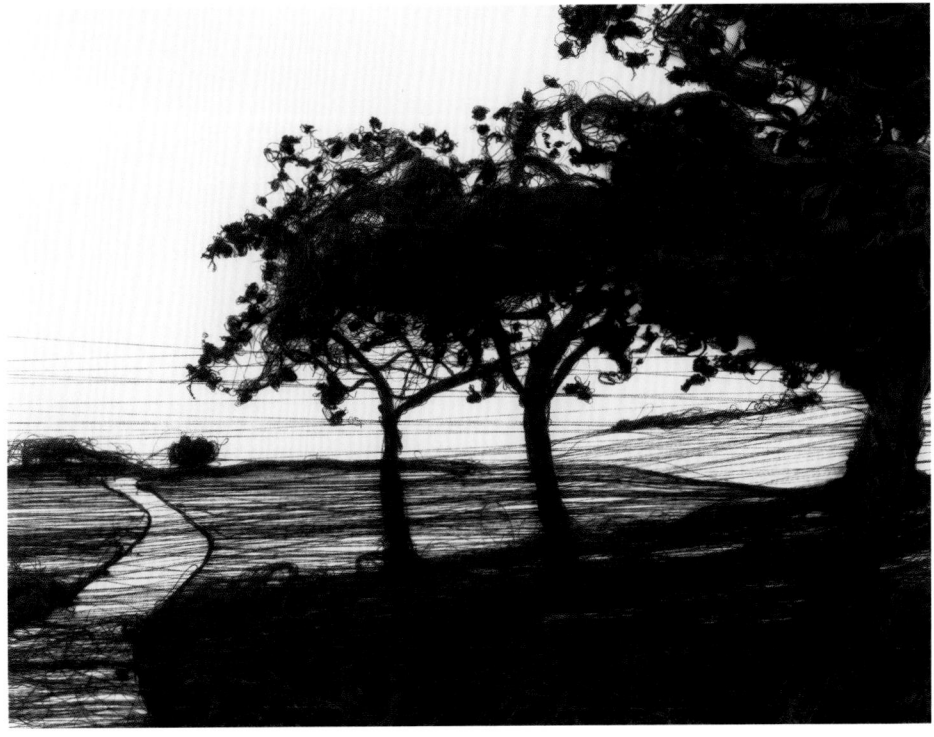

Top
Vik Muniz
*11,000 Yards (Helmingham Dell,
after John Constable),*
from *Pictures of Thread*, 1999

Bottom
Vik Muniz
*4,000 Yards (Apple Trees,
after Gerhard Richter),*
from *Pictures of Thread*, 1998

35

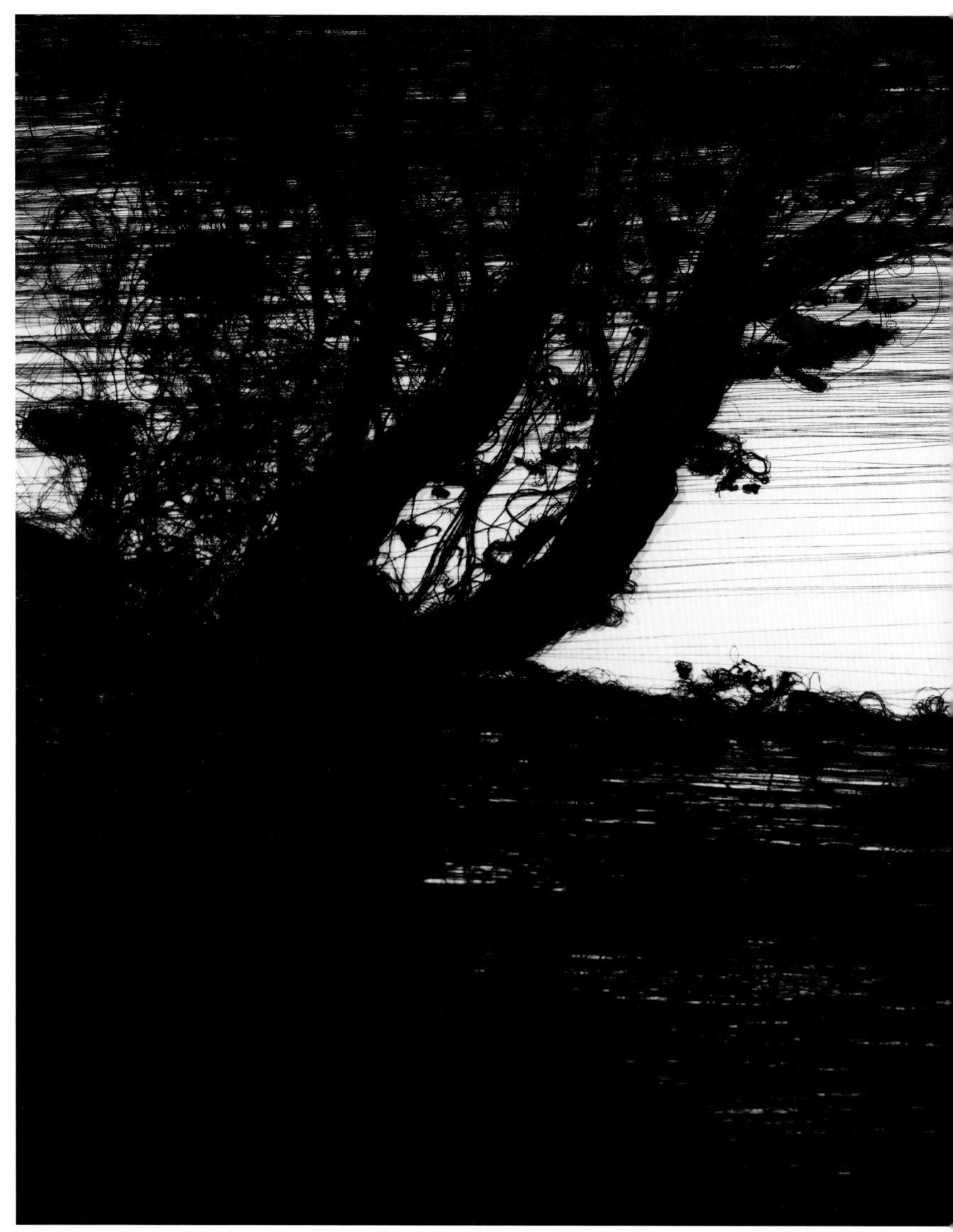

Vik Muniz
16,200 Yards (Le Songeur, after J.B.C. Corot),
from *Pictures of Thread,* 1996

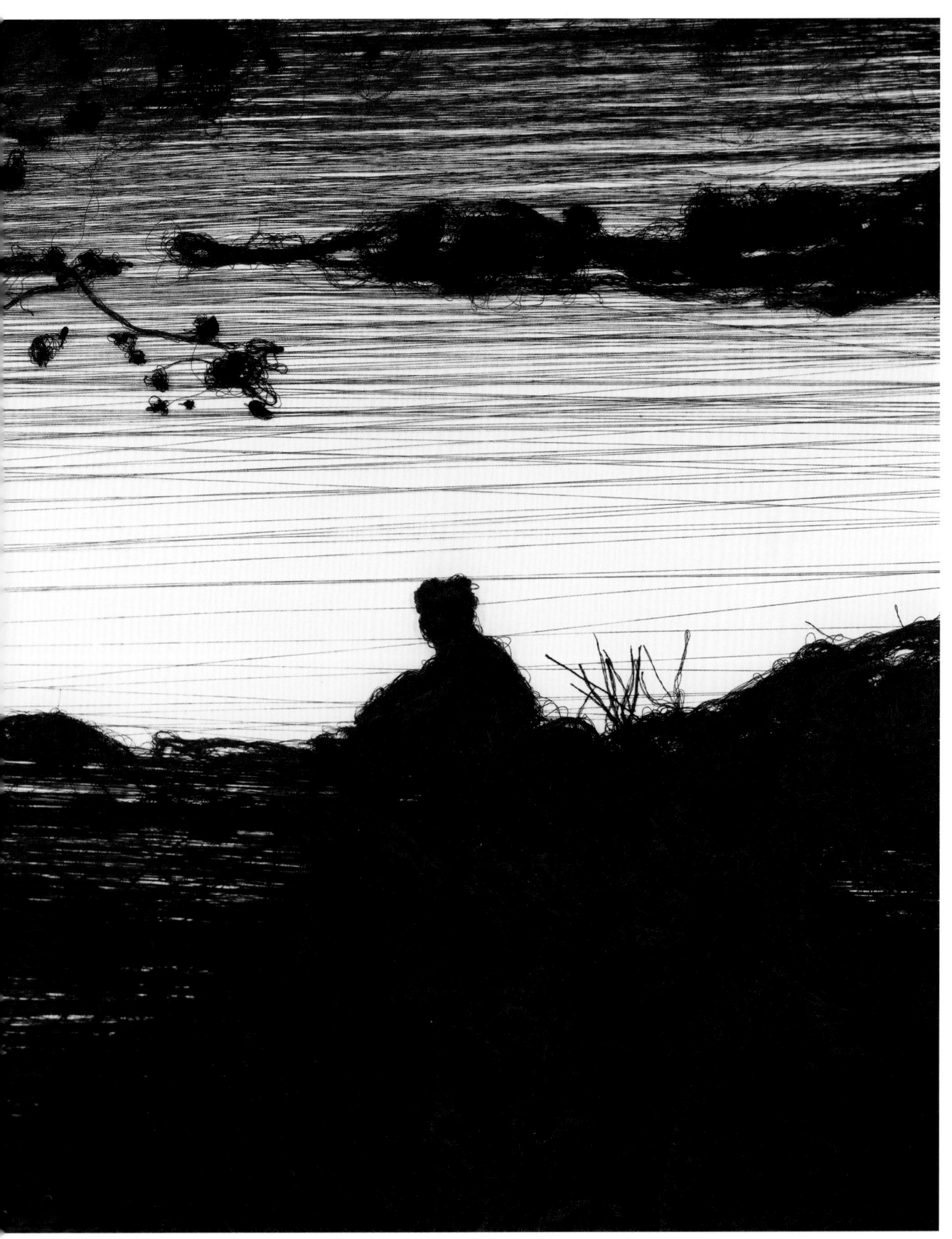

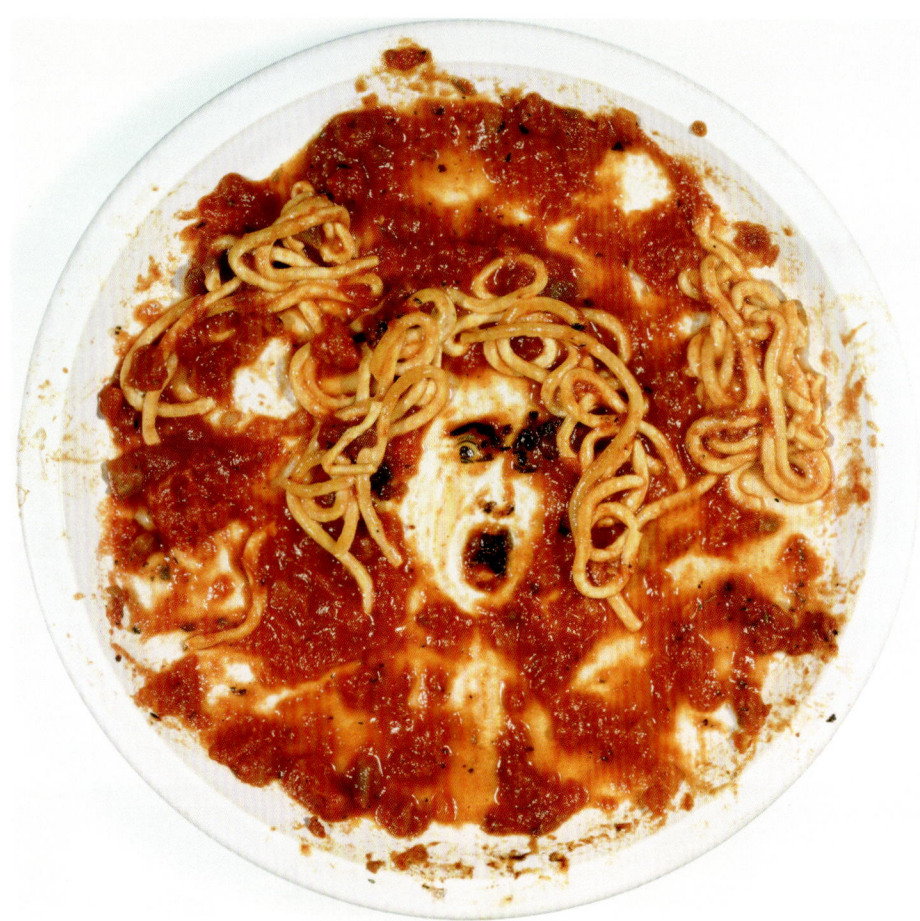

Always Play with Your Food

Wanting to make my work even more complicated by evoking more senses than just sight, I decided to draw pictures with chocolate. Chocolate is a great medium, because it has a long history that's charged with a multitude of meanings. People think it's romantic, but it's brown and gooey and melts all over your hand. I portrayed Freud first because I thought he could explain why people like chocolate so much. I also depicted Pollock doing his messy scatological thing. Crowds were a compelling subject too. The drawings were tiny, and I had to do them quickly. But the photographs are very large. I learned how to use an 8-by-10 camera, because I wanted them to look sharp.

Art should be enjoyable. I have always been a little suspicious of art that comes from pain or martyrdom. One tends to make better things when one feels good making them. It is also important to keep making, because new ideas arise in the process of making other things. I was working on a Caravaggio piece in chocolate one day, and I thought I'd make a rendition of his Medusa painting with the pasta left over from my lunch. It wasn't my intention for it to become a piece—it took me all of three minutes—but two weeks later it was on the cover of a newspaper. Art can come from anywhere, at any time, in any material, but this only happens when you're making it.

Vik Muniz
Medusa Marinara, 1997

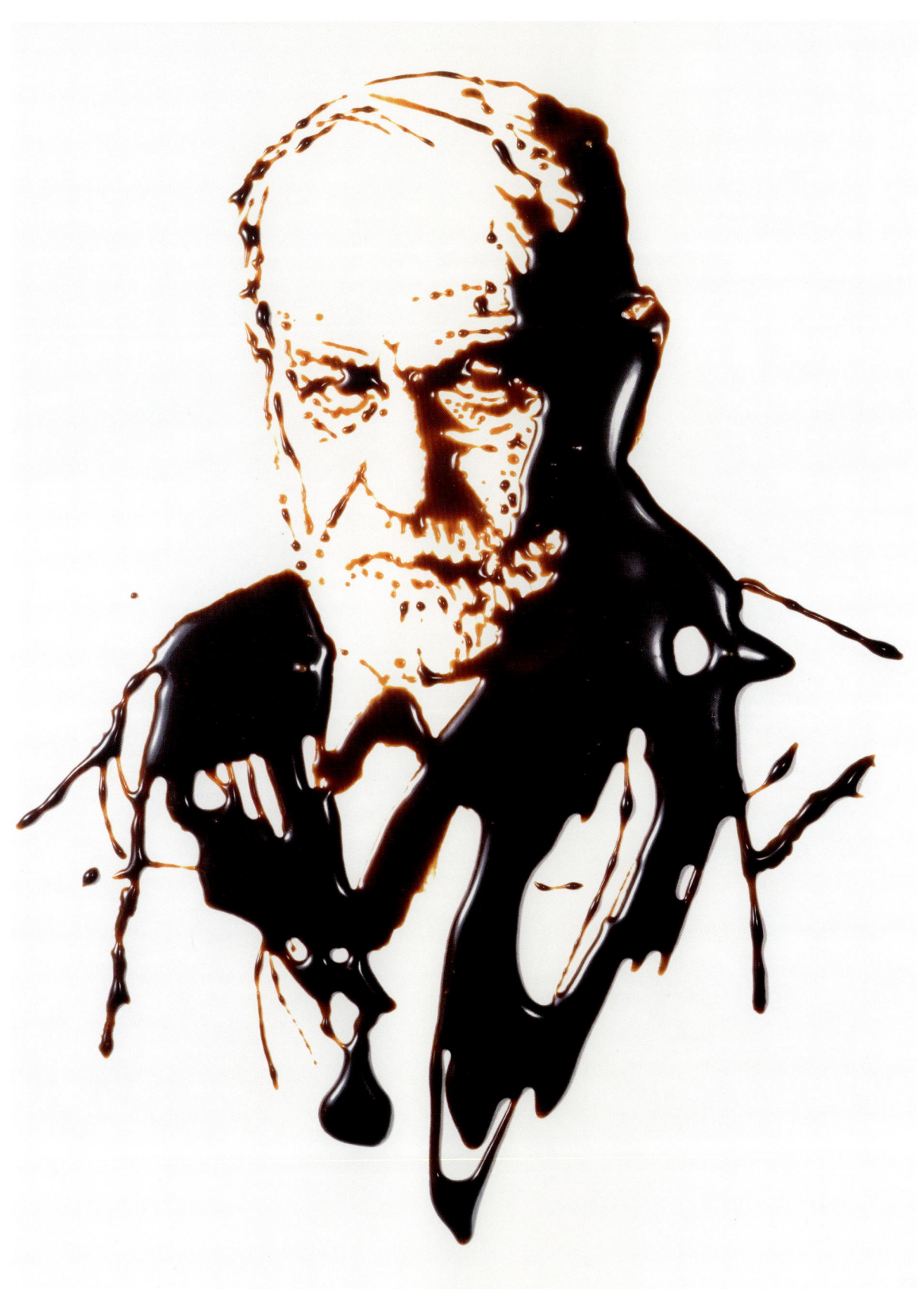

Vik Muniz
Sigmund, from *Pictures of Chocolate,* 1997

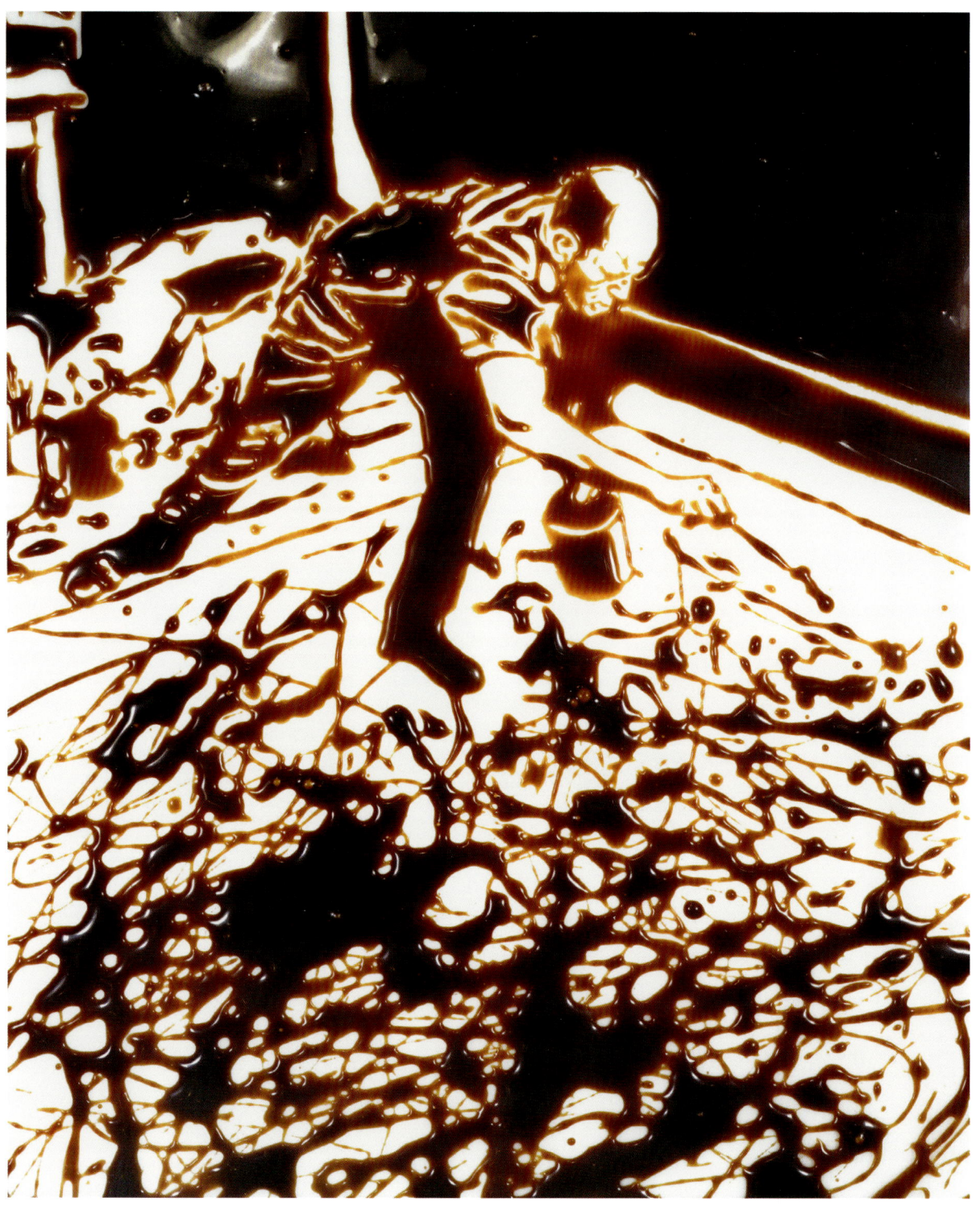

Vik Muniz
Action Photo, after Hans Namuth,
from *Pictures of Chocolate*, 1997

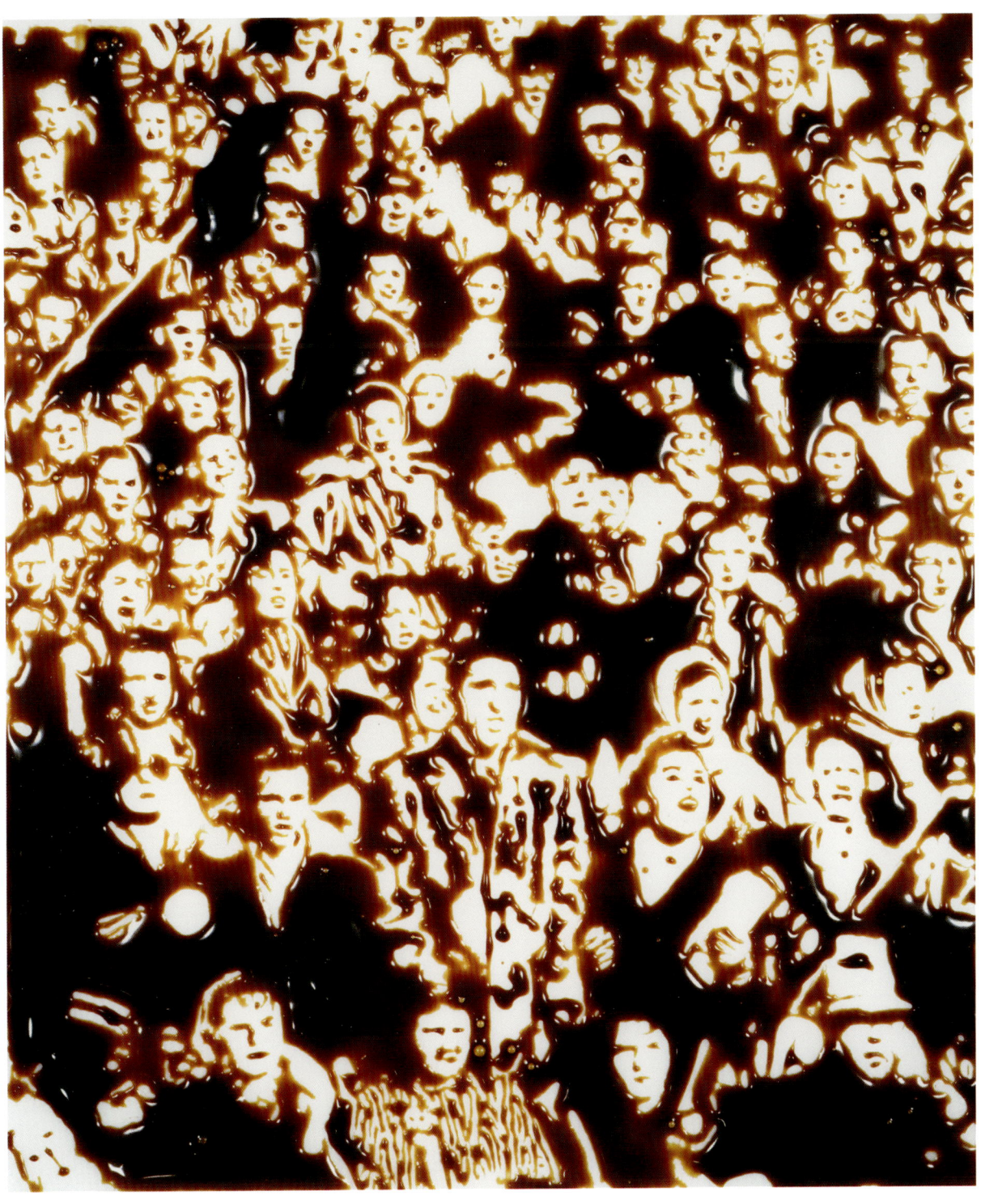

Vik Muniz
Individuals, from *Pictures of Chocolate,* 1998

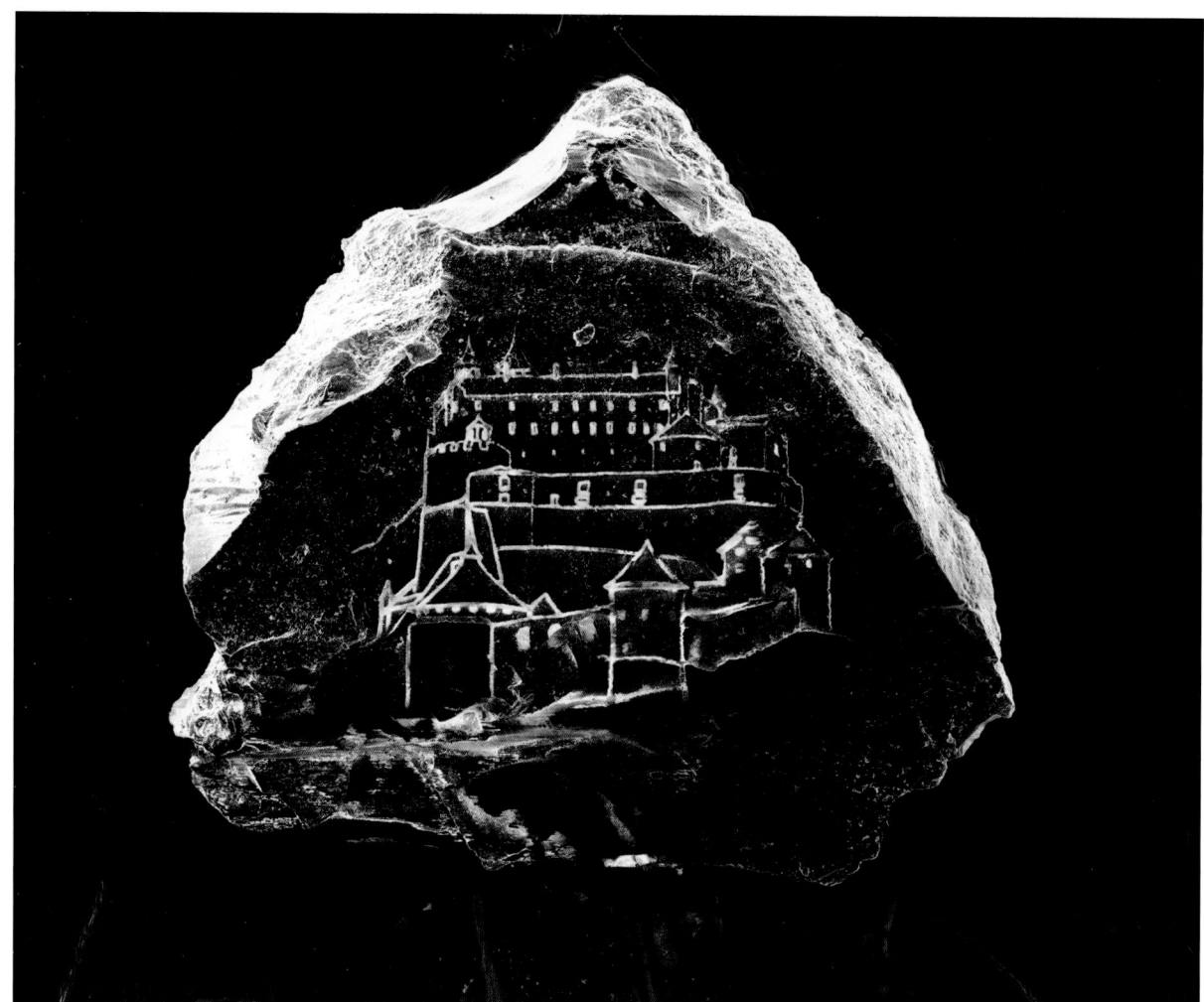

The Bigger Picture

When I travel, I sometimes take along a camera lucida to make line drawings of any castles that I might see. By 2012 I had a pile of these drawings, so when I began an artist residency at MIT, we used a Focused Ion Beam machine to etch them onto grains of sand. I had to vectorize each drawing, and then it took a single stream of ions to etch the image onto the granule. Calling it sand is an overstatement—it's more like a speck of dust. In the pictures you can see other grains, because at this scale you can't clean anything. It's way too small. I did the same thing with a picture of my daughter, Dora, and threw it into the sand at Ipanema Beach in Rio. I hope when she's sixteen and has a boyfriend, she'll say to him, "Do you really love me? Then find me there."

    While I was working with MIT's department of nanotechnology, I also started collaborating with the biogenetics department. My first idea was to work with things that grow, like fungi. But I was lucky enough to meet a guy named Tal Danino, and

Vik Muniz
Sandcastle #3,
from *Sandcastles,* 2013

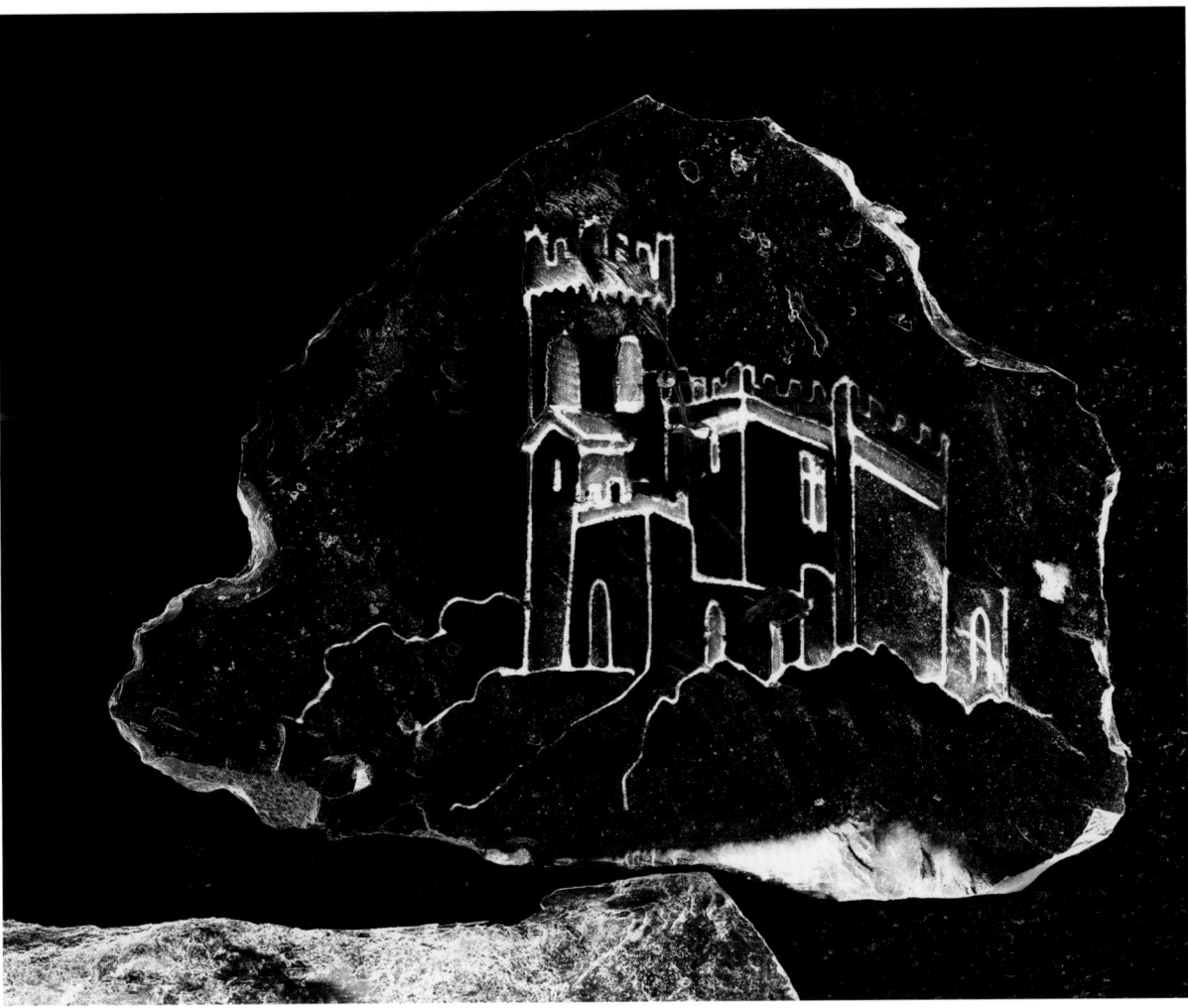

with him I figured out how to draw pictures with living cells. At first glance, the images look like swatches of wallpaper you'd find at your grandmother's house or a mandala on the wall of a macrobiotic restaurant, but the designs are actually made up of things like liver cells or cervical-cancer cells.

When we made the first one, we thought, Wow, this is wonderful—let's use different kinds of cells to make more. Liver cells are sluggish and stay in the same spot, but cervical cells have cilia and move around. Neurons, on the other hand, don't divide. So for every cell we worked with, we had to change the way we grew them, and the way we scanned them. But the fact that we could make pictures with living cells was quite fascinating. The images in *Colonies* are so sharp, you can even see the doubling of the nucleus in each dividing cell. I've always been fascinated with the idea of making works that challenge the scale of our bodies in relation to them.

43

Vik Muniz
Sandcastle #4,
from *Sandcastles,* 2013

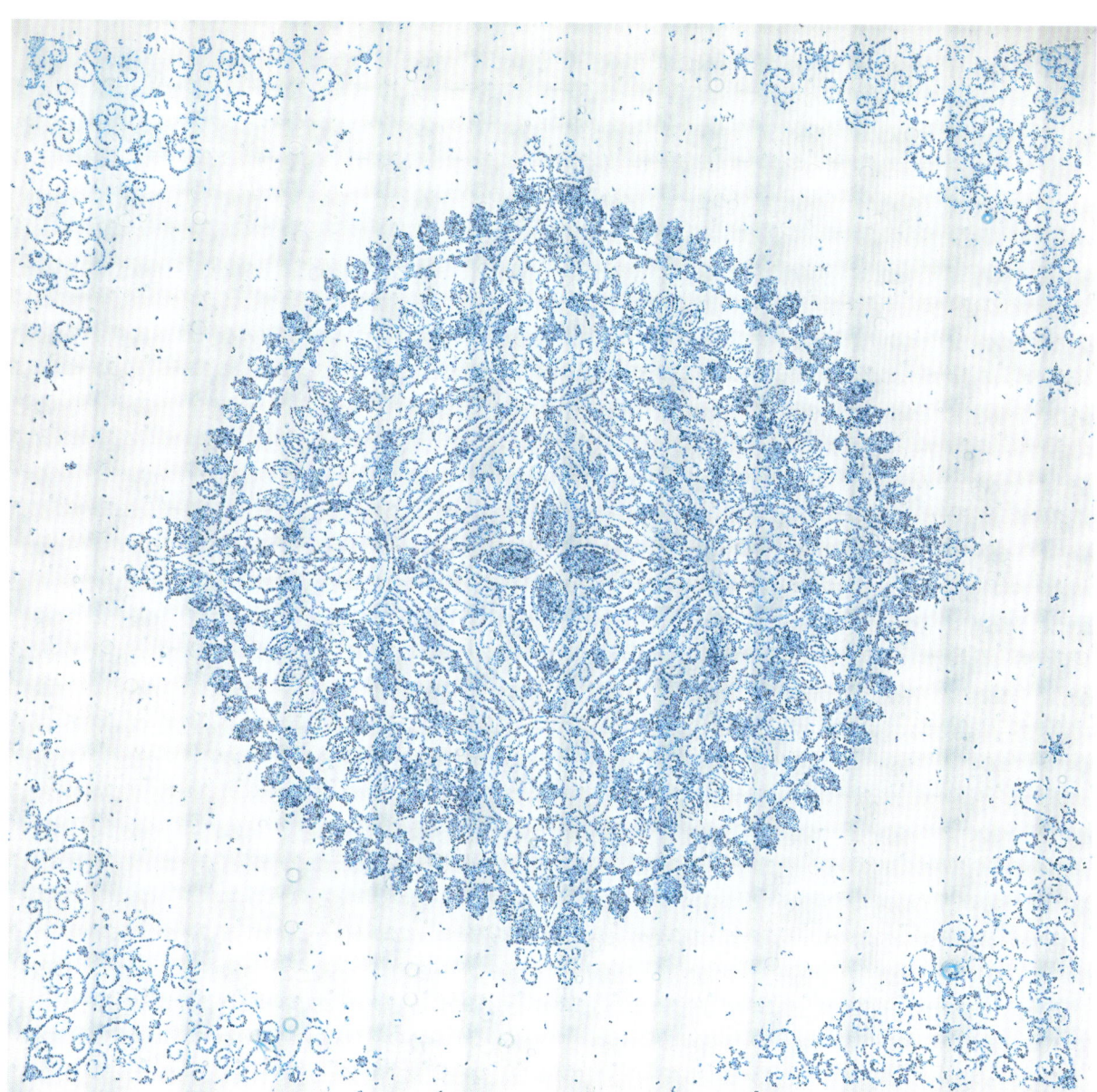

Vik Muniz
Hela Pattern 15,
from *Colonies*, 2014

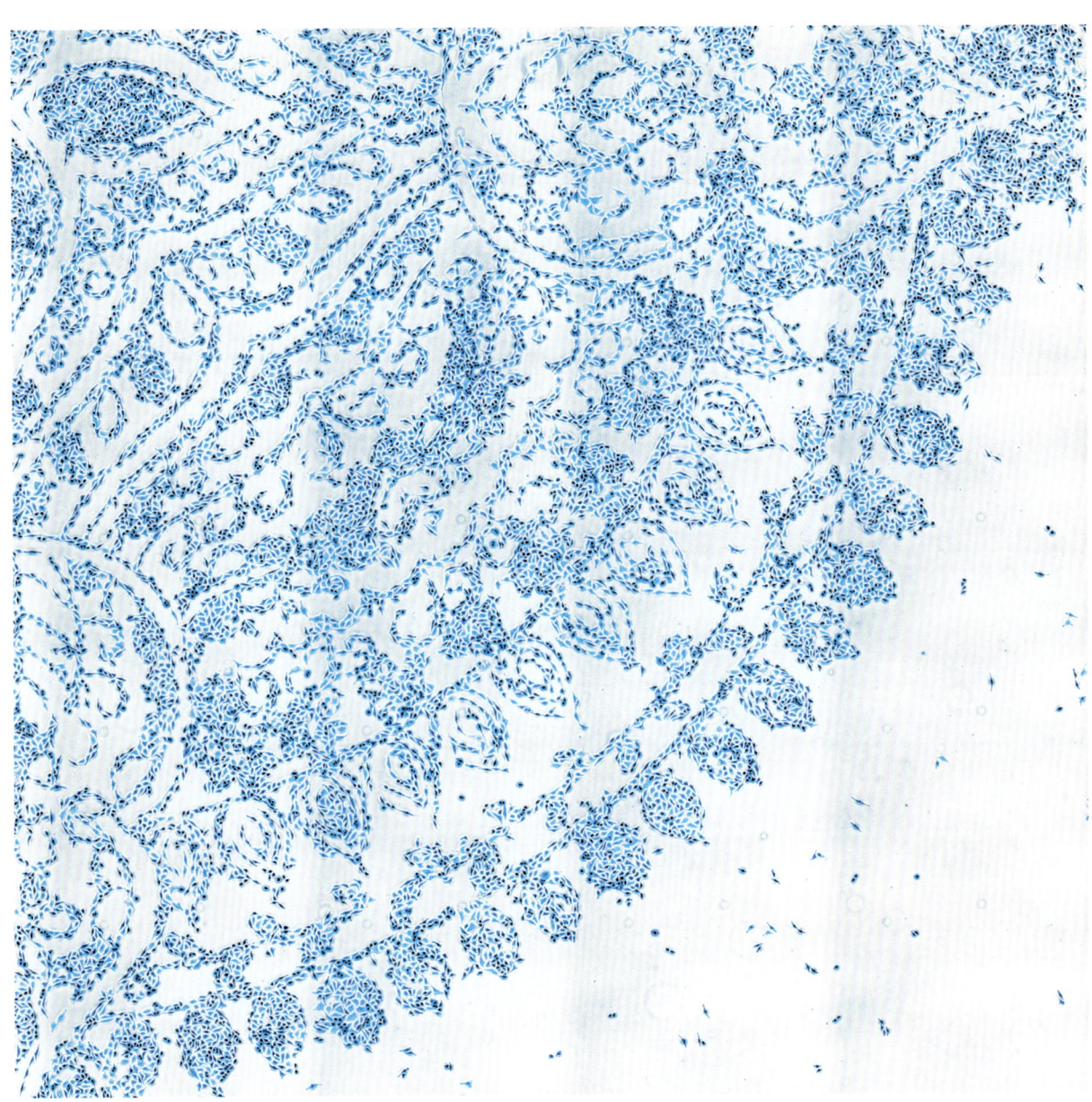

Mindworks

Even though I'm Brazilian, I'm very influenced by European and American art made during my lifetime, especially in the 1960s and 1970s. Minimalism and Land art are important to me, because their poetics of material, form, and content is what inspires most of my work. I find Robert Smithson's *Spiral Jetty*, for instance, very beautiful. By creating his earthwork in a remote place, he made a sculpture not only in the landscape but also in our minds.

I've been invited to see *Spiral Jetty* many times, but I always refuse to go because I already made the mistake of visiting the Pyramids at Giza. (They were too small, and it ruined them for me.) Because I didn't want to see *Spiral Jetty*, I tried to make something in my studio instead, to see if I could create a work for this mind place. It ended up being boring and lonely, so I decided to devise something grander. I spent years convincing a Brazilian mining company to let me use their facility and equipment to make *Pictures of Earthworks (The Sarzedo Drawings)*. (I can be very persuasive if given enough time.) Iron mines have huge flat spaces that are perfect canvases, and they have tractors and excavators. We plotted the drawings using GPS and then photographed them from the company's helicopters. They were incredibly large, up to a quarter mile long (four hundred meters). Some could even be seen from commercial aircraft. Most of the land artists of the 1960s and '70s used geometric forms, some more symbolic than others. But I wanted to use really stupid images, like clip art, to deemphasize the idea of subject and instead go back to the idea that art is about *process*. In this case, a process that took me three and a half years.

When Creative Time asked me to make a project for New York City in 2001, there was something I'd wanted to do for a long time: use a plane to draw clouds in the sky. A cloud is something you expect to see in the sky, but never in the shape of a drawing. And it moves!

The first one I made looked too much like a Mexican sombrero, unfortunately, but the later drawings were much better. After New York, we also made clouds over Miami. When a drawing is that big, you can't see it because you're in it. You're part of a bigger picture. Come to think of it, we're all part of a vast panorama. We're placed in it together. That's as true for gigantic things as it is for infinitely small ones.

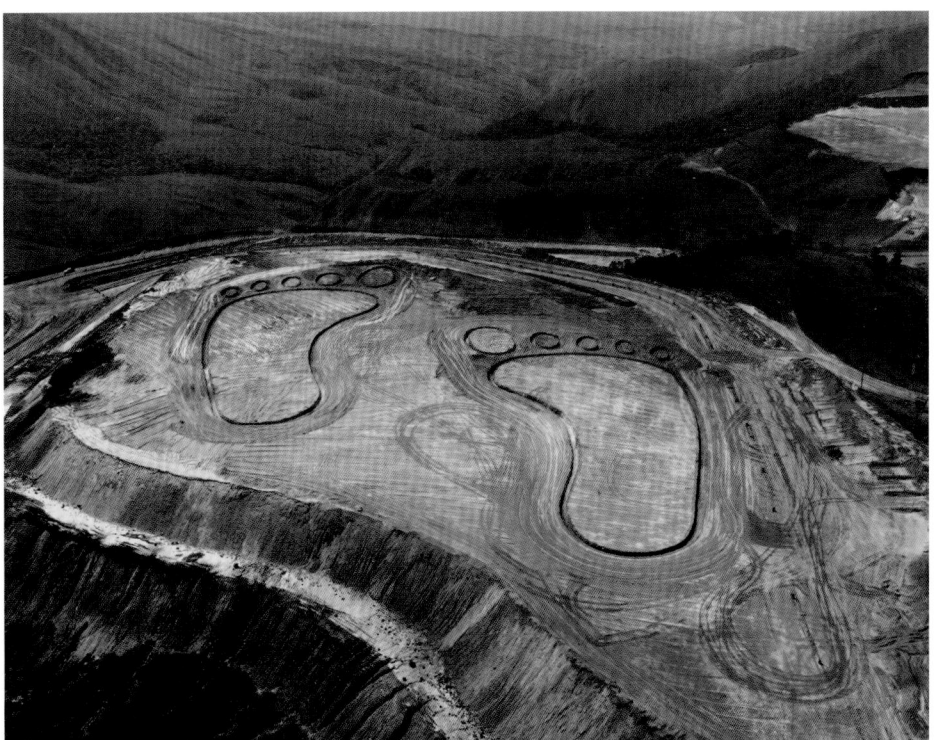

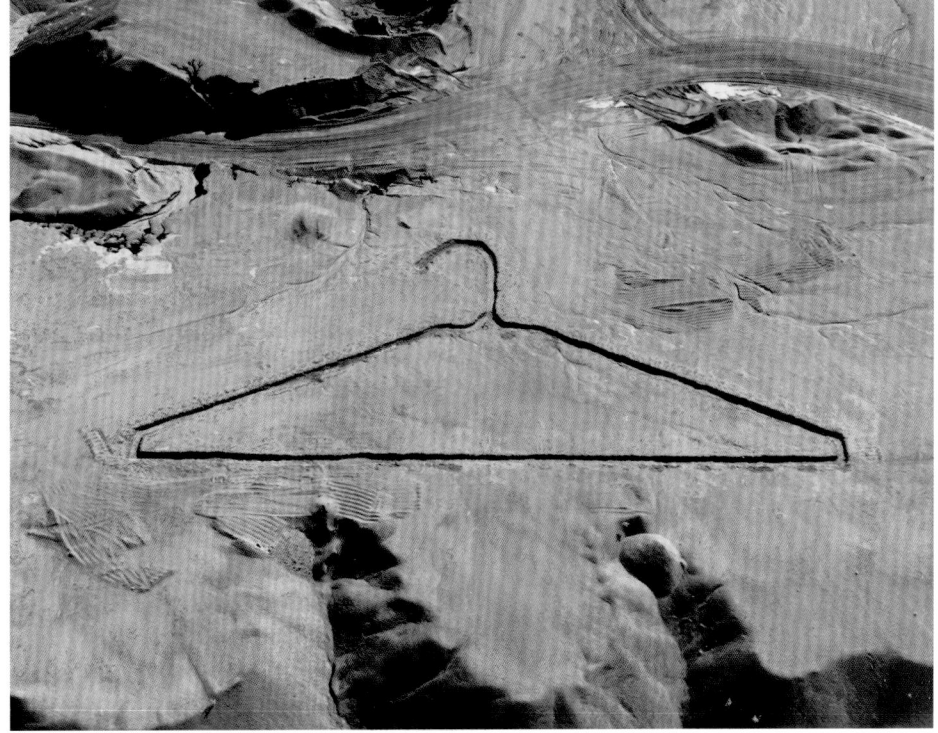

Top
Vik Muniz
Footsteps (João Pereira, Iron Mine),
from *Earthworks*, 2006

Bottom
Vik Muniz
Hanger (The Sarzedo Drawings),
from *Earthworks*, 2002

47

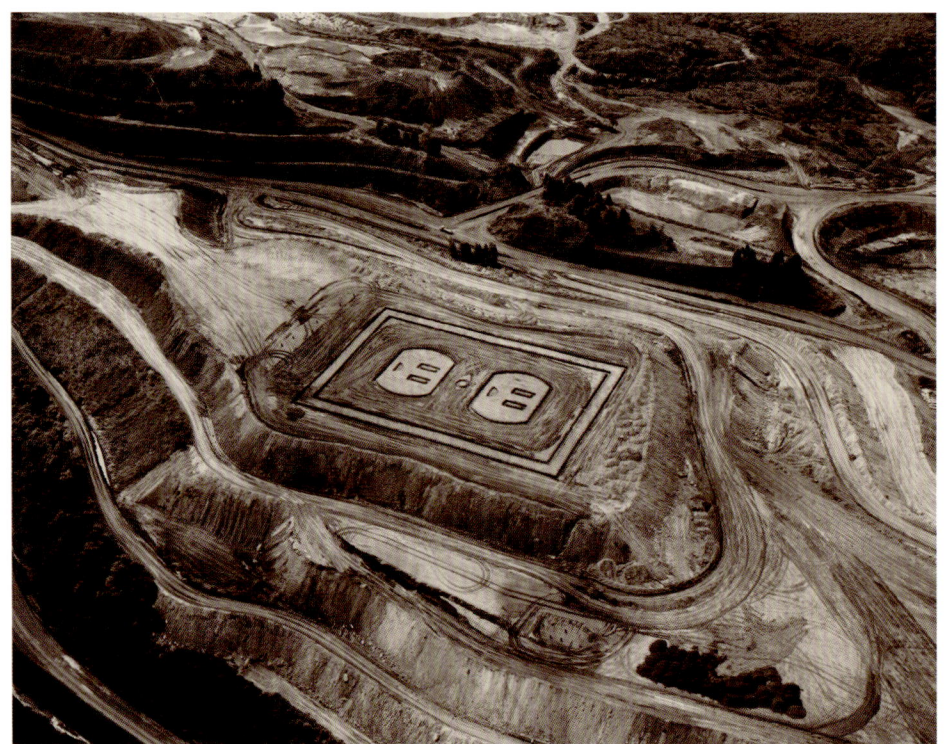

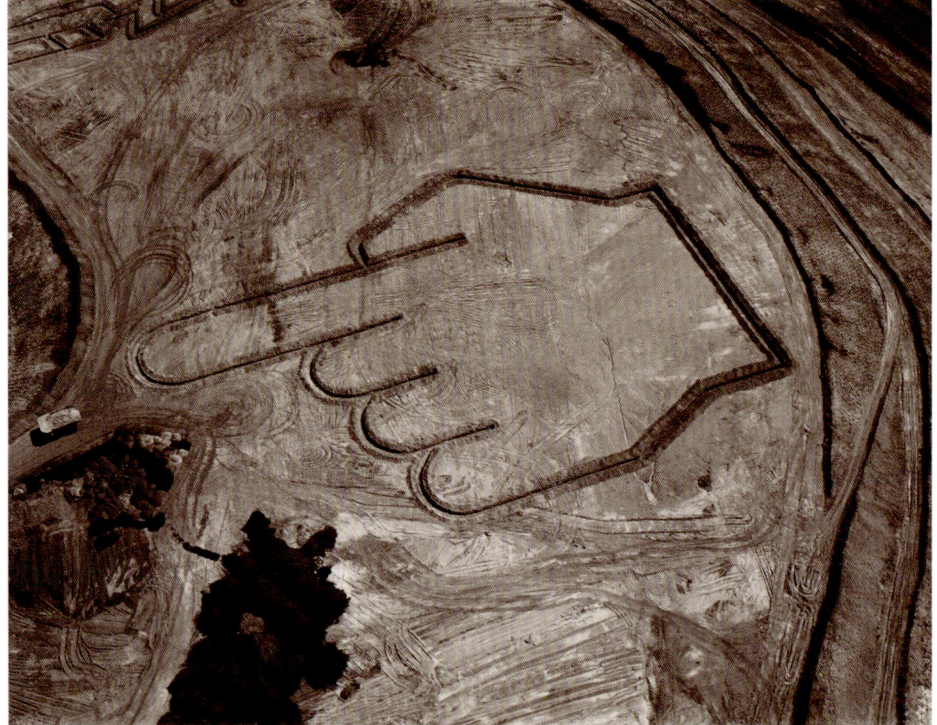

Top
Vik Muniz
Outlet (Fabrica, Iron Mine),
from *Earthworks*, 2005

Bottom
Vik Muniz
Pointing Hand (Itabira, Iron Mine),
from *Earthworks*, 2006

48

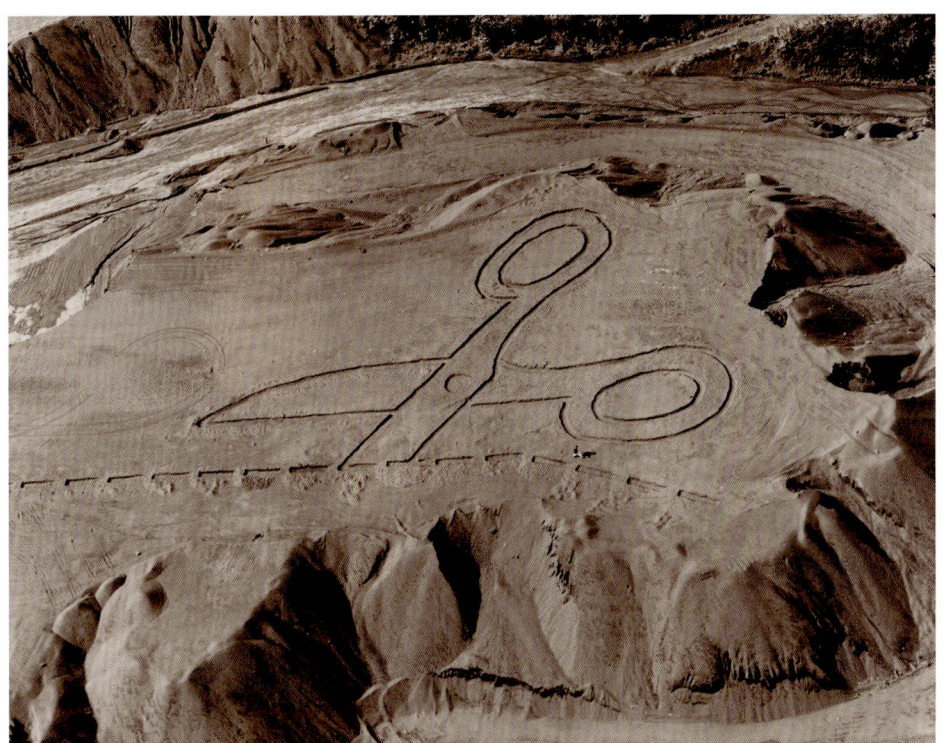

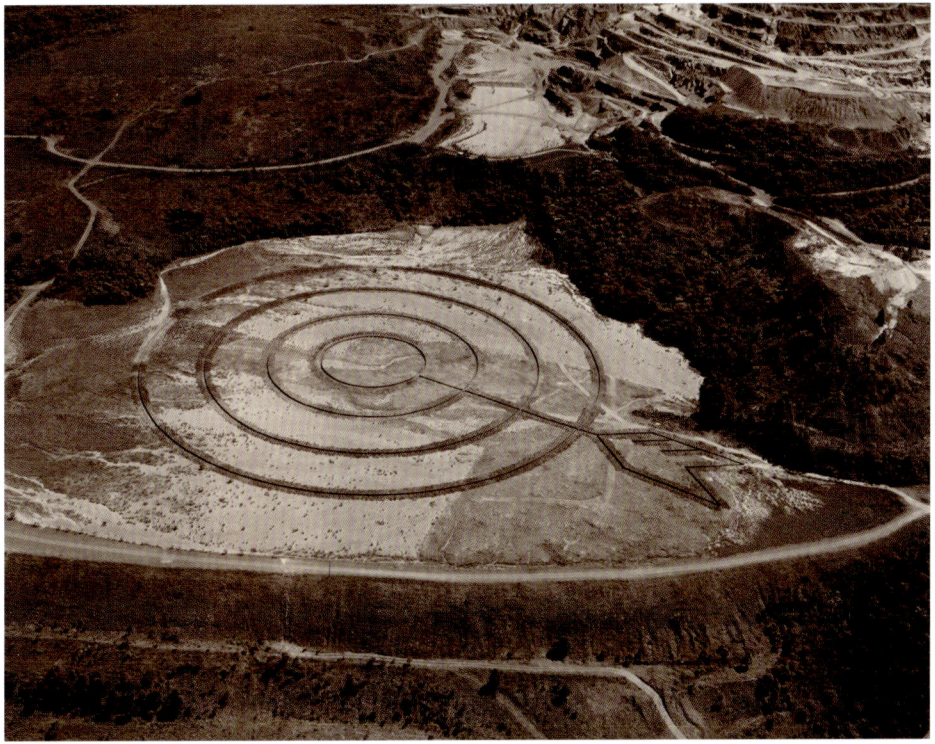

Top
Vik Muniz
Scissors (The Sarzedo Drawings),
from *Earthworks,* 2002

Bottom
Vik Muniz
Target (Fazendão, Iron Mine),
from *Earthworks,* 2005

49

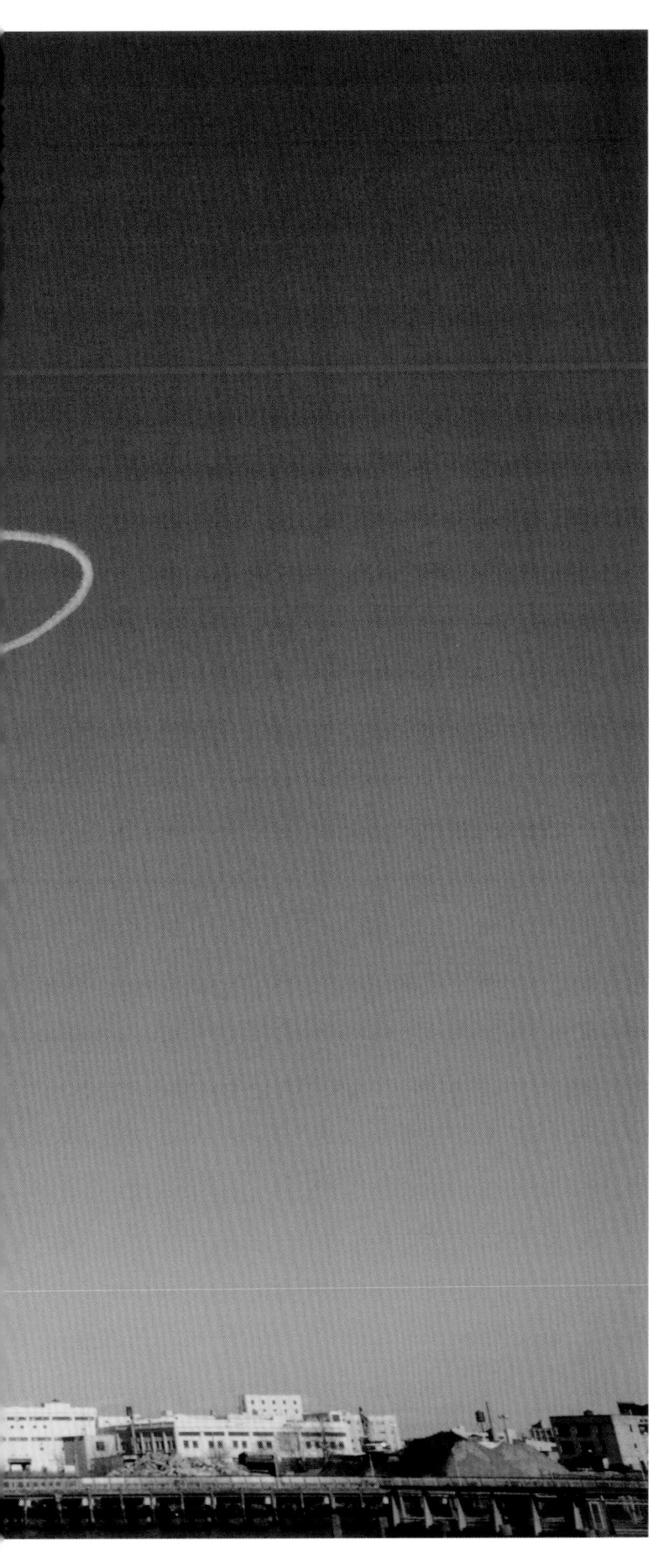

Vik Muniz
Cloud Cloud, 59th Bridge,
from *Pictures of Clouds*, 2002

Inside and Out

When I first saw Cindy Sherman's film stills, I was new to contemporary art, but I understood that she was someone, like me, who was trying to find herself, who was navigating the limbo between our inner lives and the dreams we see projected in movie theaters or glistening on television screens. Her work was about the concept of aesthetic distance, which had become a primary concern of the first generation of artists to grow up entirely under the spell of television. This idea of representation's outside and inside has always been present in my work as well.

I decided to become an artist one afternoon at the Metropolitan Museum of Art. There was a show called *Liechtenstein: The Princely Collections*, which included a lot of works by Peter Paul Rubens. Rubens was the Jeff Koons of his time—he had at least as many assistants, and his paintings reflected the zeitgeist. There was nudity, abundance, luxury. At the museum I saw people look at one part of the painting, then another, like they were switching channels. His art was the kind that makes TV seem obsolete.

In an adjacent room, there was a long line of people. Like any good Brazilian, when I see a line, I go stand in it. Finally I reached the head of the line, and there was the portrait of a little girl named Clara Serena, Rubens's five-year-old daughter.

Anyone who draws knows that when you make a portrait of someone you know well, you overlook certain things. You see the drawing as a symbol of what they represent to you affectively. It's hard to dispassionately draw a person you know and love. In this picture, however, Rubens drew his beloved daughter, a beautiful girl, with all her imperfections, all the little dissymmetries—one eye is slightly lower than the other, an eyebrow is slightly longer, the mouth is a little crooked—without sacrificing an ounce of his affection for the subject.

I waited in that line ten times, until the museum closed. And I knew that this was what I wanted, to make art that relied on the separation between inside and outside.

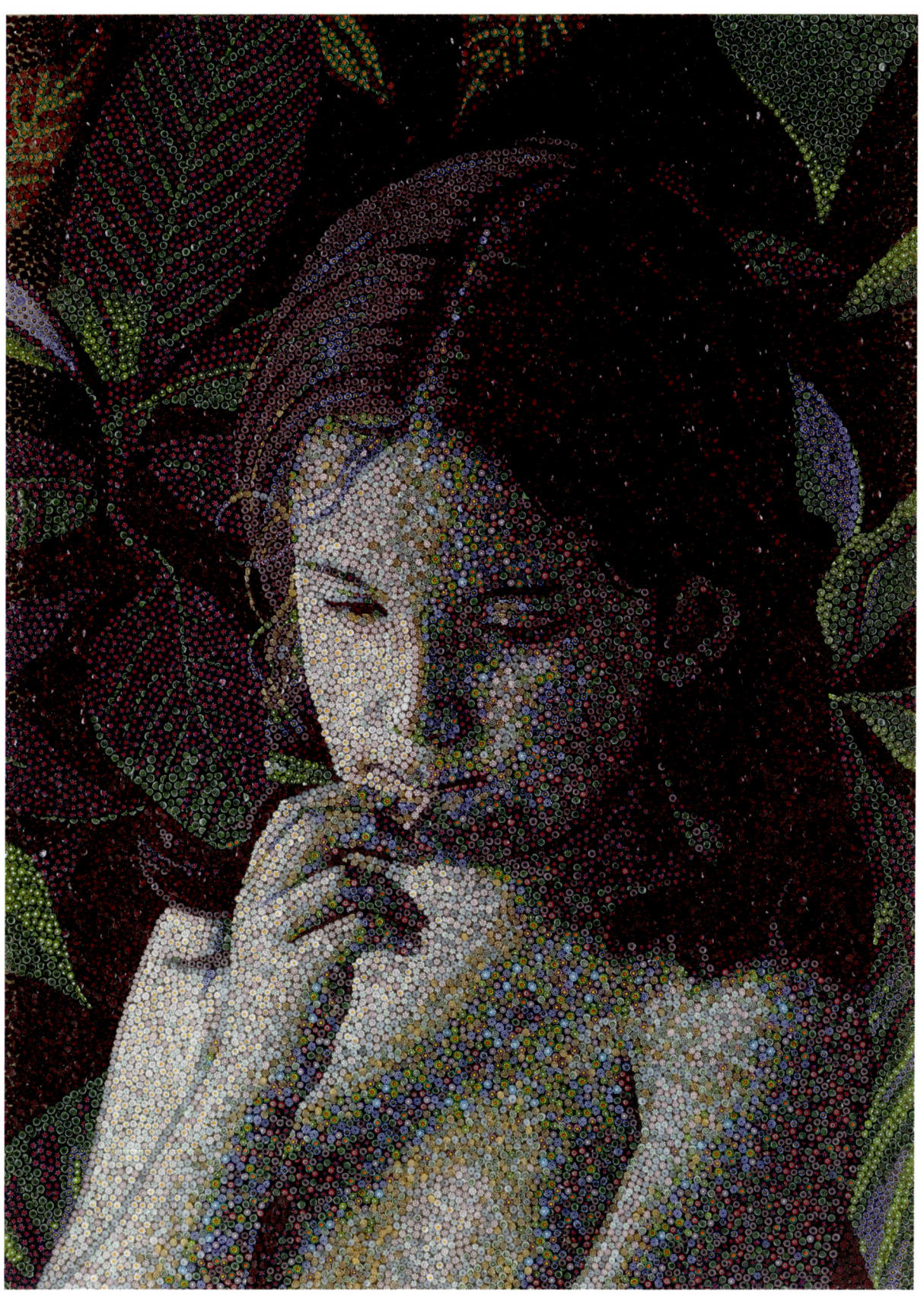

Vik Muniz
Dora (Murrine), 2019

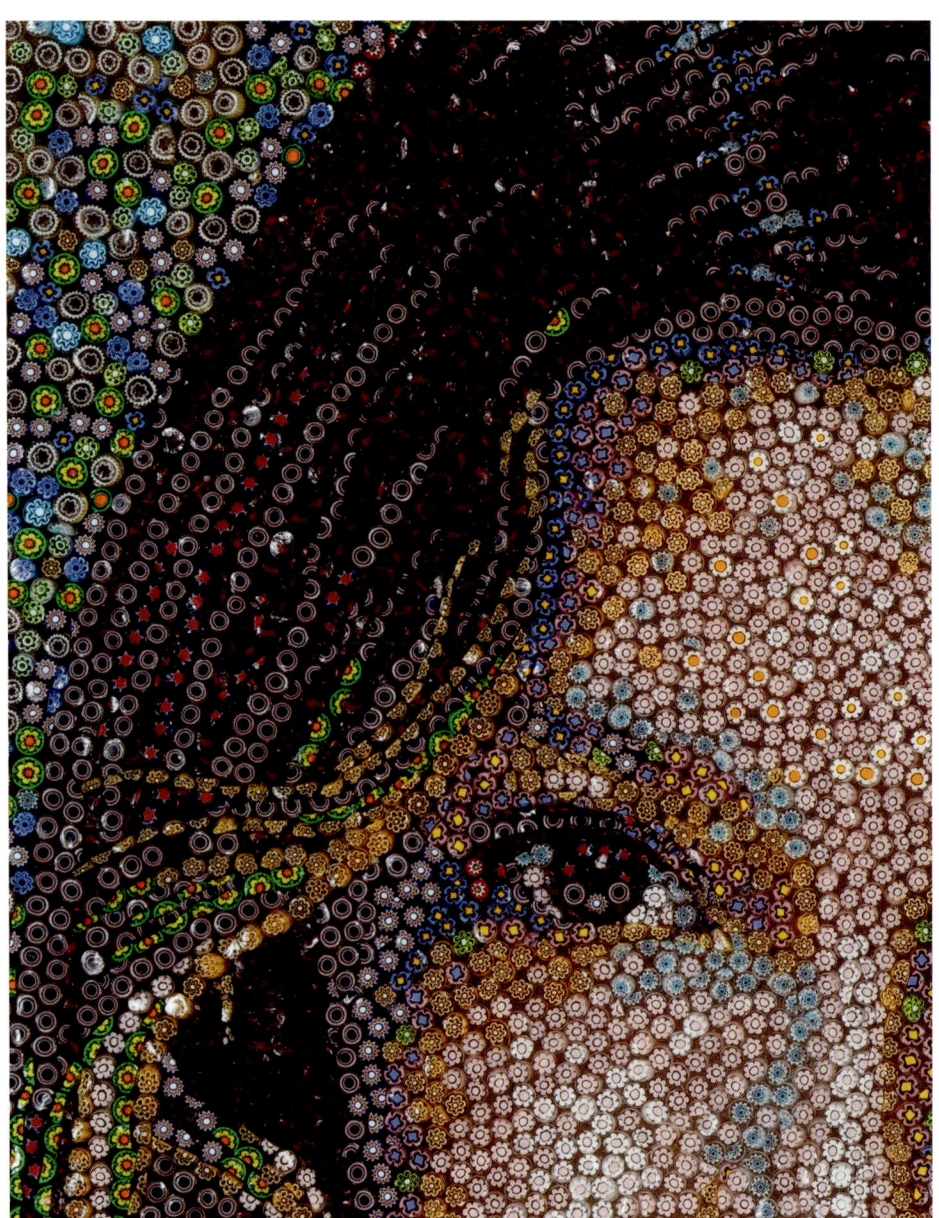

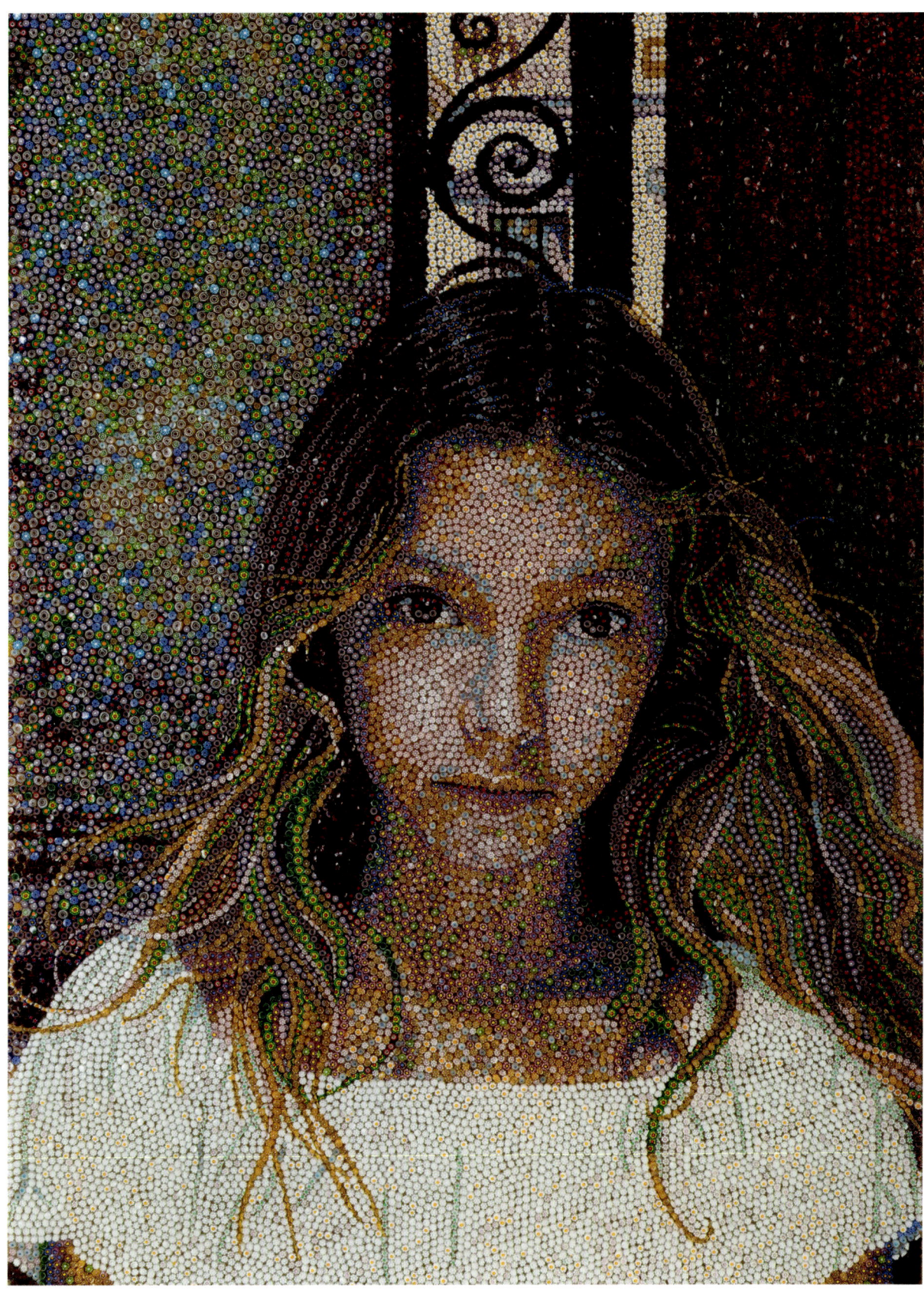

Vik Muniz
Mina (Murrine), 2019

Connection

In the early 1990s there was a deep recession, and I thought about leaving art. First, though, I did something all artists should do when they start having doubts: take a vacation. I flew to Saint Kitts in the Caribbean and spent fifteen days on a beach. I got to know some of the kids who played there, and I took their pictures. On my last day, a girl named Valentina took me to meet her parents. They were completely different from her or the other kids—they were weary, sad, heavy people because they spent sixteen hours a day harvesting sugar cane.

When I went back to Brazil, I read "Sugar," a poem by Ferreira Gullar that asks, Where does sugar come from? Does it come from a store? From a warehouse? The poem ends, "In dark mills / men with hard / and sour lives / produced the pure white sugar / I'm about to use / to sweeten my coffee / this morning / in Ipanema" I was drinking coffee, and I decided to get some sugar and a piece of black paper to draw portraits of the kids from my vacation photos.

I first showed this work at the back of a gallery in SoHo. Somehow a reporter from the *New York Times* saw it, and three weeks later I was invited to participate in the show *New Photography 13* at the Museum of Modern Art. Seven months later I had a midcareer retrospective at the International Center of Photography (ICP), which was funny because I had just begun my career as an artist. Around the time of that show, I noticed curators were categorizing me as a photographer. I was self-conscious about it, because I had never studied photography. And although I felt really good about the show, something was missing.

There's a UPS driver, a fellow from Jamaica named William, who used to deliver packages to my third-floor studio. Every time he came up, he would ask, "What are you working on, man?" One day I had one of my big thread pieces hanging on the studio wall, and he said, "Hmm, I don't like this one." I asked why. "Because, before, when you were making them small, there was a relationship between the size of the thread and the size of the picture. Now that you've blown it up, it's not good."

I had to put the same picture in a group show that afternoon. After the opening, I sat across from a famous art critic. He looked at me and said, "You're Vik, right? I've been following your work. I like it a lot, but your latest stuff I don't like." I asked why. "Because, before, when you were making it small, there was a relationship between the size of the thread and the size of the picture. But now you've blown it up." I said, "You must be right, because my UPS driver said exactly the same thing."

While I was preparing to show the six *Sugar Children* pictures for the first time, William noticed them on my studio wall. "What is this?"

"What do you think it is?" (I like to answer a question with a question.)

"Is it art or something?"

We went on like this for a while, and by the end of the conversation, he seemed to really like the work. This whole story is to say that when William came to my opening at ICP, he brought along a seventh sugar child: a portrait I had made of his child. To know that this series was hanging at the ICP, in a museum in Saint Kitts, and on the mantelpiece of William's home—that it was pleasing people in all of those places—was one of the most complete experiences I've ever had as an artist.

From then on, I resolved to make art that pleases people like my mother. You know a show is good when the museum's maintenance people get excited. It affects people physically first. You can pile any theory you want on top, but first you must achieve a response in the viewer that's entirely instinctive, primal, and perceptive.

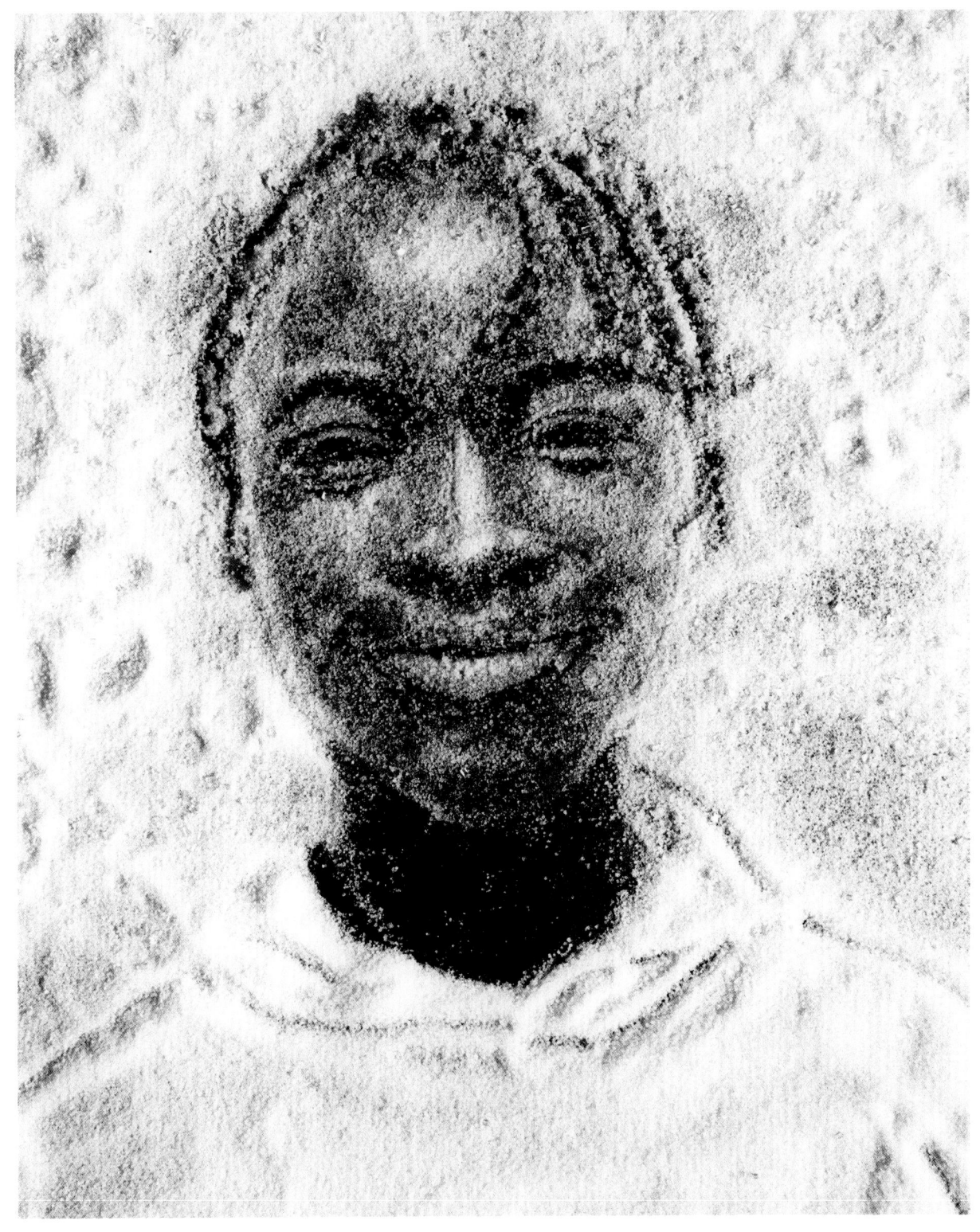

Vik Muniz
Valicia Bathes in Sunday Clothes,
from *Sugar Children*, 1996

57

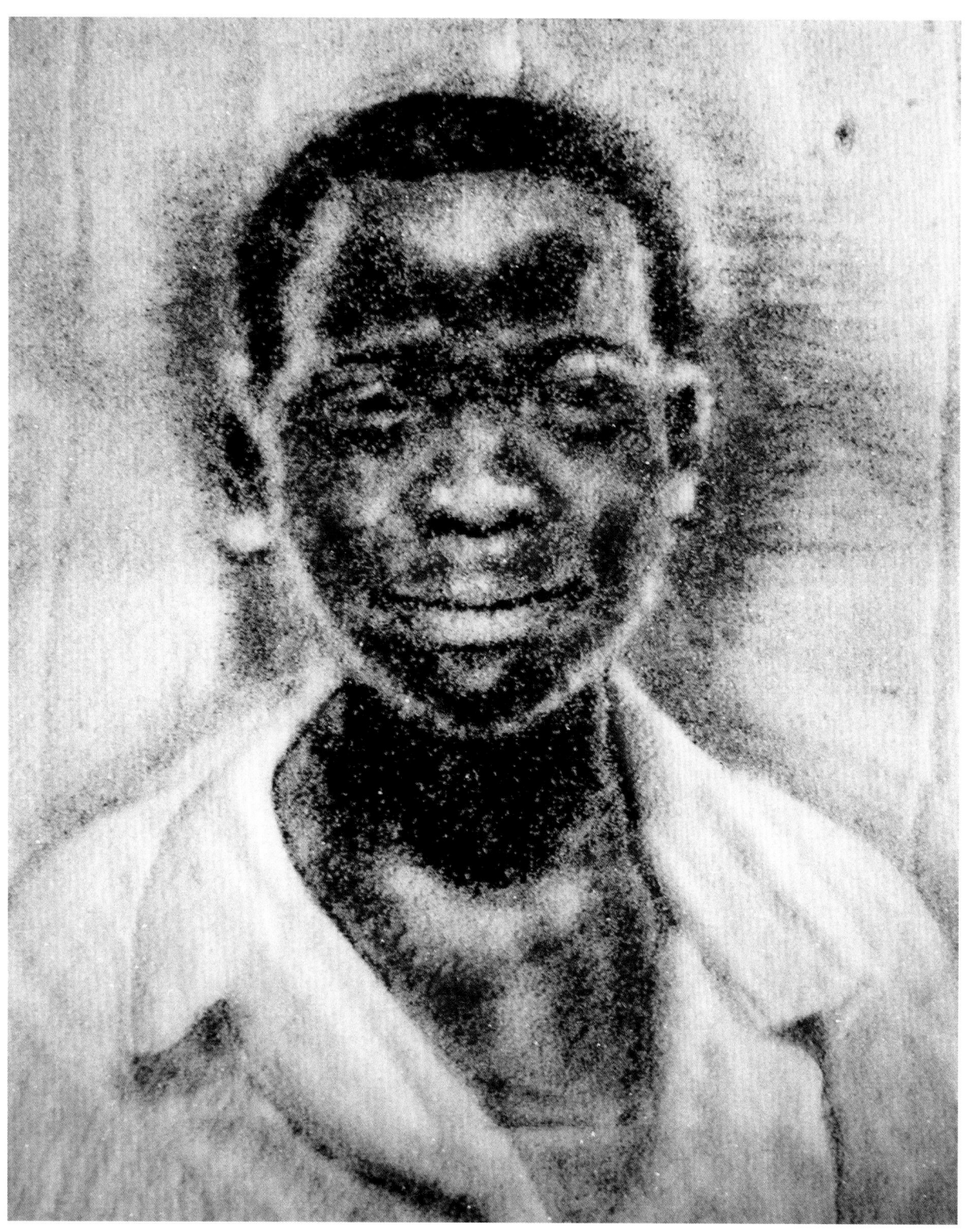

Vik Muniz
Lil' Calist Can't Swim,
from *Sugar Children*, 1996

58

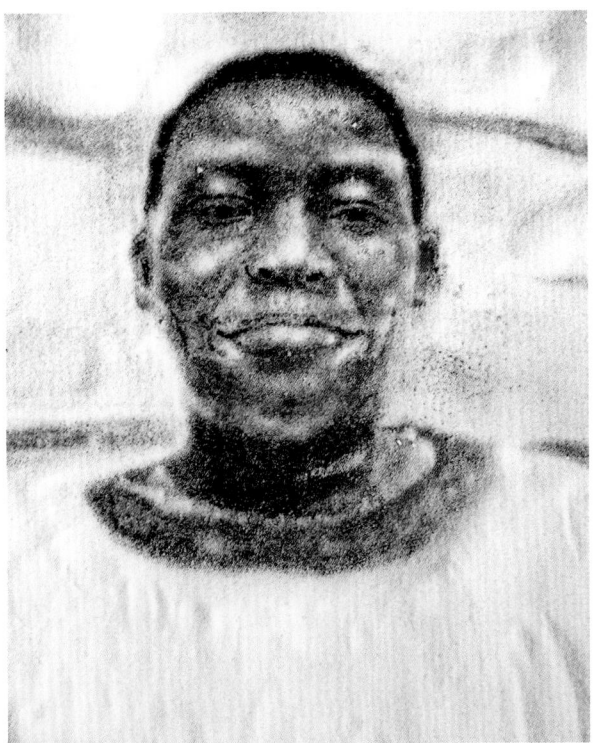

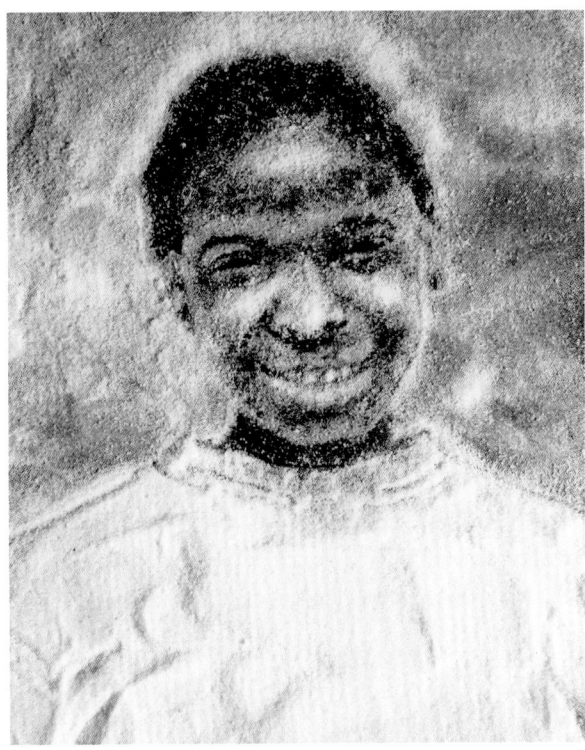

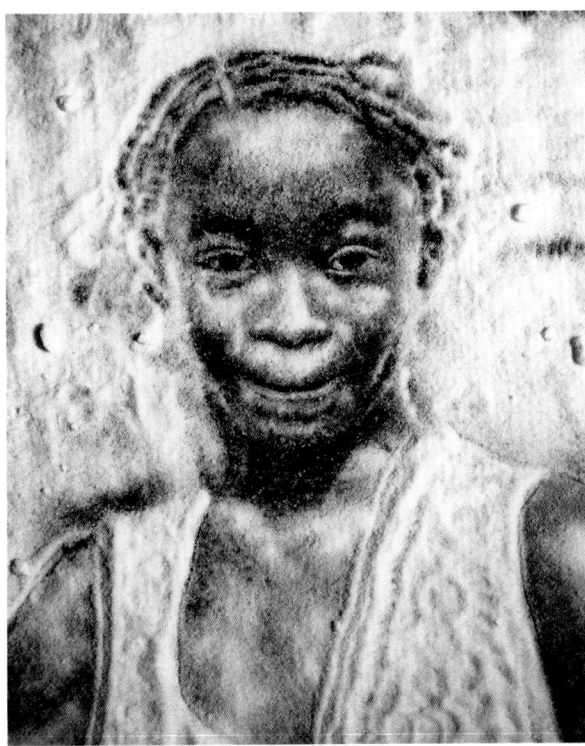

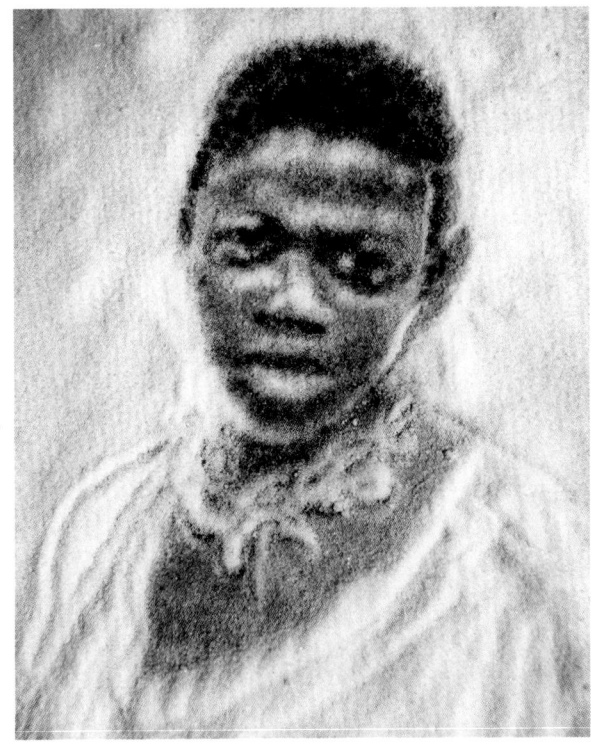

Top left
Vik Muniz
Big James Sweats Buckets,
from *Sugar Children*, 1996

Top right
Vik Muniz
Jacynthe Loves Orange Juice,
from *Sugar Children*, 1996

Bottom left
Vik Muniz
Valentina, the Fastest,
from *Sugar Children*, 1996

Bottom right
Vik Muniz
Ten Ten's Weed Necklace,
from *Sugar Children*, 1996

59

Objects with an Identity Crisis

When I first became an artist, I rented a studio, painted the walls white, and sat down in a chair. "Now I am going to make some art," I said. "Art, come!"

But art is not a thing. Art is a process. I realized that the only creative experience I'd had up to that point was with advertising and psychology. So I decided to make objects that had an identity crisis, objects with a discrepancy between what they were and what they represented.

I made *Clown Skull*, a remnant from a long-ago generation of Brazilian entertainers, and the Ashanti Joystick, which is so old it was made for Atari. I made a "travel" edition of the *Encyclopedia Britannica* bound in a single volume. I made *Pre-Colombian Coffee Maker* (in New York City a lot of the coffee is Colombian, but this is pre-Colombian). I made *Tupperware Sarcophagus* for people who think the afterlife is going to be a long journey. I made the Mickey Mouse *Nail Fetish*. And I made half of a tombstone for people who are not dead yet.

The apotheosis of this project was when a photographer came to document the sculptures. He arrived with lights and two assistants. All the attention was on the objects. It was amazing. When I saw the pictures he took, they were so sharp and beautiful, I didn't care about the objects anymore.

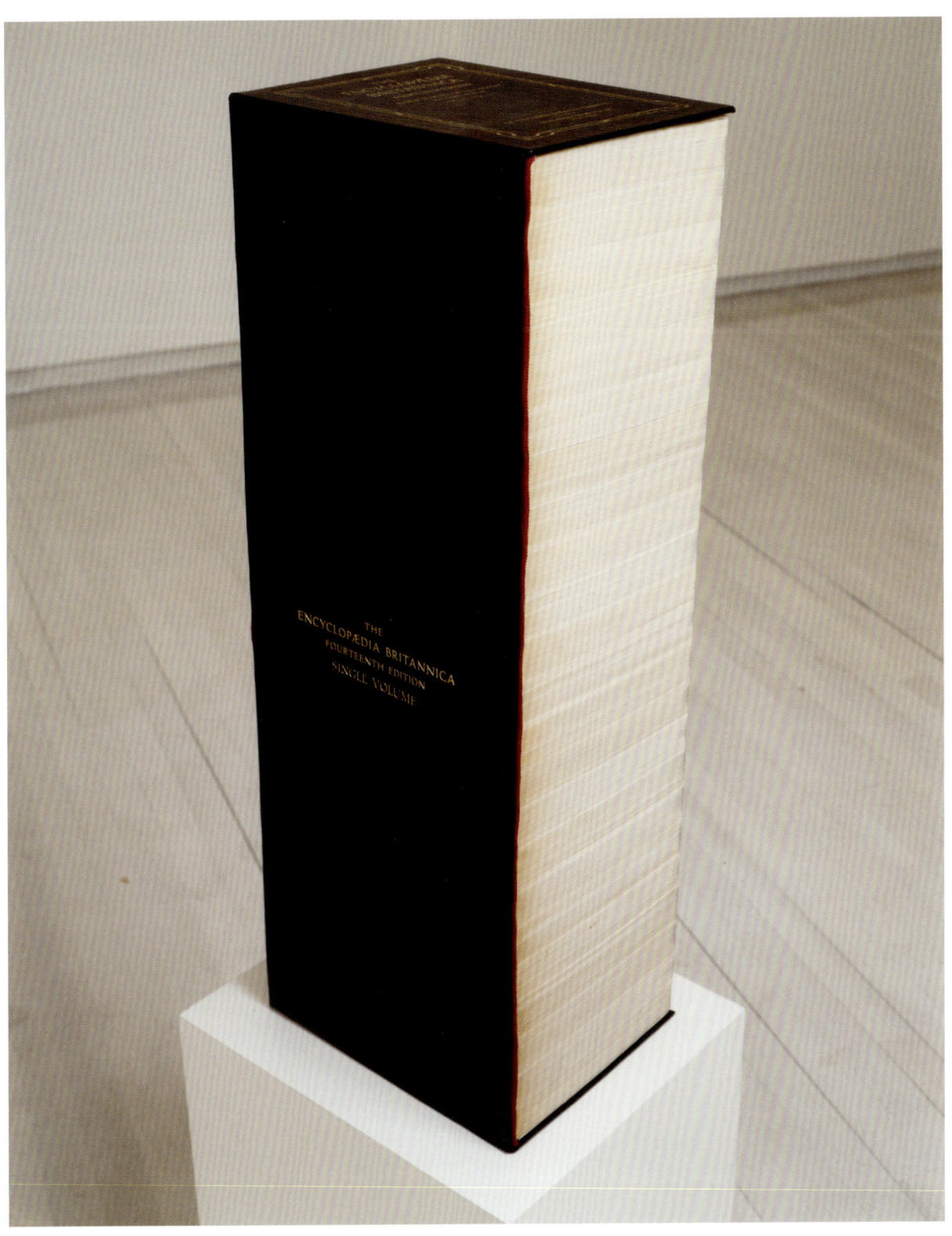

Vik Muniz
The Big Book, 1989

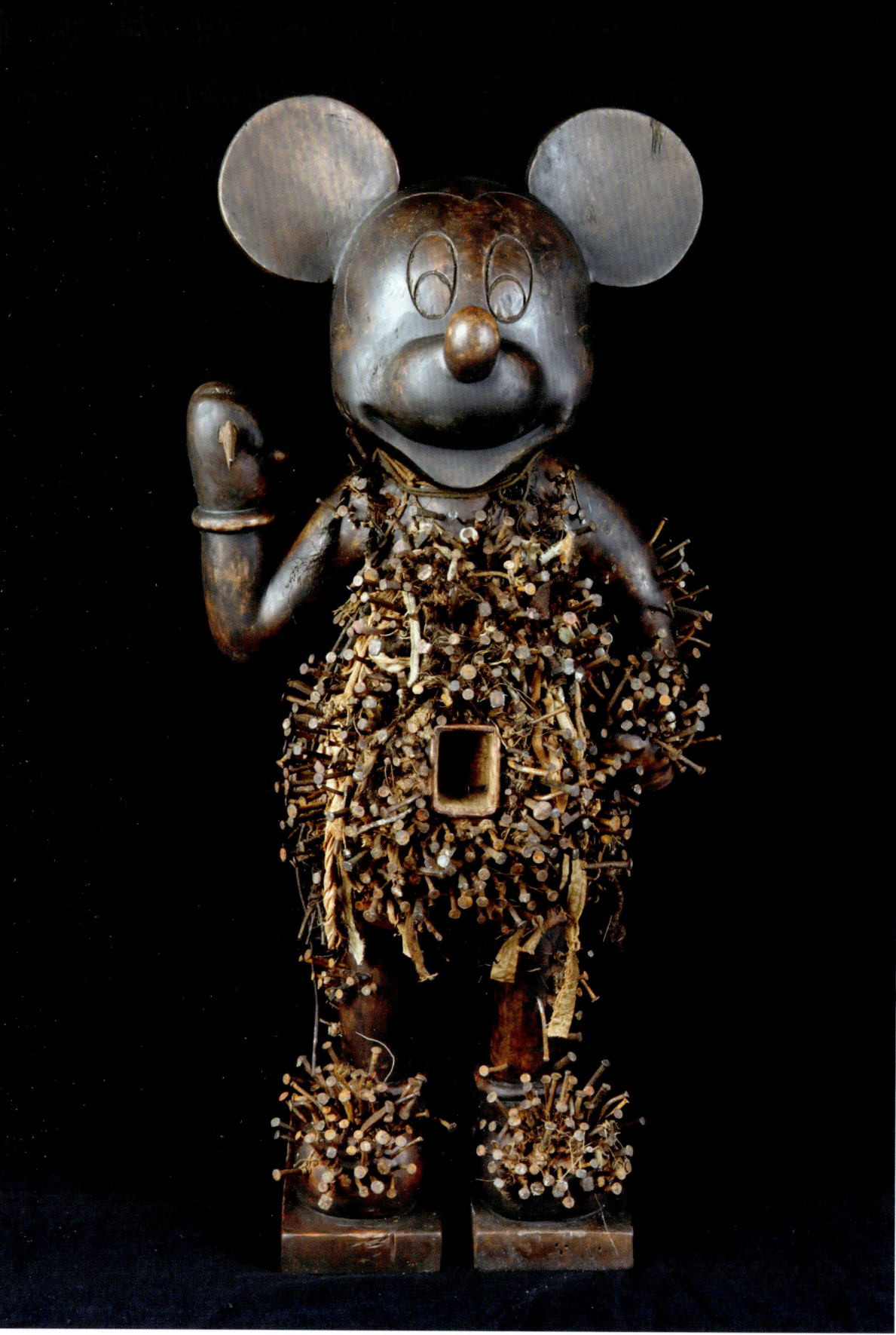

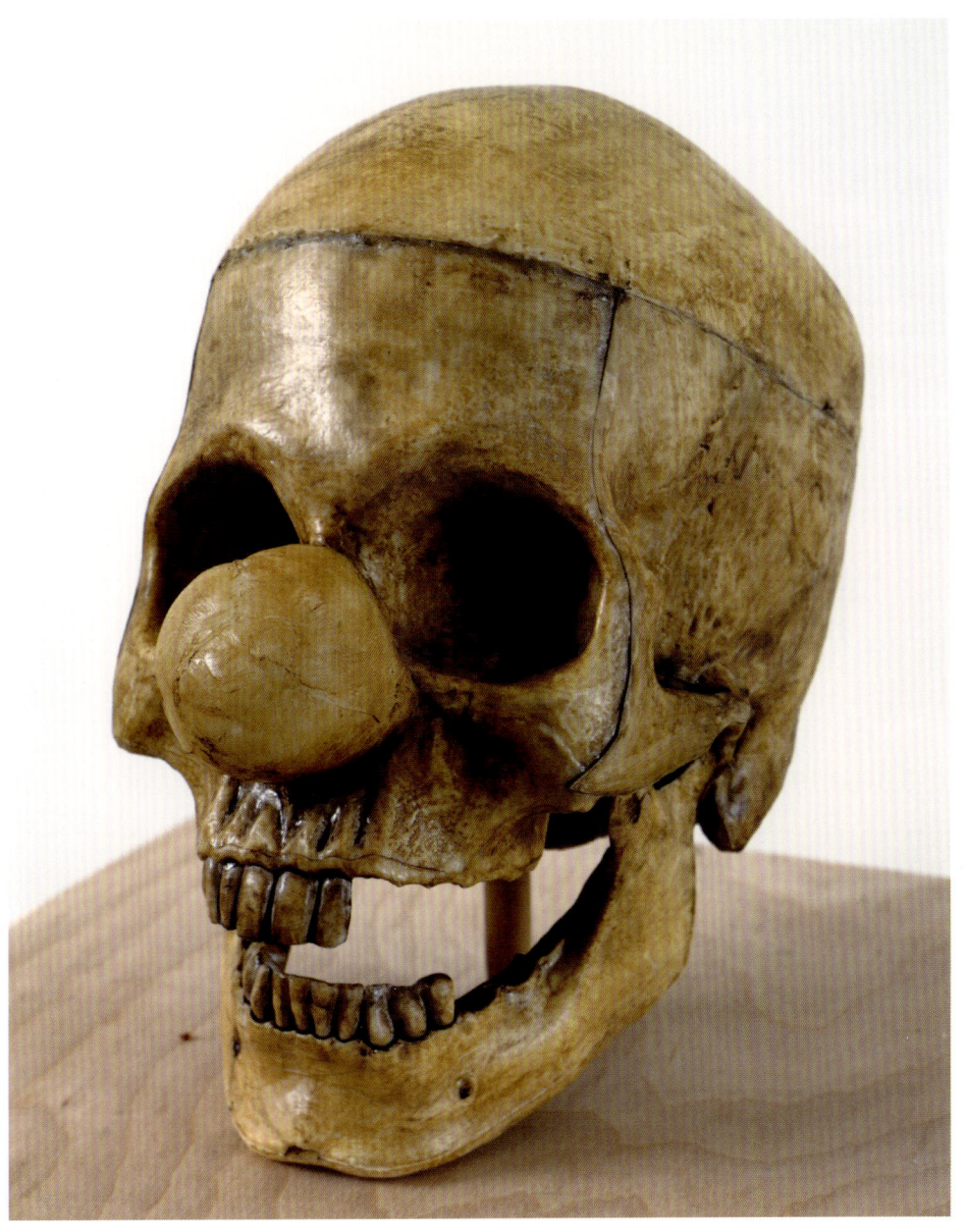

Left
Vik Muniz
Nail Fetish, 2010

Top
Vik Muniz
Clown Skull, 1989

63

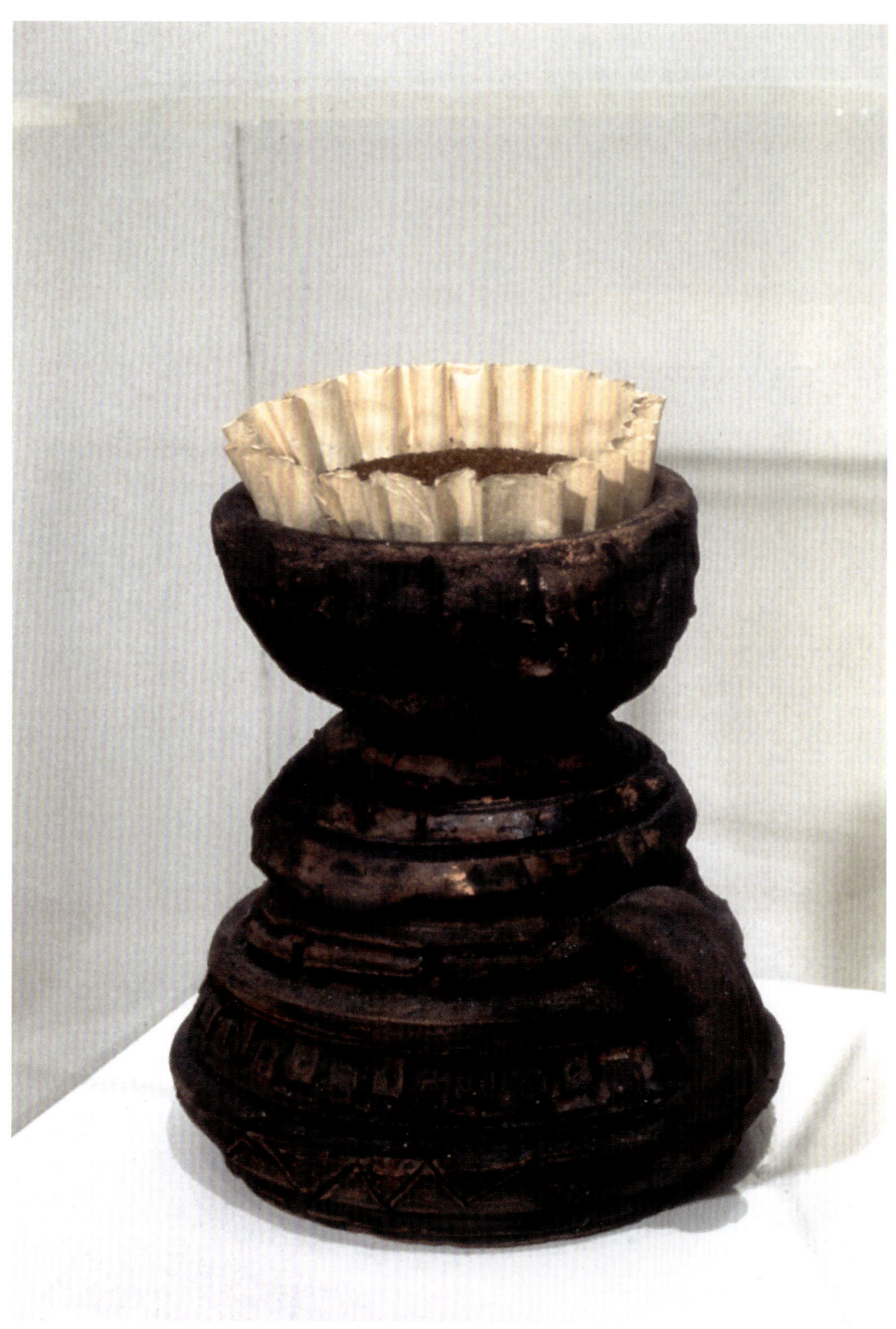

Vik Muniz
Pre-Colombian Coffee Maker, 1989

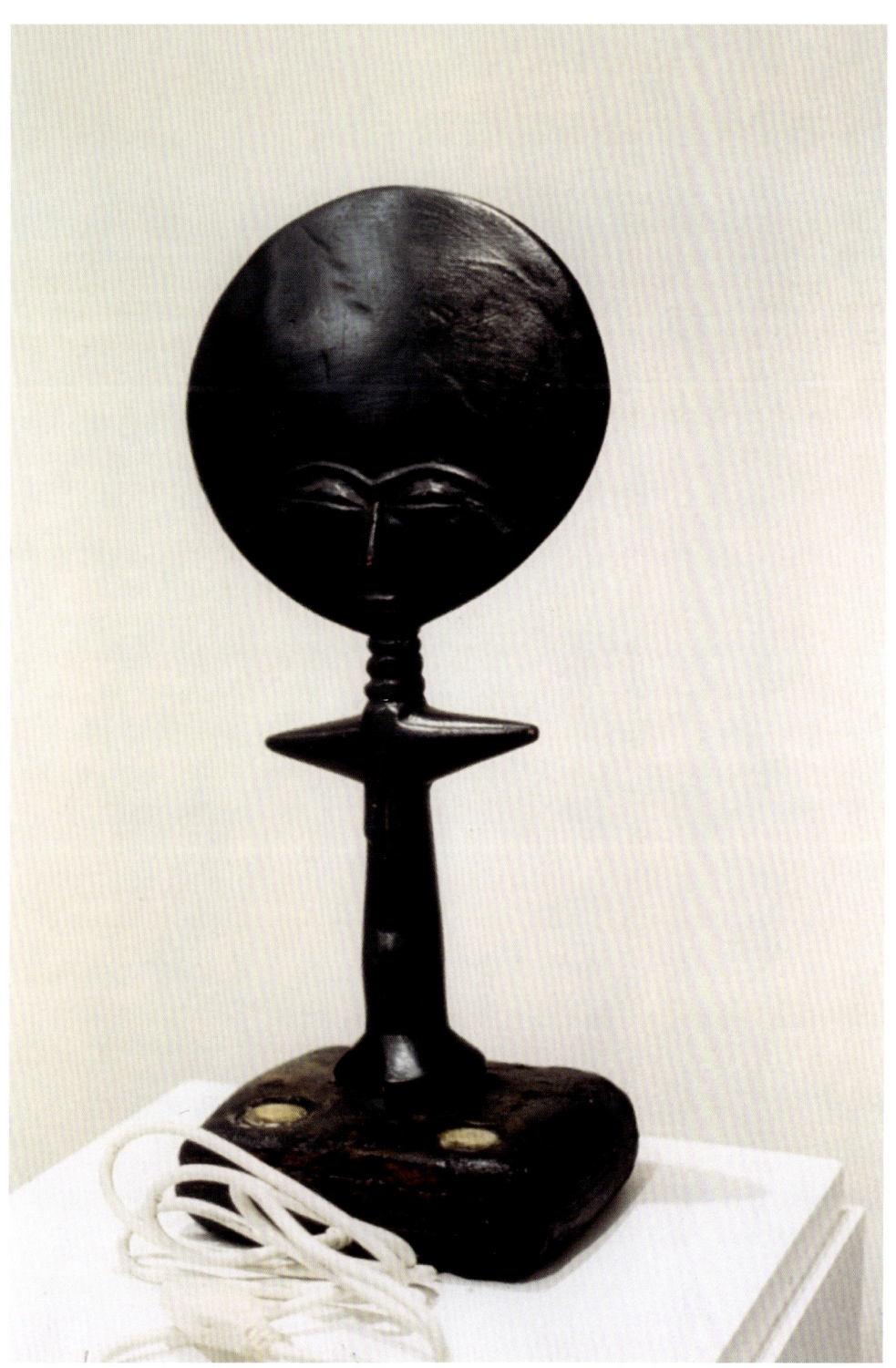

Vik Muniz
Souvenir #18 (Ashanti Joystick), 1989

An Artwork
Is a Mechanism

In 2002, I was at the Guggenheim while they were rehanging a display of paintings from the permanent collection, and I saw the back of Picasso's *Woman Ironing*, from 1904. Somehow it made me think of an experience I'd had forty years before, at the Museu de Arte de São Paulo. The museum's architect, Lina Bo Bardi, had decided that the paintings would be hung on glass panels. As a seven-year-old visiting the museum for the first time, I wasn't as interested in the pictures as I was in the hardware, the cobwebs, and all the other things I could see on the backs of the paintings.

At the Guggenheim, I turned to the curator. "Wow, can I take a picture of the back of that Picasso?" She said I could do it the next day, so I returned and ended up taking a whole bunch of pictures. Then I asked Kirk Varnedoe at the Museum of Modern Art if I could take a picture of the back of Picasso's *Les Demoiselles d'Avignon*. He said "Sure, Vik." He didn't take much persuading, which made me feel important, I must admit.

I took photographs of the backs of famous paintings for years before I decided to turn them into objects. When I had all the information I needed, I started with Van Gogh's *Starry Night*.

Process—what actually *moves* media—is just as important as the images themselves. When you look at the back of a painting, it tells you a story. It's dirty. It bears traces of the studio where the artist painted it. When I first exhibited these *Verso* objects, people would walk into the gallery and think the installation hadn't happened yet. But when they stepped closer and saw that the painting might be a Van Gogh or a Picasso or a Rembrandt, they'd say, "Wait—it can't be!"

It took six years of bugging the people at the Louvre before they let me photograph the back of the Mona Lisa. The painting only comes out of its vault on the first Monday of November each year. On that day, no staff are allowed inside the museum. We were given badges that allowed us to walk through the building by ourselves, which was its own privilege, but when we arrived at the painting, the guards didn't trust us. The conservators became an important part of this project, because they began to help out. The entire panel around the Mona Lisa is state of the art, with a thick pane of glass that pops out. The devices on the back make it look like something from a James Bond film. There's an electronic band that monitors a vertical gap on the panel that was fixed in place with a butterfly joint in the nineteenth century; if the gap widens even one micron, somebody gets a text message. The same guy who designed the band also designed the one for my Mona Lisa. During its annual maintenance the following year, the Louvre invited me to compare my creation to the real painting in front of the conservators and students. My work was brought in during a break. After shuffling both pieces, we asked everyone which back was real, and which one was fake. More than half of the viewers thought mine was the real one.

This idea of what lies on the other side of a work makes me think of time. There are watches that tell you the time, and there are watches that are so beautiful they make you *think* about time. Just like a clock, a work of art has a function. The verso is part of a larger mechanism, as intricate as the painting itself. The mechanics, the supports, whatever is on the back, is just as important as what's on the front. To really understand media, we have to consider both sides of the coin.

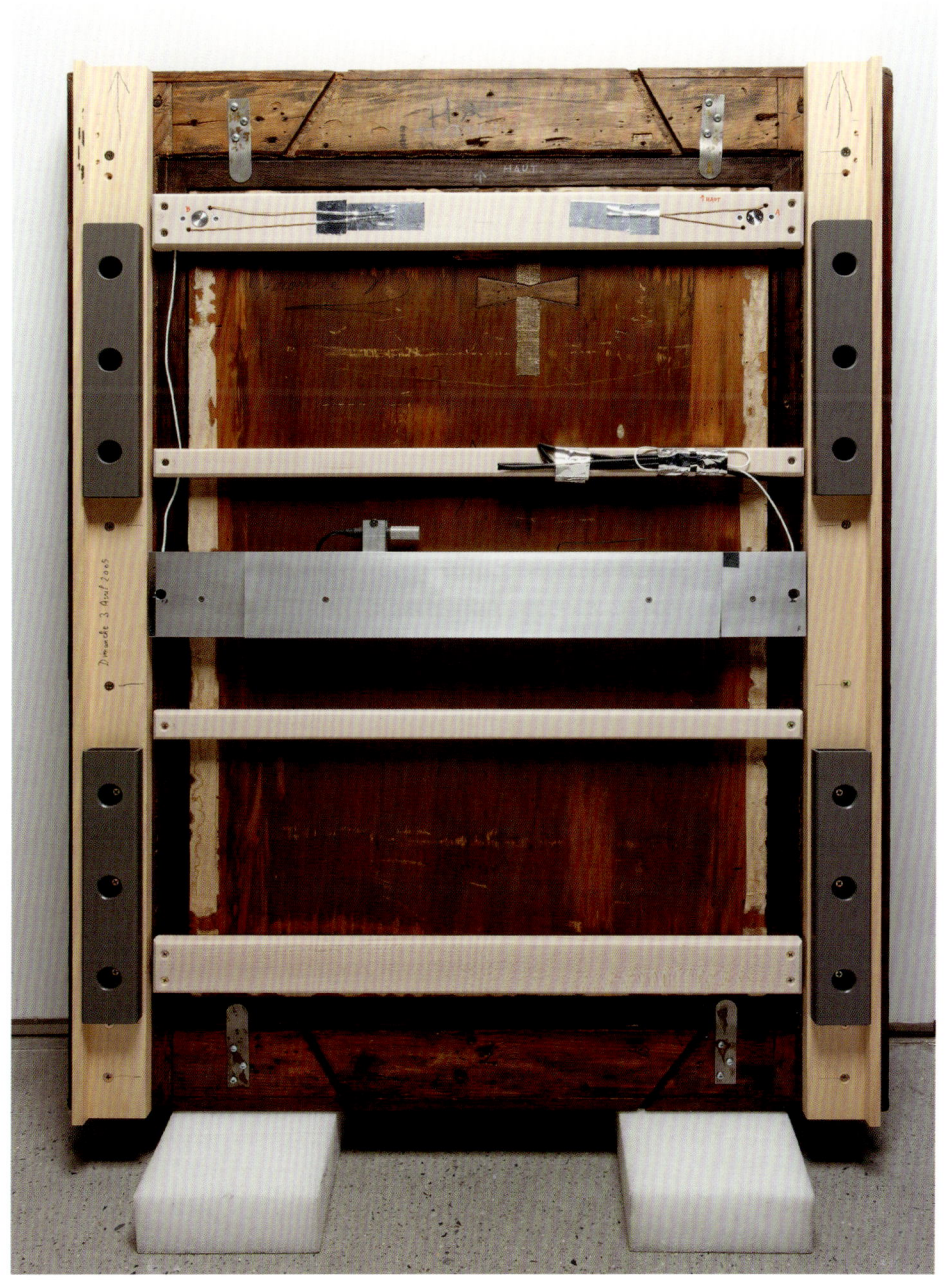

Vik Muniz
La Gioconda, from *Verso*, 2012

pp. 68–69
Exhibition view of *Vik Muniz: Verso*
at the Mauritshuis, The Hague,
Netherlands, 2016.
Photograph by Ivo Hoekstra

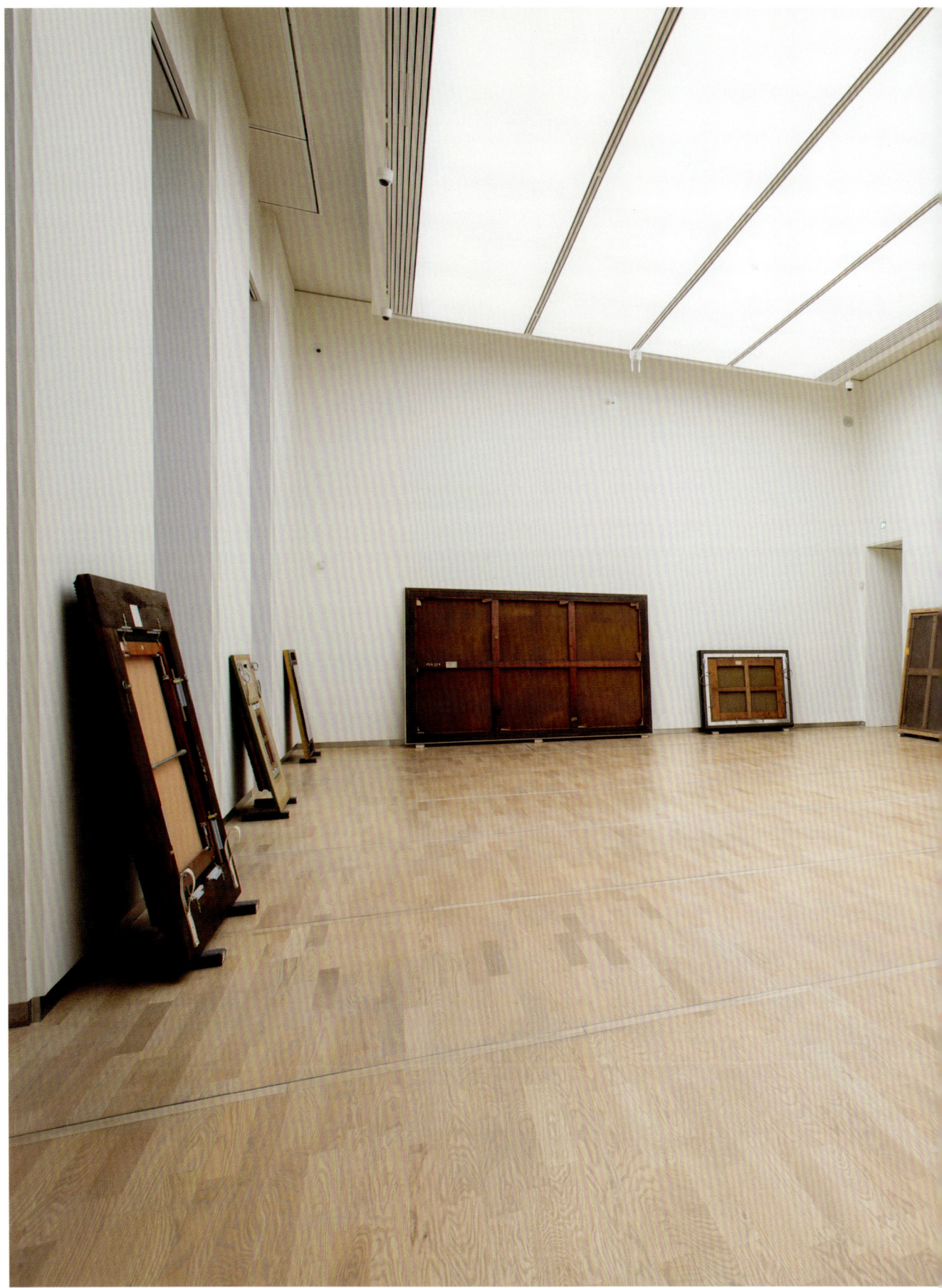

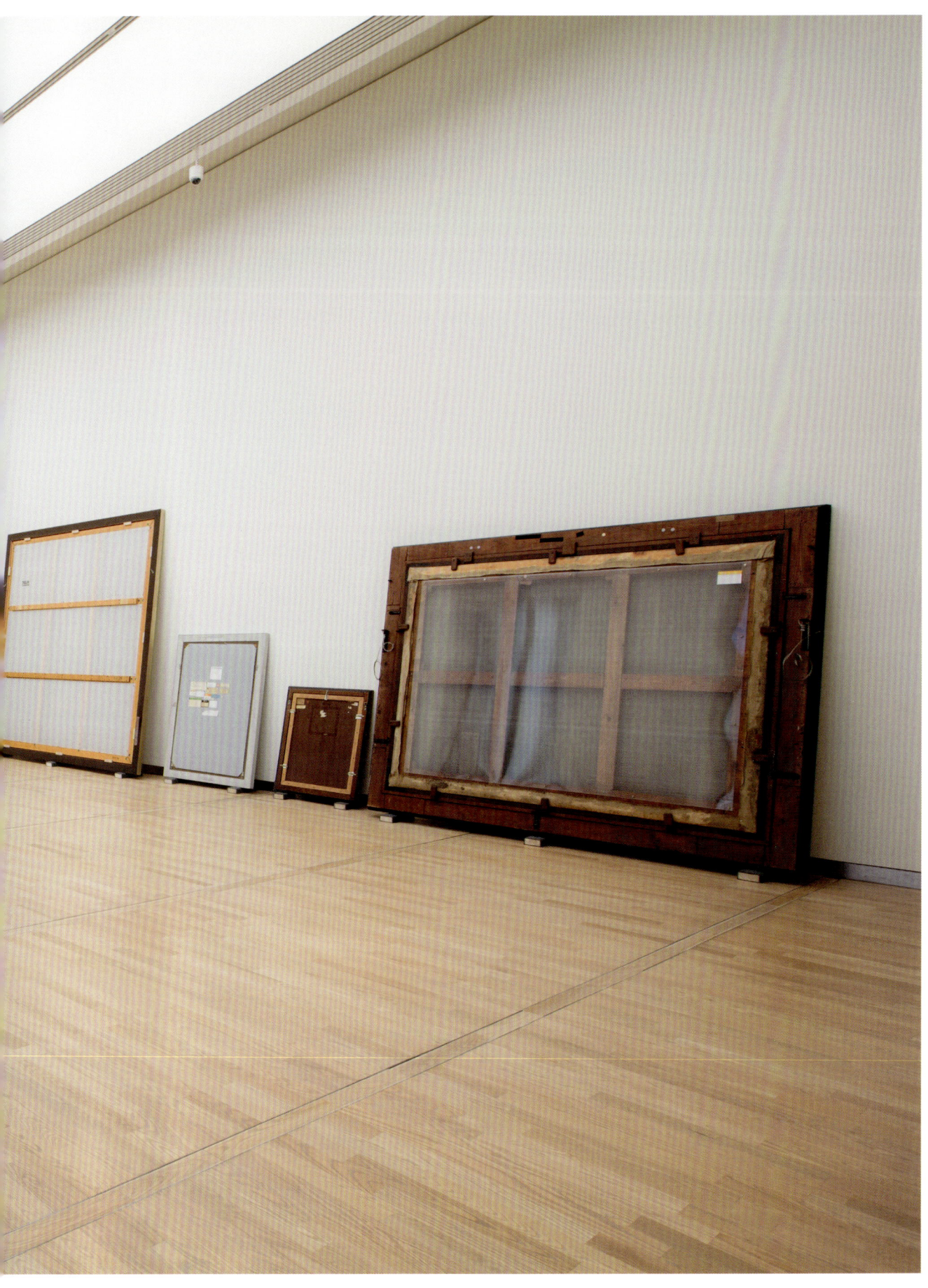

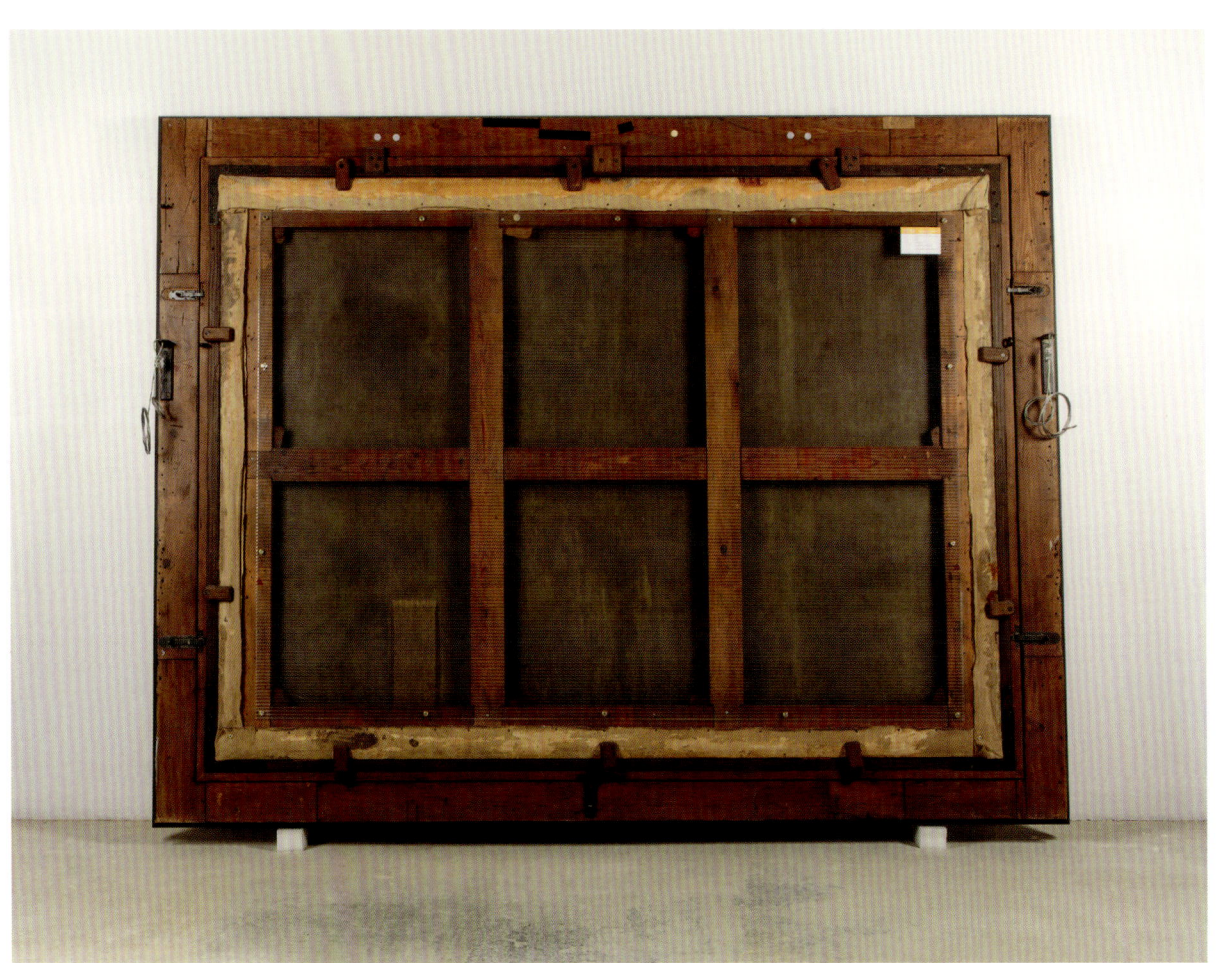

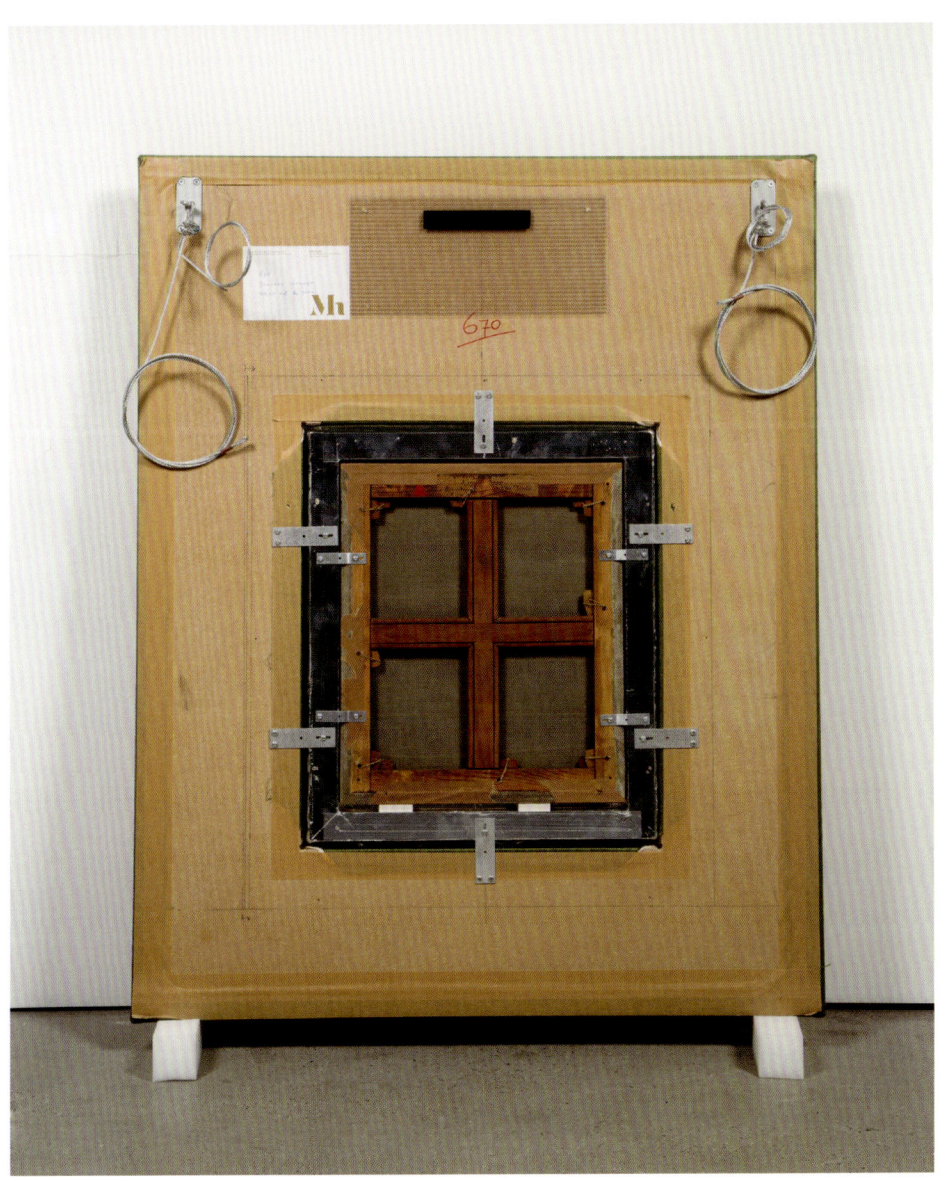

Vik Muniz
The Girl with a Pearl Earring,
from *Verso*, 2016

Perspective

The more space you have, the bigger your work becomes. As soon as I moved into a larger studio, I stopped working with materials like cotton or chocolate and began to make art out of objects. Toys had always fascinated me. They're a way for kids to interact with reality—we play with cars before we learn to drive, and we pretend to cook with plastic food before we do any actual cooking. When I made my first piece with objects, *Toy Soldier*, I was thinking of the direct relationship between the subject and the material. It was also a great excuse to go to toy stores.

People often say to me, "You're that guy who makes art out of weird things." But the truth is, when you put yourself in absurd situations, like making art with toys, you're exposed to different processes, and you find different paths to get to the artwork. I'll give myself this task of using something strange to draw a picture, something I haven't used before, so that I can put myself in a new mindset.

While I was making these pictures with toys, I wondered if I could go larger. I rented an even bigger space next to the largest landfill in Rio, in a dangerous neighborhood nicknamed the Gaza Strip. And I had the idea to make pictures out of garbage, with the help of people who lived there.

With these works, there's an ergonomic recognition. As soon as you notice an oil drum or a piano in the photograph, it gives you a clue about the perspective of the image. These works are shot at an angle from a tower sixty-five feet (twenty meters) high. The drawing on the floor is elongated, which means you can't see the picture until you climb the tower. Unless you change your vantage point, it looks like a meaningless pile of junk.

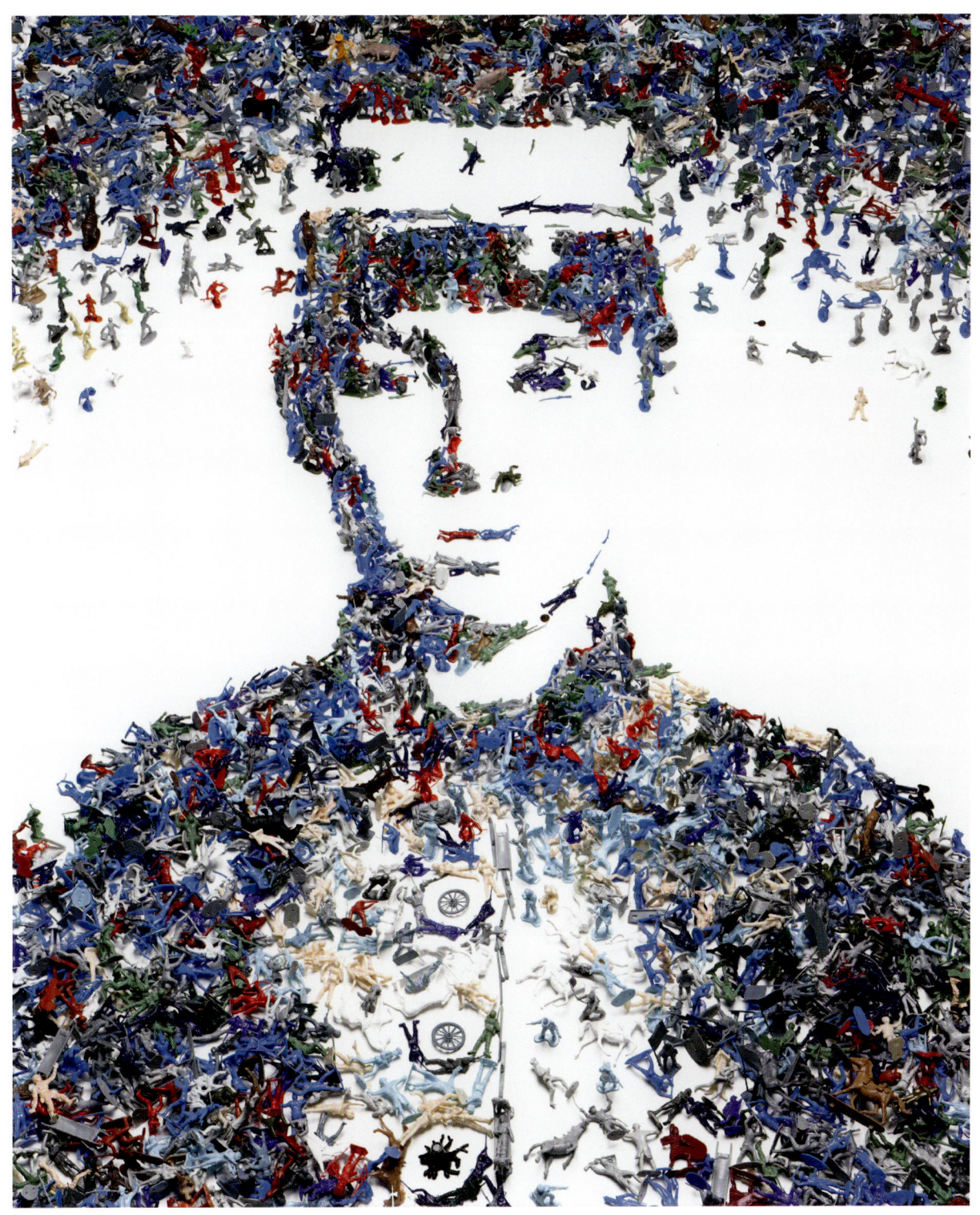

Vik Muniz
Toy Soldier, from *Monads*, 2003

73

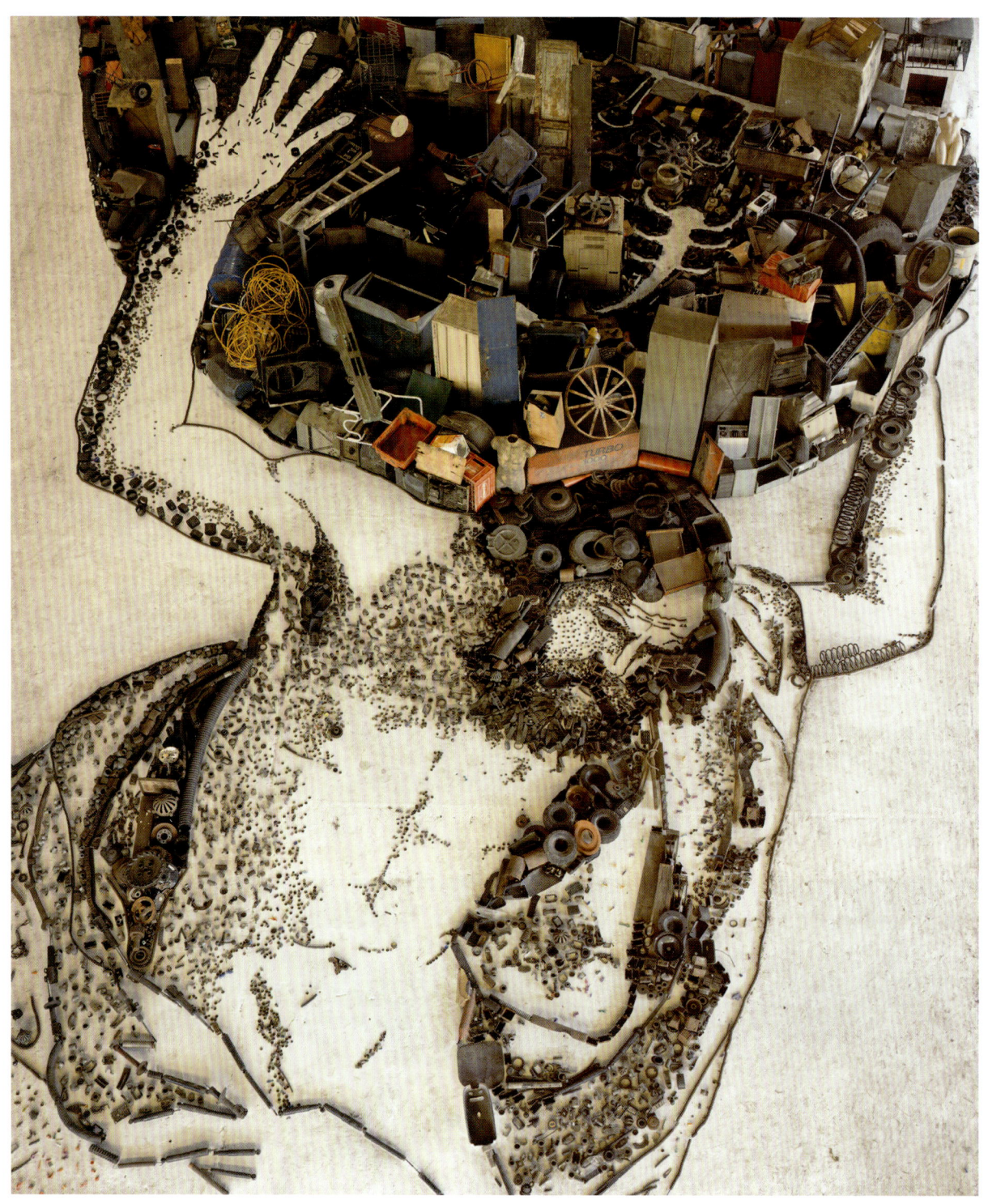

Vik Muniz
*Atlas, after Giovanni Francesco
Barbieri (Il Guercino),*
from *Pictures of Junk*, 2007

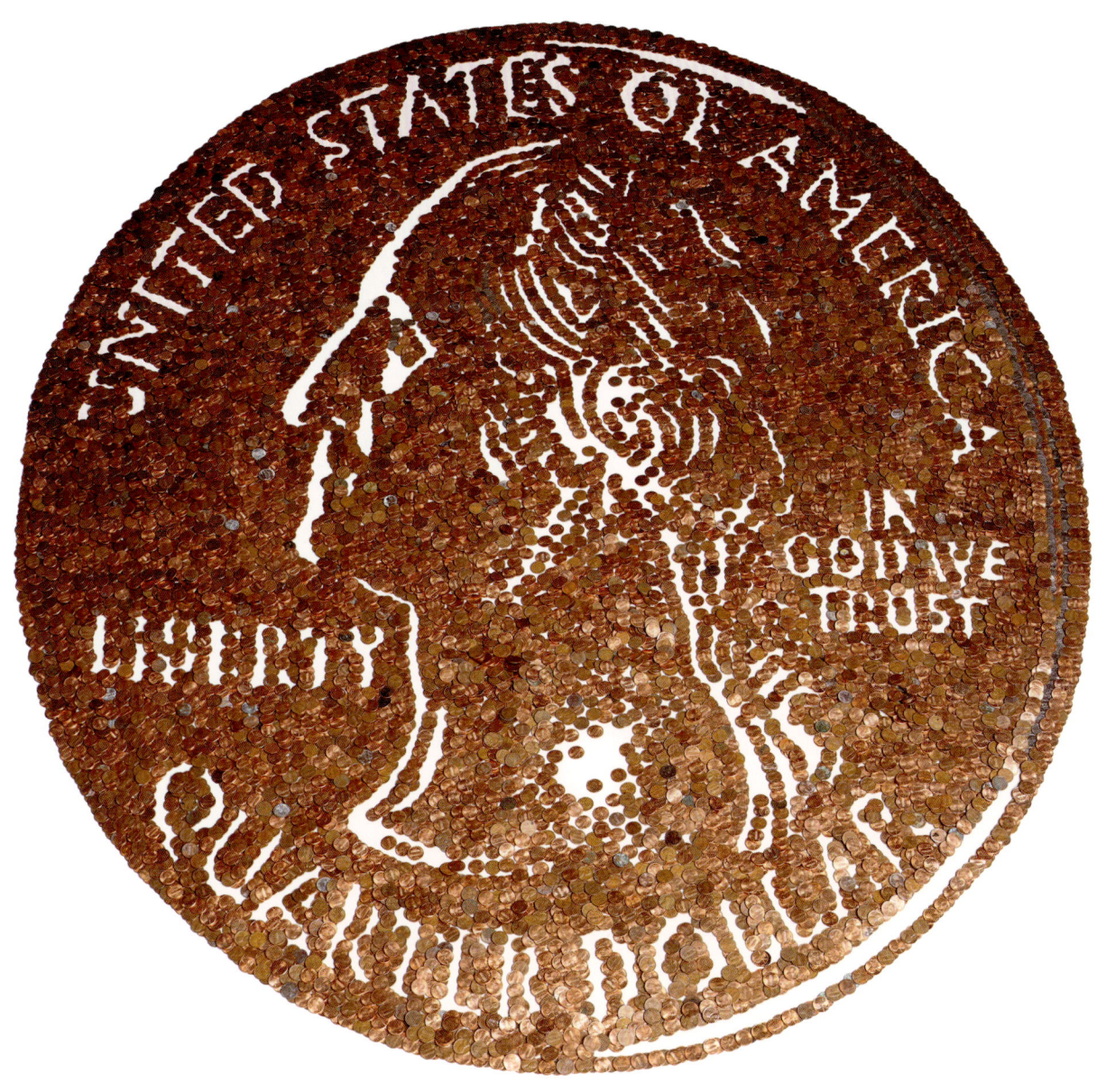

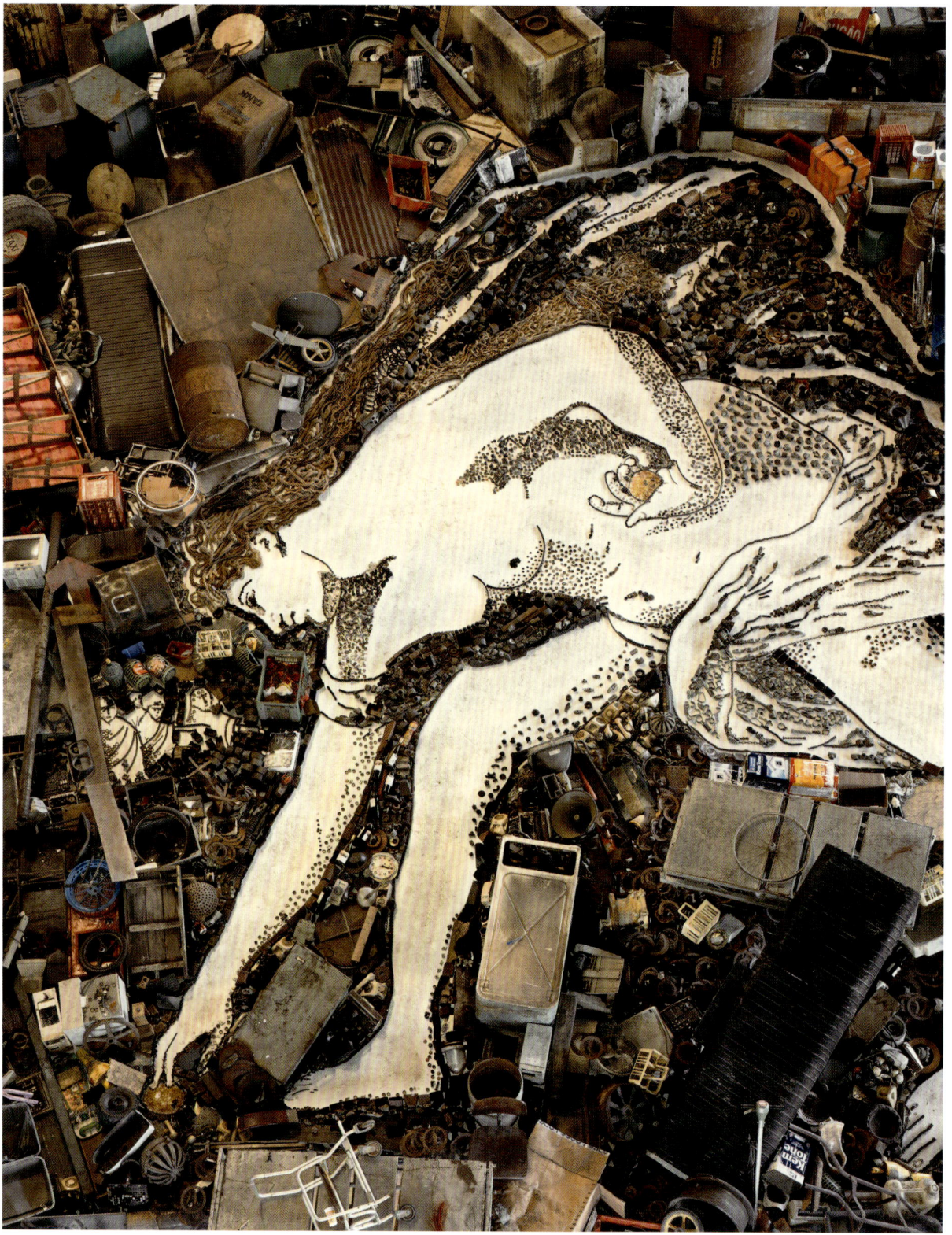

76

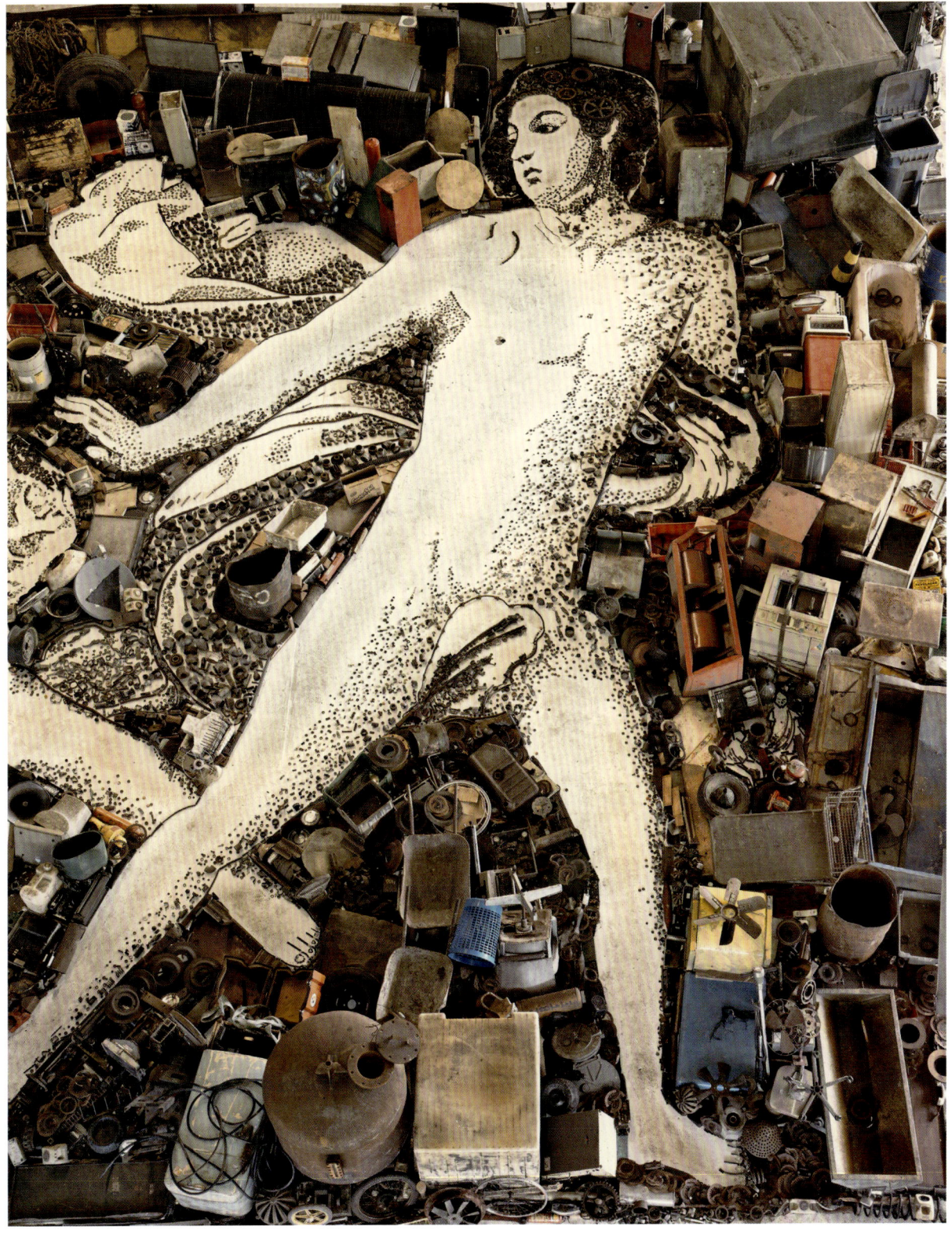

Vik Muniz
*Atalanta and Hippomenes,
after Guido Reni* (diptych),
from *Pictures of Junk*, 2006

The Impossibility of a Pure Image

The junk pictures are high contrast—there are clean areas and dirty areas. In our subconscious, where we actually mine meaning from the vast landfill that is our image memory, we don't have the luxury of cleanliness.

I wanted to make pictures the same way we think about them, so I started cutting up magazines to externalize that confusion. Every piece of the image is made from another image. It's very distracting when you encounter one of these works. Wherever you look, you are led to another train of thought, and they all have meaning.

After working with magazines, I did something similar with family photo-albums. For a century, family albums were passed along from generation to generation like genetic information. But now that this is no longer true, it's interesting for me to work with the idea of photography as physical evidence of someone's existence. I only have nine pictures of myself growing up. When I see pictures of other people for sale, I buy them, because I don't want them to be orphaned. Now I own 250,000 of these photo-albums. I didn't know what do with them, so I decided to use them so that they could continue to be seen.

Every photo-album tells exactly the same story. Only the characters change. Weddings, birthday parties, vacation photos—I depicted them with individual pictures, creating something universal with something very particular. Every photograph depicts a collage of hundreds, possibly thousands, of photographs that are reassembled to represent a photograph. Later, I did the same thing with postcards, which I also collect. When you think about Paris, you picture the Eiffel Tower, the Seine. But every single building in that mental picture may not be from Paris; some of them could be from Detroit, from London. The Paris-like image is just something you make in your head.

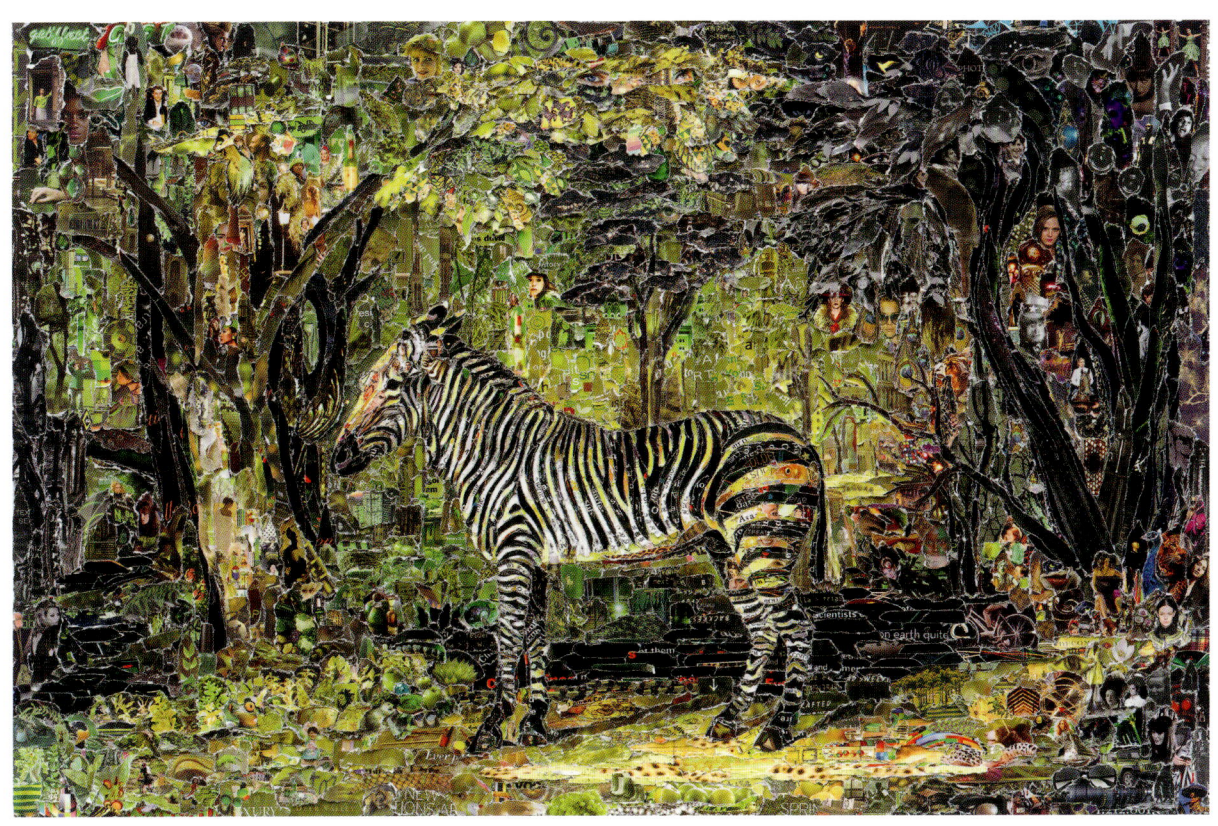

Vik Muniz
Zebra, after George Stubbs,
from *Pictures of Magazines 2*, 2011

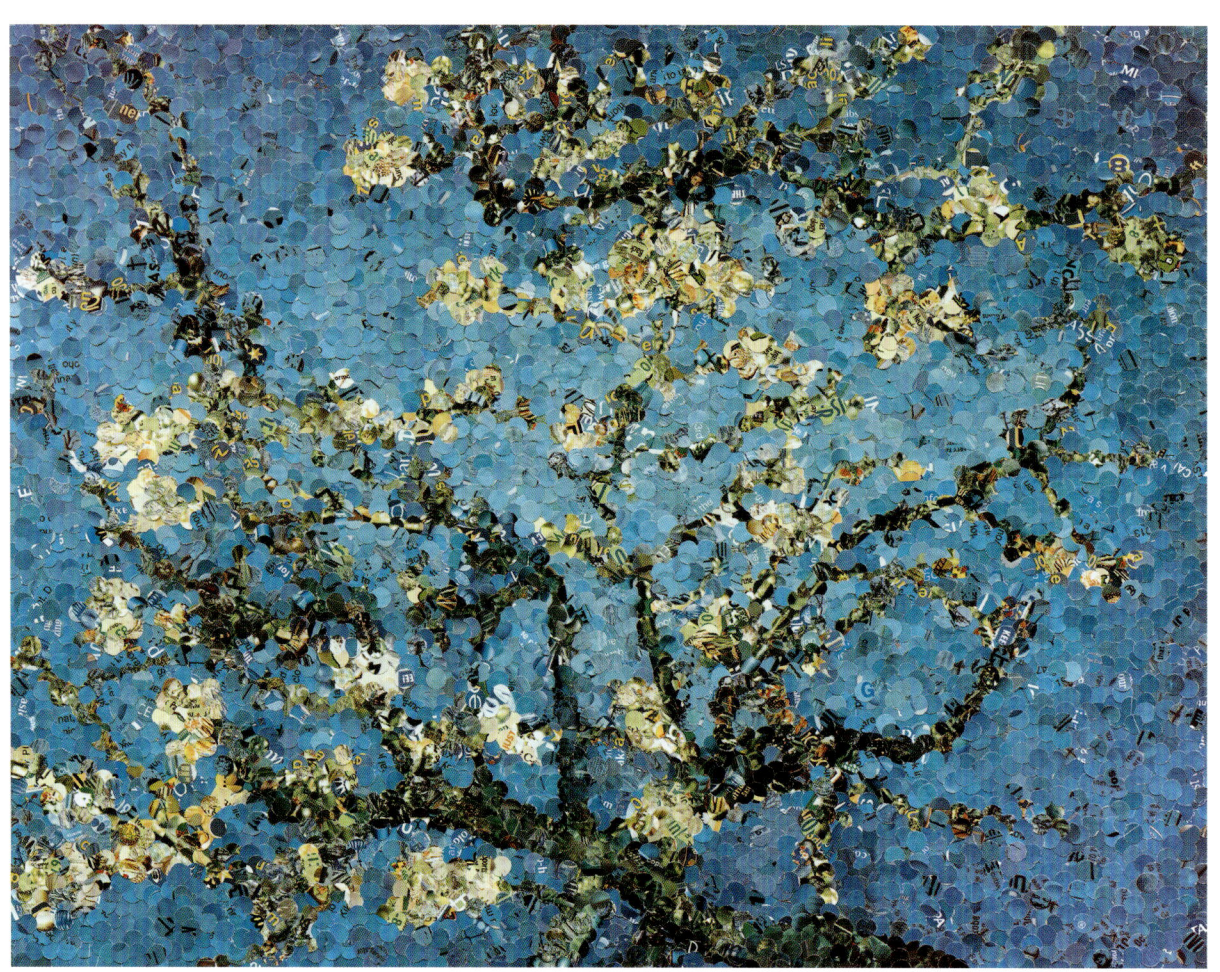

Vik Muniz
Almond Blossom, after Van Gogh,
from *Pictures of Magazines 2,* 2005

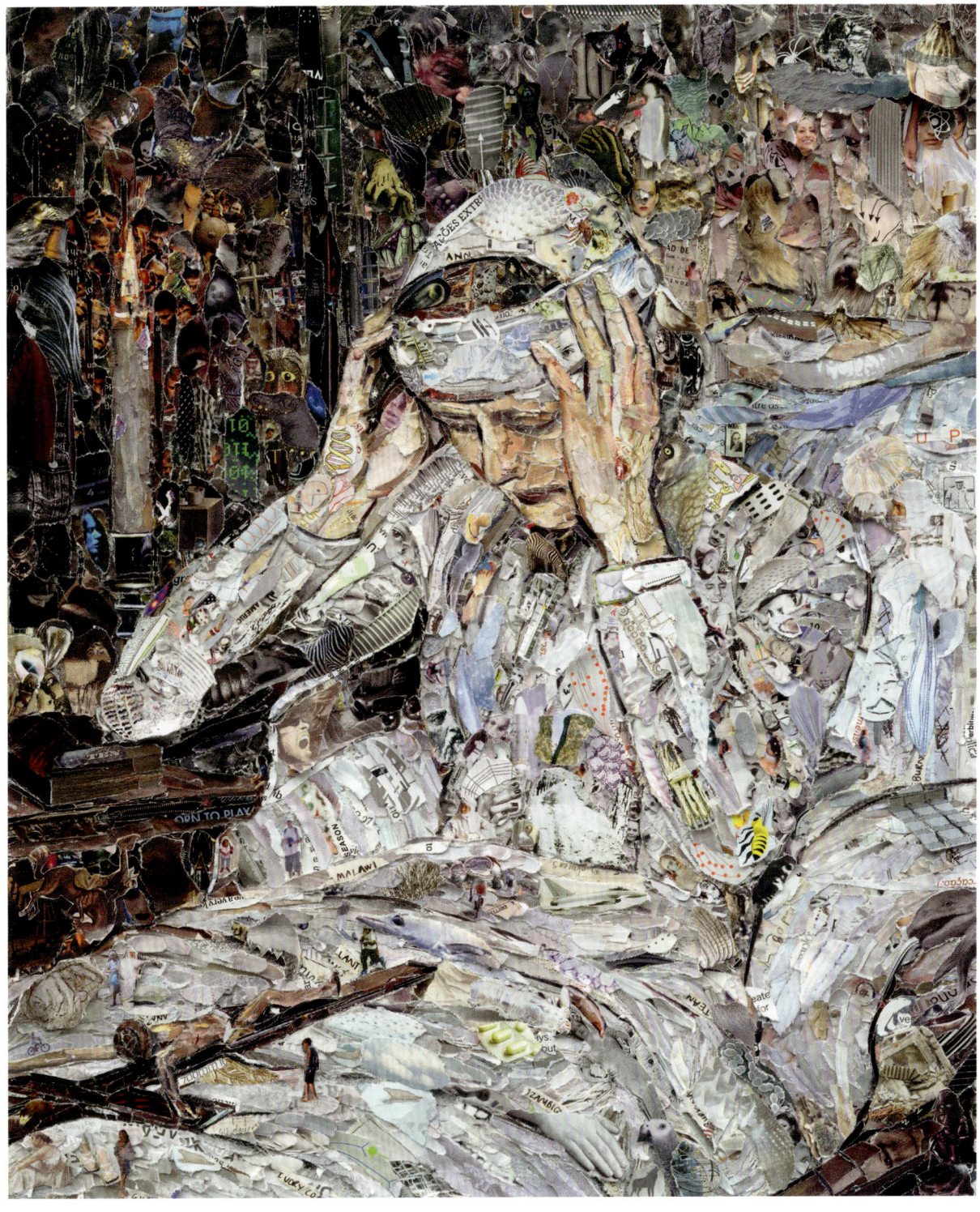

Vik Muniz
The Ecstatic Virgin Anna Katharina Emmerich,
after Gabriel Cornelius Ritter von Max,
from *Pictures of Magazines 2,* 2013

81

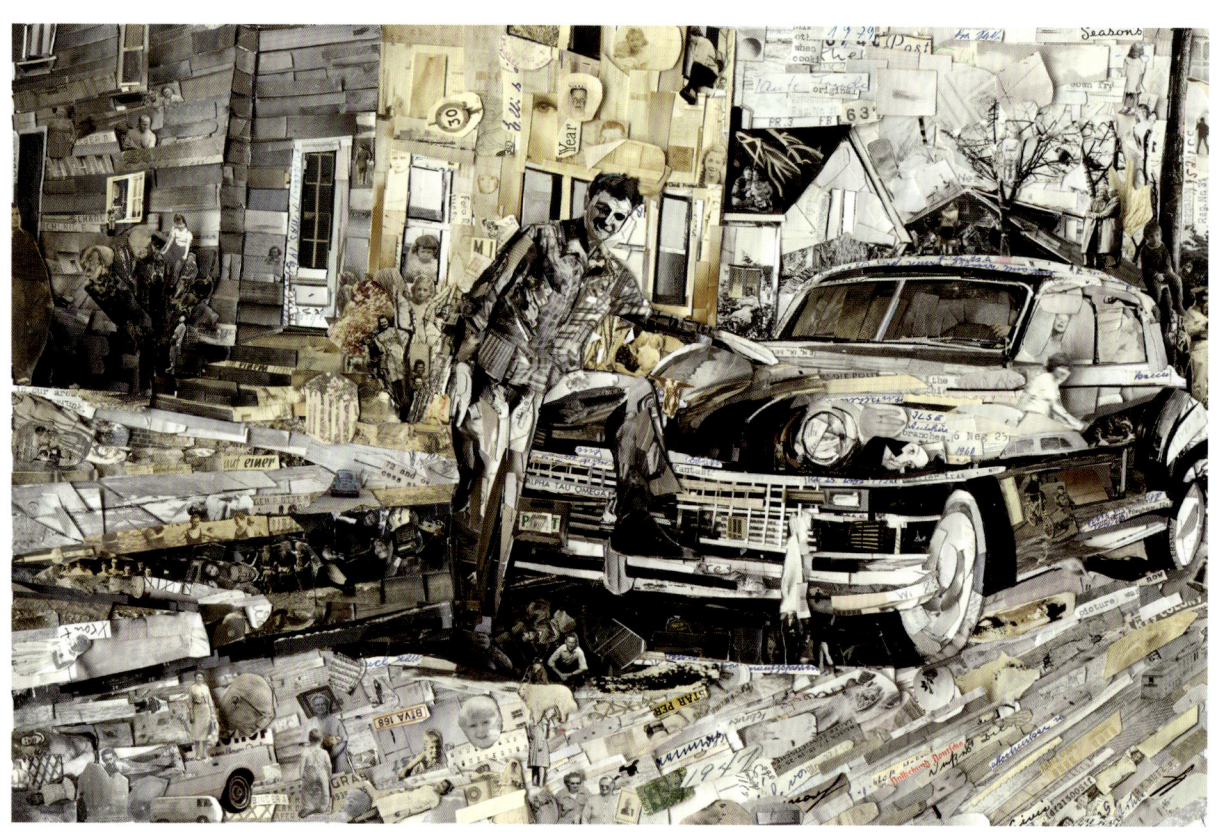

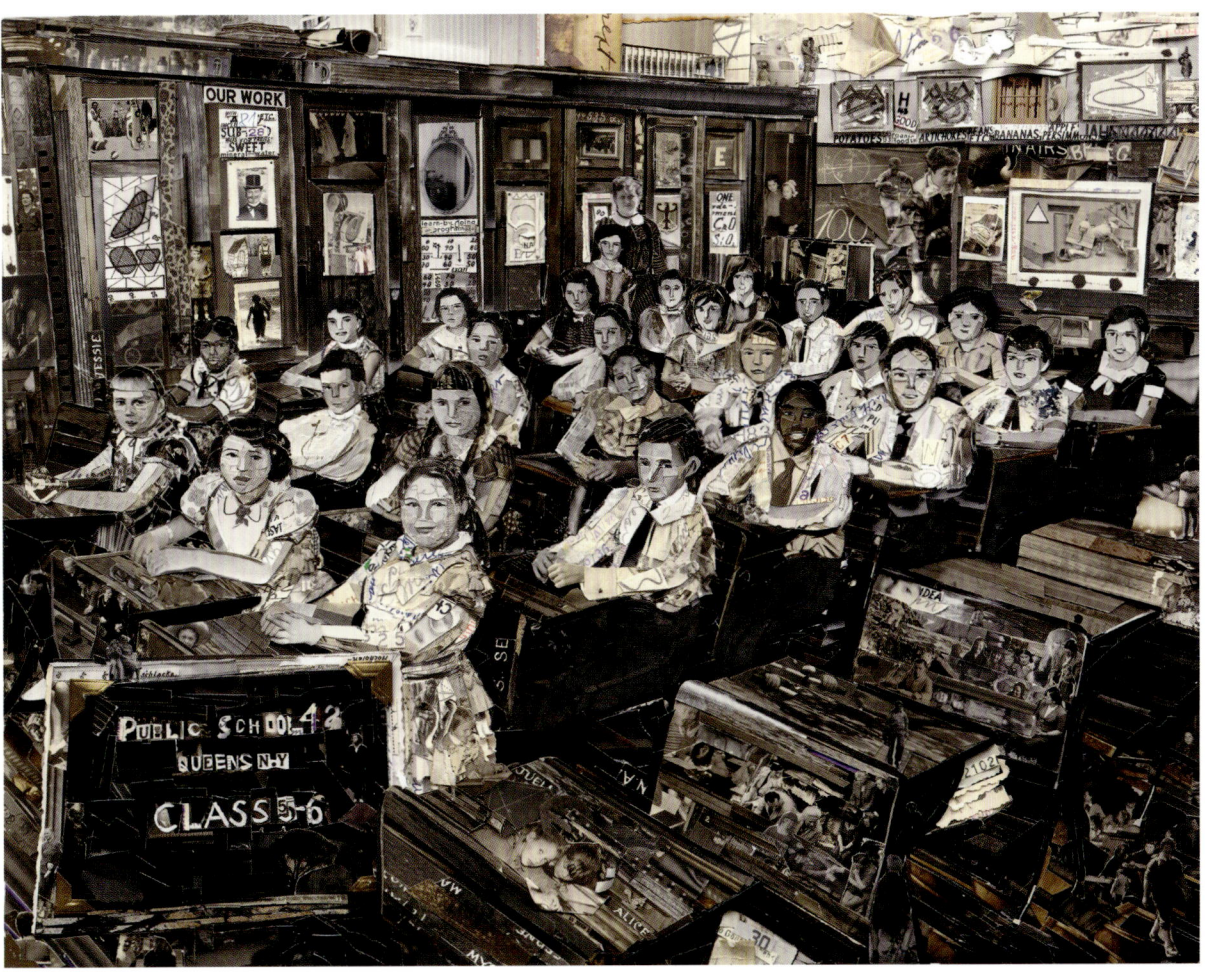

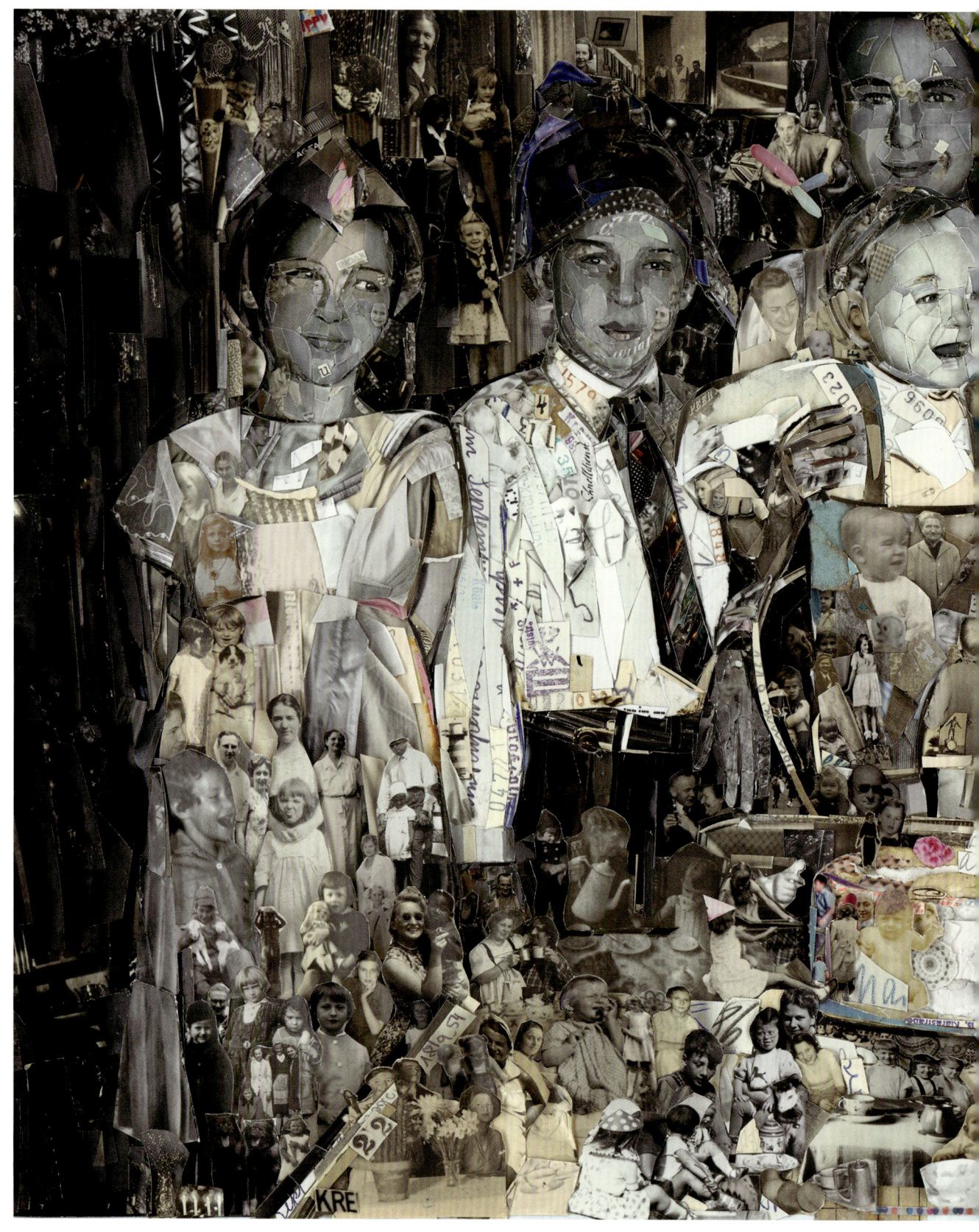

Vik Muniz
First Birthday, from Album, 2014

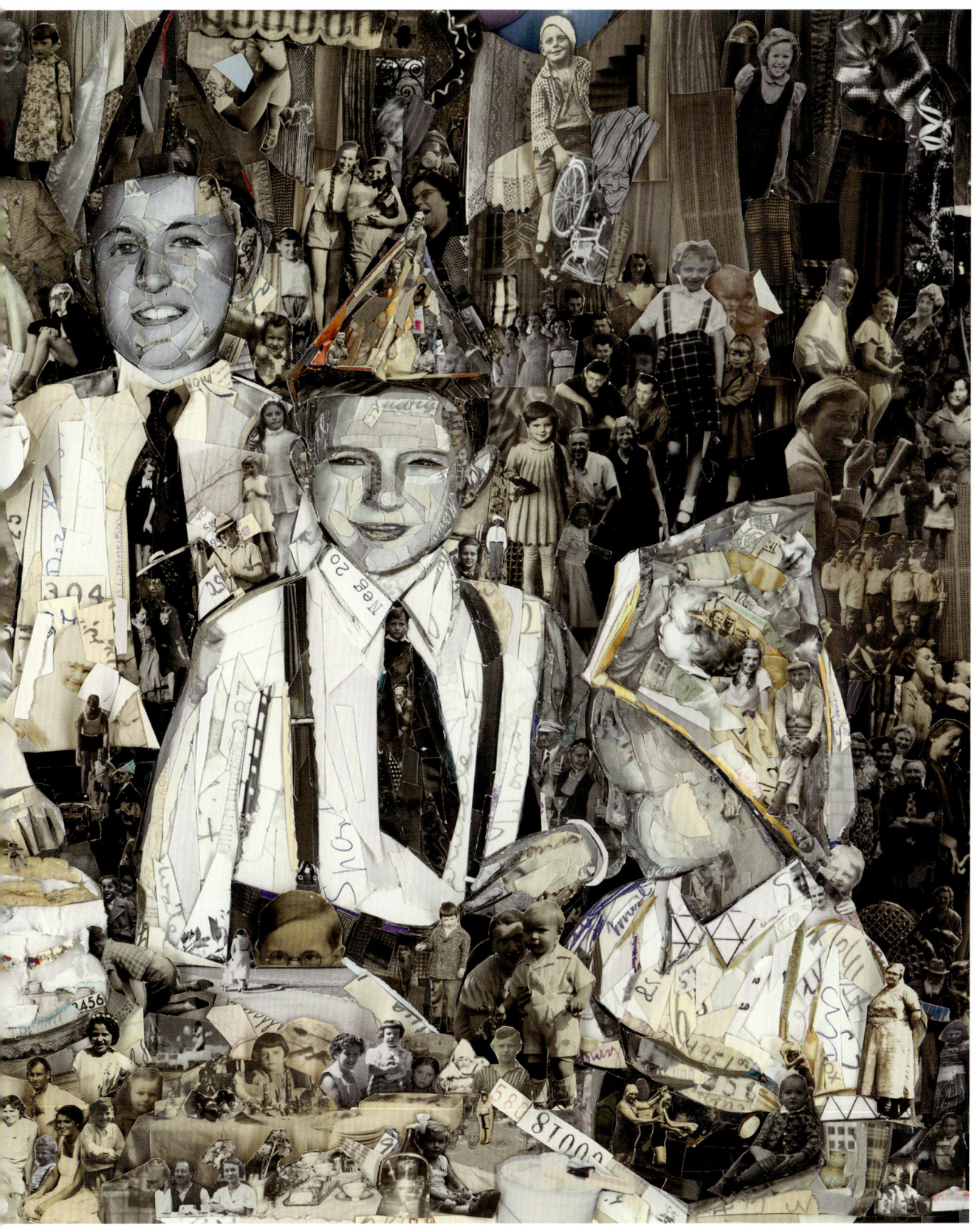

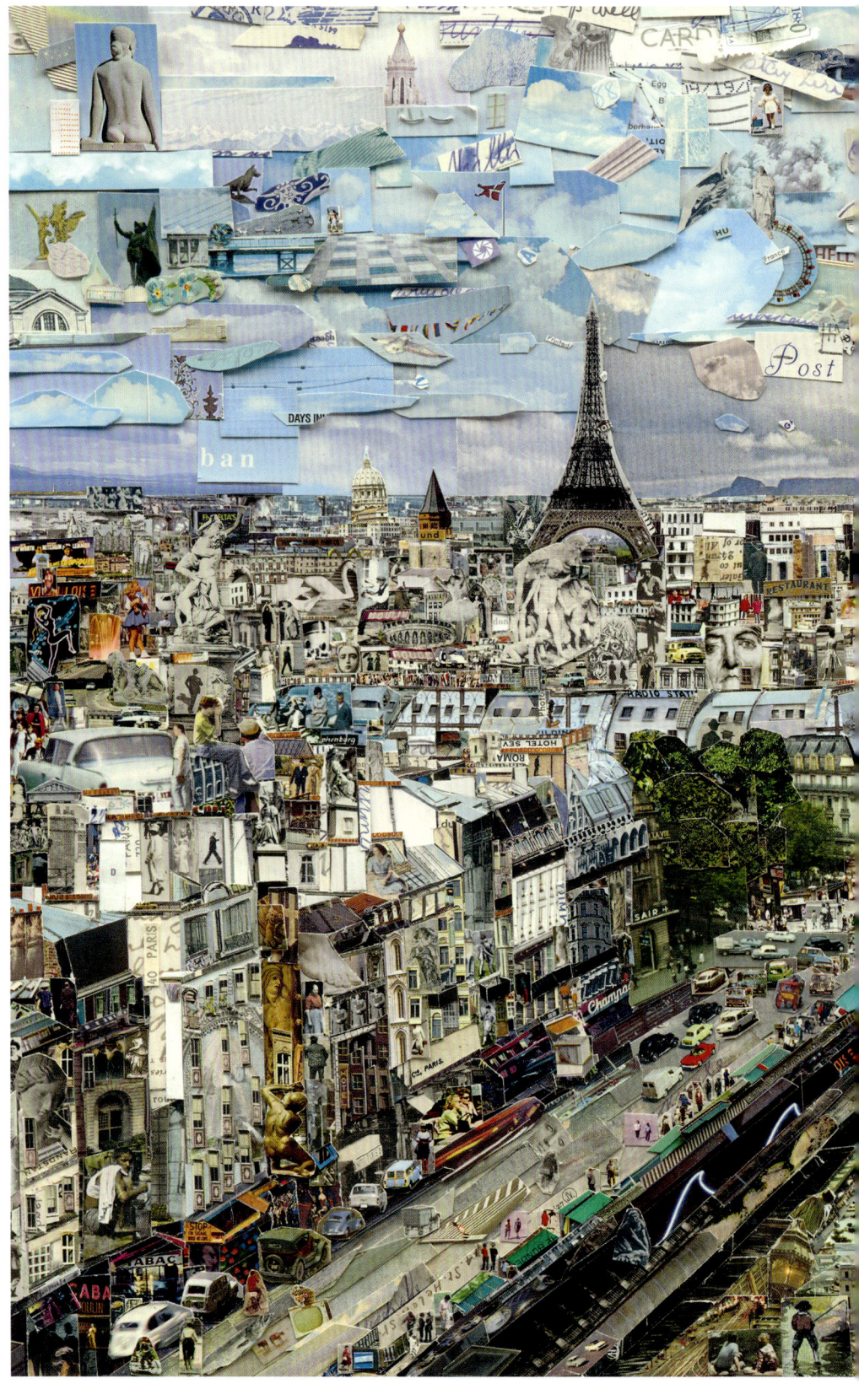

Vik Muniz
*Paris, from Postcards
from Nowhere,* 2013

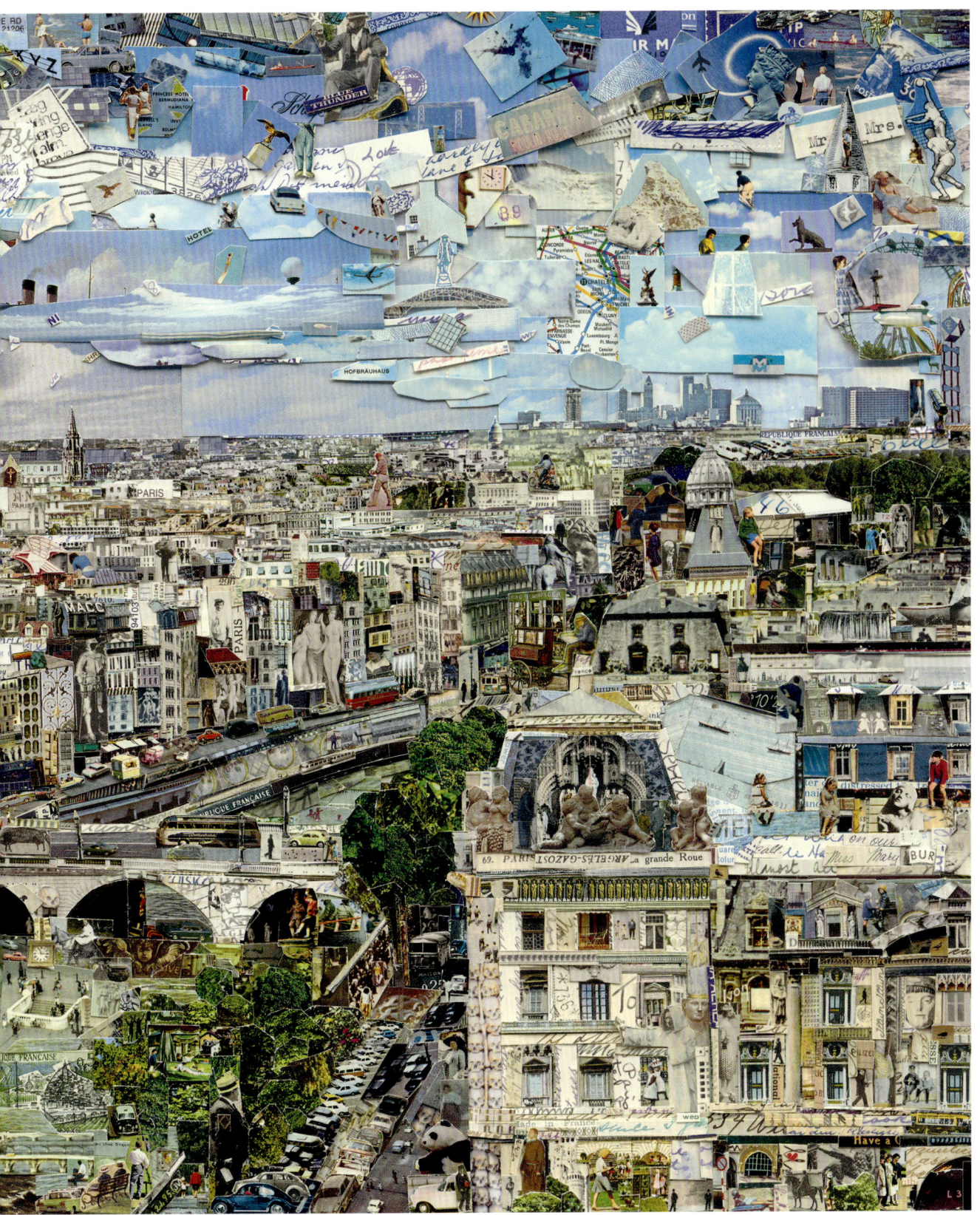

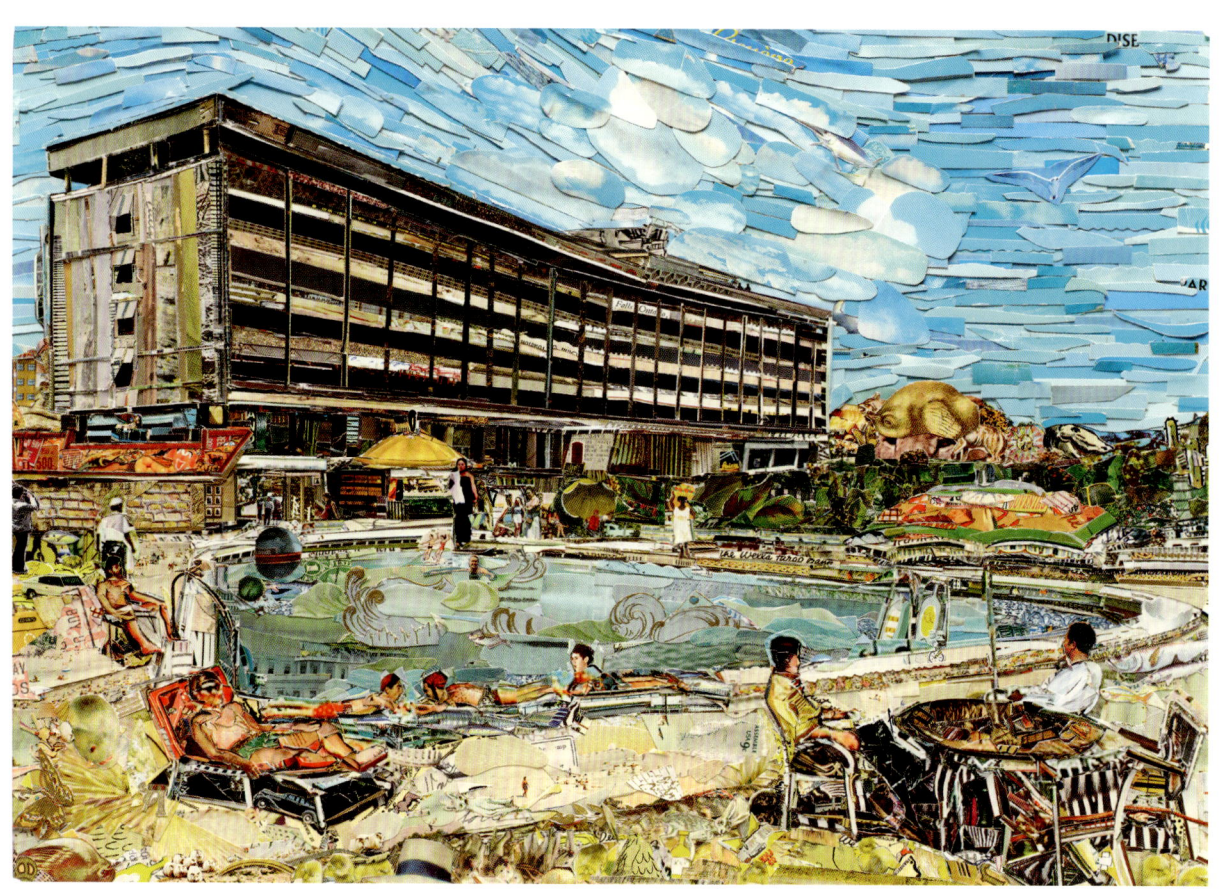

Vik Muniz
Kabul, from *Postcards from Nowhere*, 2023

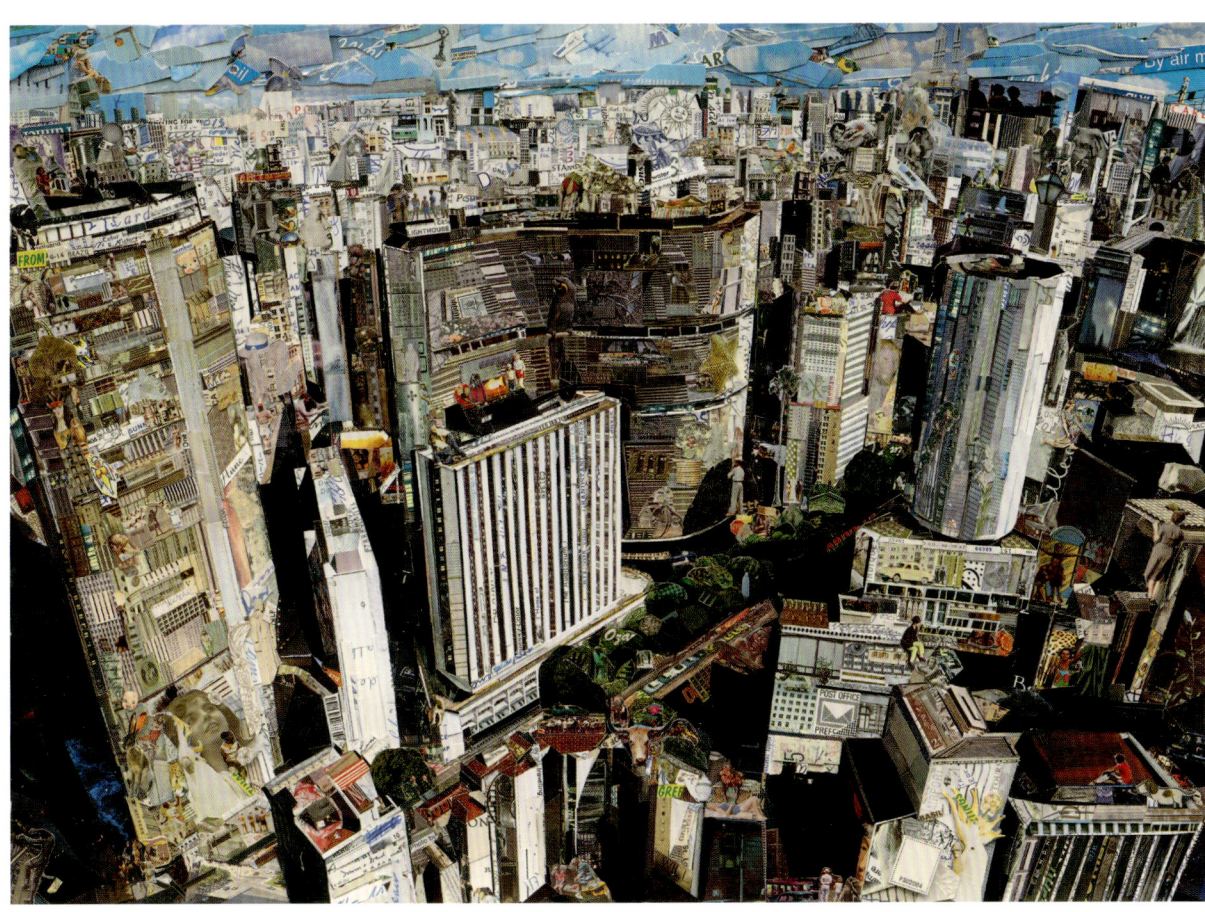

Vik Muniz
São Paulo, from *Postcards from Nowhere*, 2013

The Roles of Paper

Something curious about my work from the 2000s was its concern with the materiality of paper. This may have been a result of the technological shifts sweeping the photography world at the time. Analog media were becoming precious commodities, and professional photographers, sensing the dramatic change in the way photographs were produced, rushed to purchase film and paper stocks, fearing their imminent discontinuation. (I still have a garage full of expired film and photographic paper.) I think we did this out of a fear of being discontinued ourselves.

The significance of paper has shifted considerably in the last twenty-five years, and not just photographic paper—these days it can be hard to find a newspaper. Because our relationship to paper is changing so rapidly, the idea of exploring its physicality became very intriguing to me. I tried many times to create collages using different kinds of paper. First, I tried using only white paper, but that didn't work. Then I tried to make collages using different grays. But if you put a gray jacket in front of a white wall, it will look completely different from a gray jacket on a black wall. The collages I wanted to produce were impossible to construct without digital imaging— I just didn't know it yet. When computers finally did make it possible, I was able to break a picture down into five tonalities, from white to black and three different grays. I initially thought this would be a short exercise in slowing down my thinking about a medium that was so rapidly evolving. Little did I know that, almost twenty years later, I would still be working with this amazing material and continuing to learn about our indelible relationship to it.

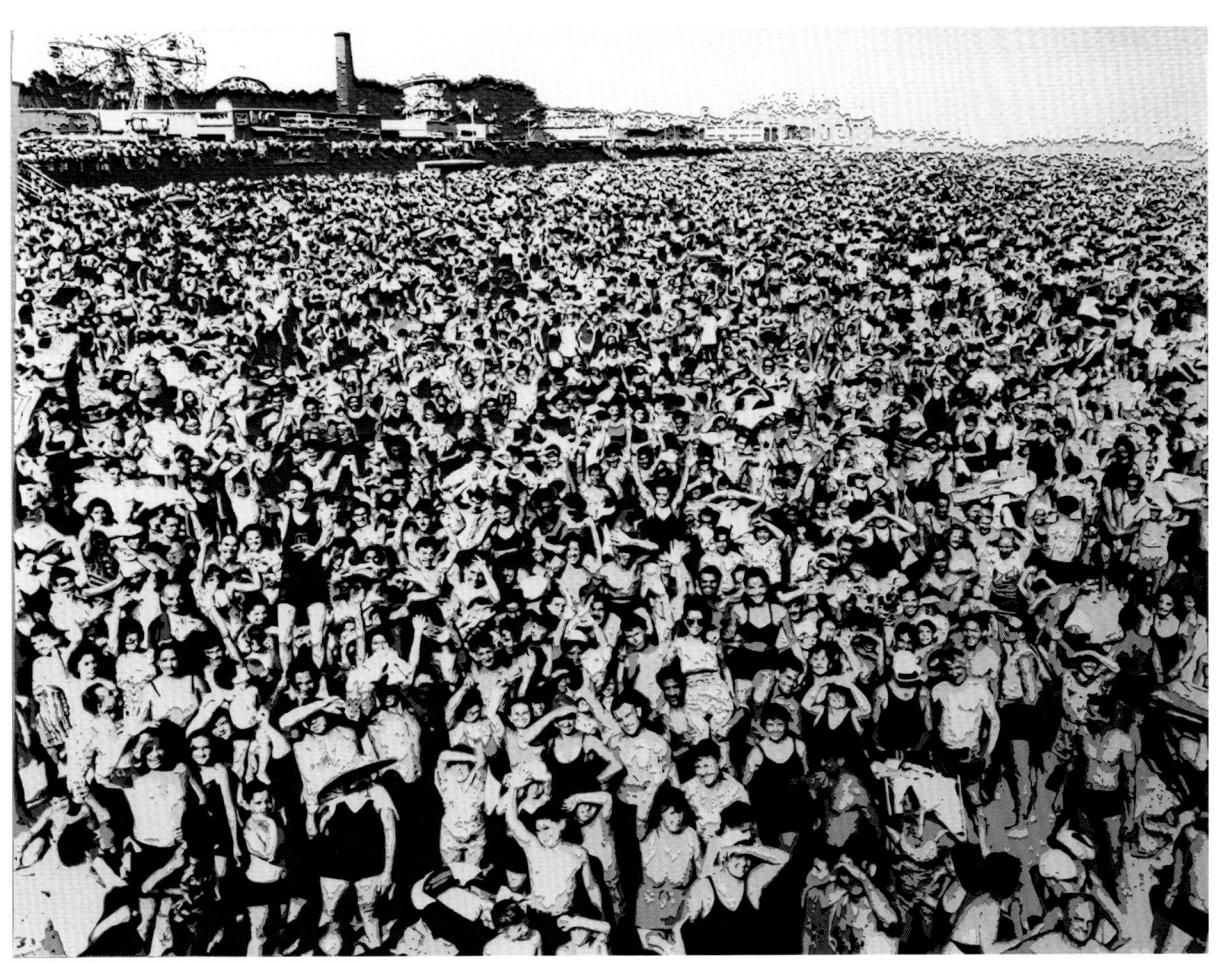

Vik Muniz
Crowd at Coney Island, 89°, They Came Early
and They Stayed Late, July 1940, after Weegee,
from *Pictures of Paper*, 2009

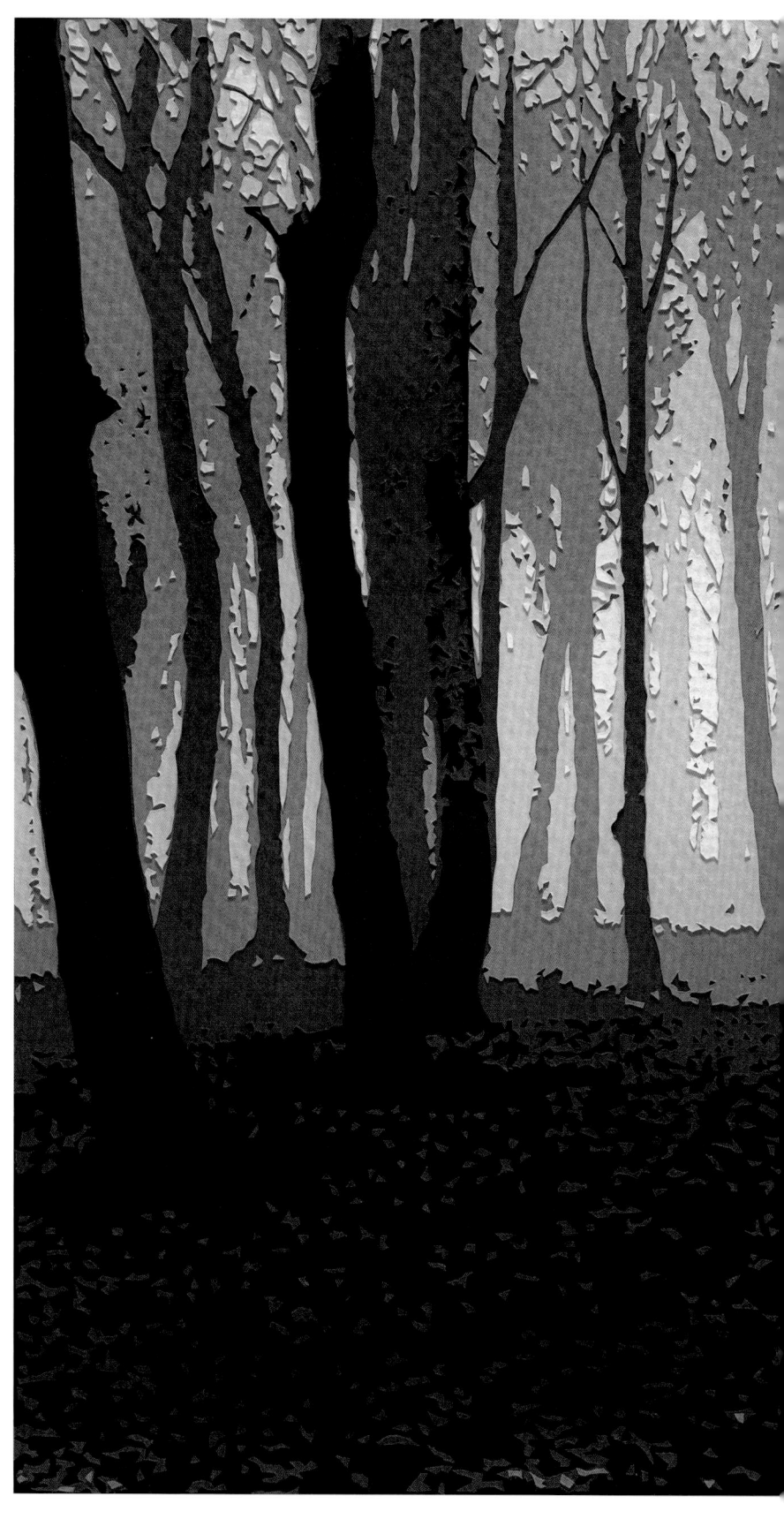

Vik Muniz
*Woods in November, after Albert
Renger-Patzsch,* from *Pictures
of Paper,* 2008

92

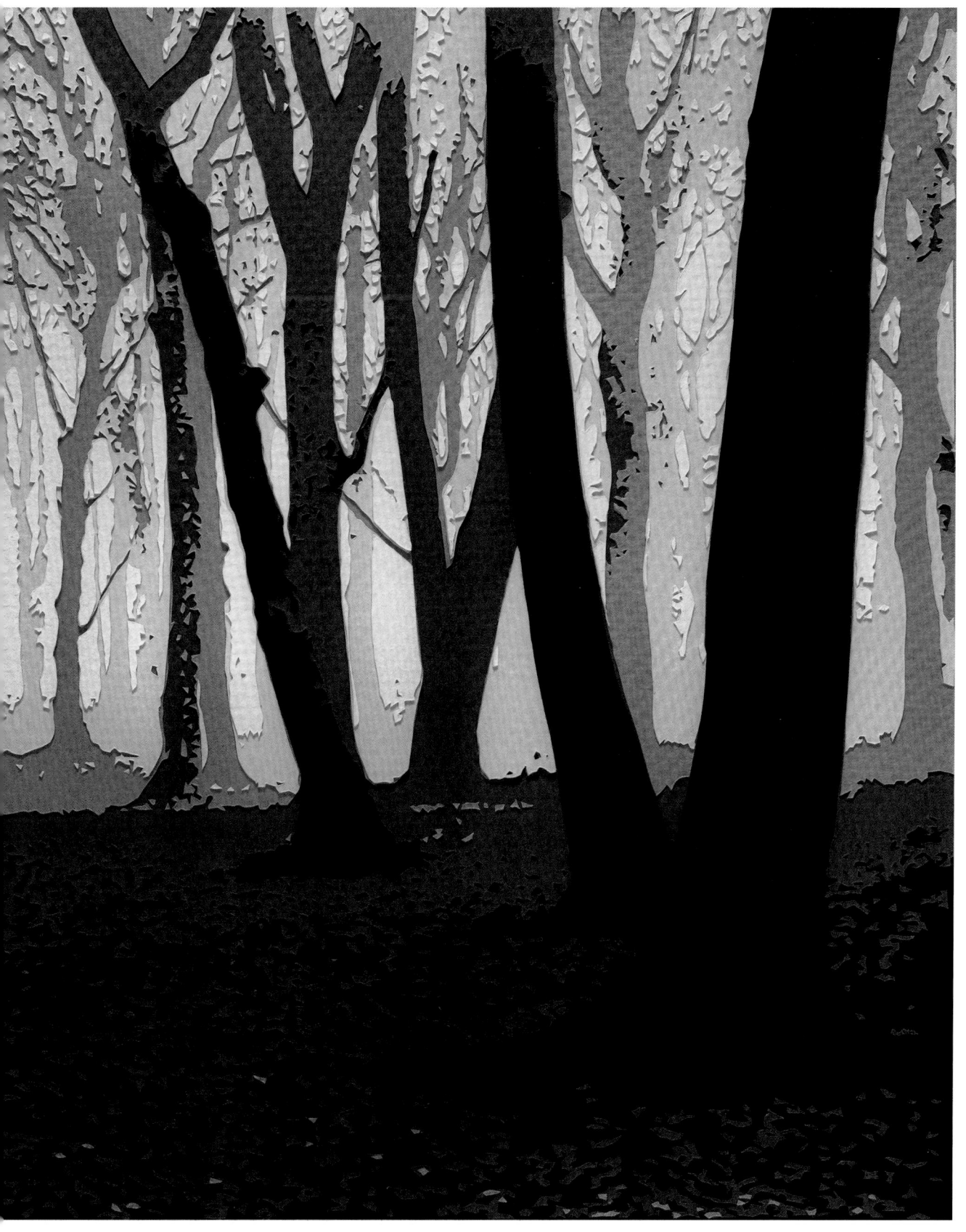

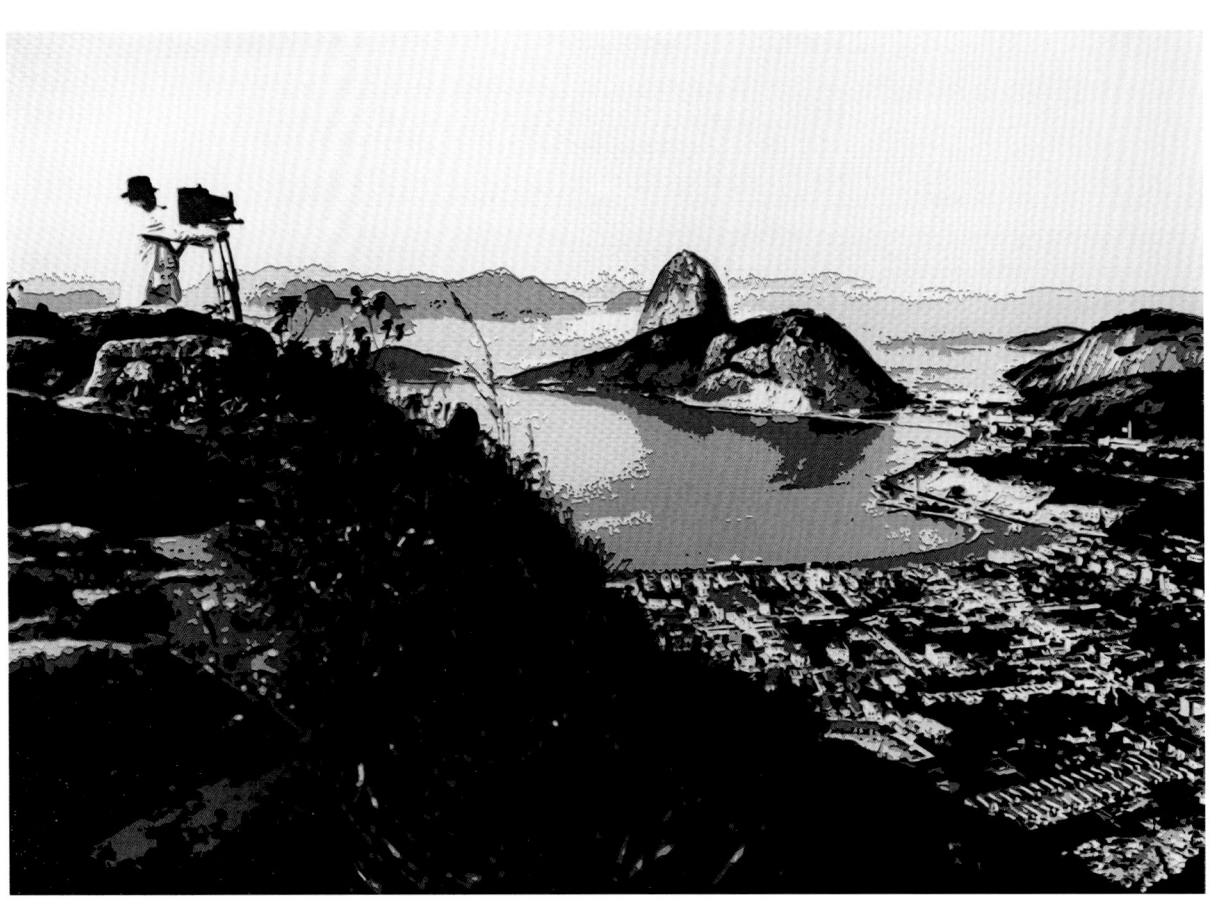

Vik Muniz
View of Rio from Niterói, after Marc Ferrez, from *Pictures of Paper*, 2009

94

Value and Destruction

Money, hard currency, is a lot of different things, but most importantly it's an efficient means of communication that's in rapid decline. This is partly what makes it an interesting artistic medium.

Between 2010 and 2023, as the shift from chemical to digital imaging accelerated, a lot of things were changing in my studio. My attention had returned to paper, specifically to images that rely on it as a support vehicle. Somewhat fortuitously, Brazil's national mint, the Banco Central do Brasil, approached me with an opportunity to work with banknotes that it had removed from circulation and then shredded.

Every Brazilian banknote has a depiction of a native animal on the back, a different one for each denomination, from one real all the way up to a hundred reais. I decided to focus on these animals, because several of them are, like paper money itself, at risk of becoming extinct. This gave me a finite number of subjects to work with. Of course, once I got started, I realized I could explore the idea further, so I began incorporating landscapes painted by traveling artists during the eighteenth and nineteenth centuries, the era of European scientific expeditions in Brazil. One of them is a painting from the end of the Industrial Revolution by Félix Taunay, *Mata Reduzida a Carvão* (Forest Reduced to Charcoal), about 1830. Funny how time passes but ideas persist, like the idea that forests are worthless until they're turned into something useful.

You may not think about this, but when you sketch a tree, you're drawing it with another tree. The pencil, for example, is made of wood and graphite, which is carbon from ancient trees. Even the sheet of paper was once a tree. The landscapes in the *Live Cash* series have this same quality: a thing that represents the value extracted from the very thing that it depicts. In this way, the series complements other works of mine that deal with paper as a vehicle for mediating our evolving relationship with images.

A couple years later, I obtained some shredded dollar bills from the Federal Reserve Bank of New York. Looking at a different currency got me thinking about the national archetypes that commonly appear on a country's banknotes, elastic concepts that can shift with sociopolitical trends. In the United States, for example, there was an initiative in 2015 to remove Andrew Jackson from the twenty-dollar bill and replace him with Harriet Tubman. This story became the starting point for *Legal Tender*.

After using the shredded bills to make a portrait of Tubman, I turned to examples from American history that also brought together its triumphs and tragedies— animal species hunted almost to extinction (bald eagles, bison), vibrant communities destroyed by hate (the Tulsa race massacre of 1921), and people who courageously fought against discrimination (Oglala Lakota Chief Wašíčuŋ Tȟašúŋke a.k.a. American Horse the Elder, Amelia Earhart, Frederick Douglass). We don't often get a chance to decide which parts of our history we want to commemorate. And on those rare occasions when we do decide—in the case of the Tubman twenty-dollar bill, approved through a poll of six hundred thousand Americans—sometimes the opportunity is still snatched away from us.

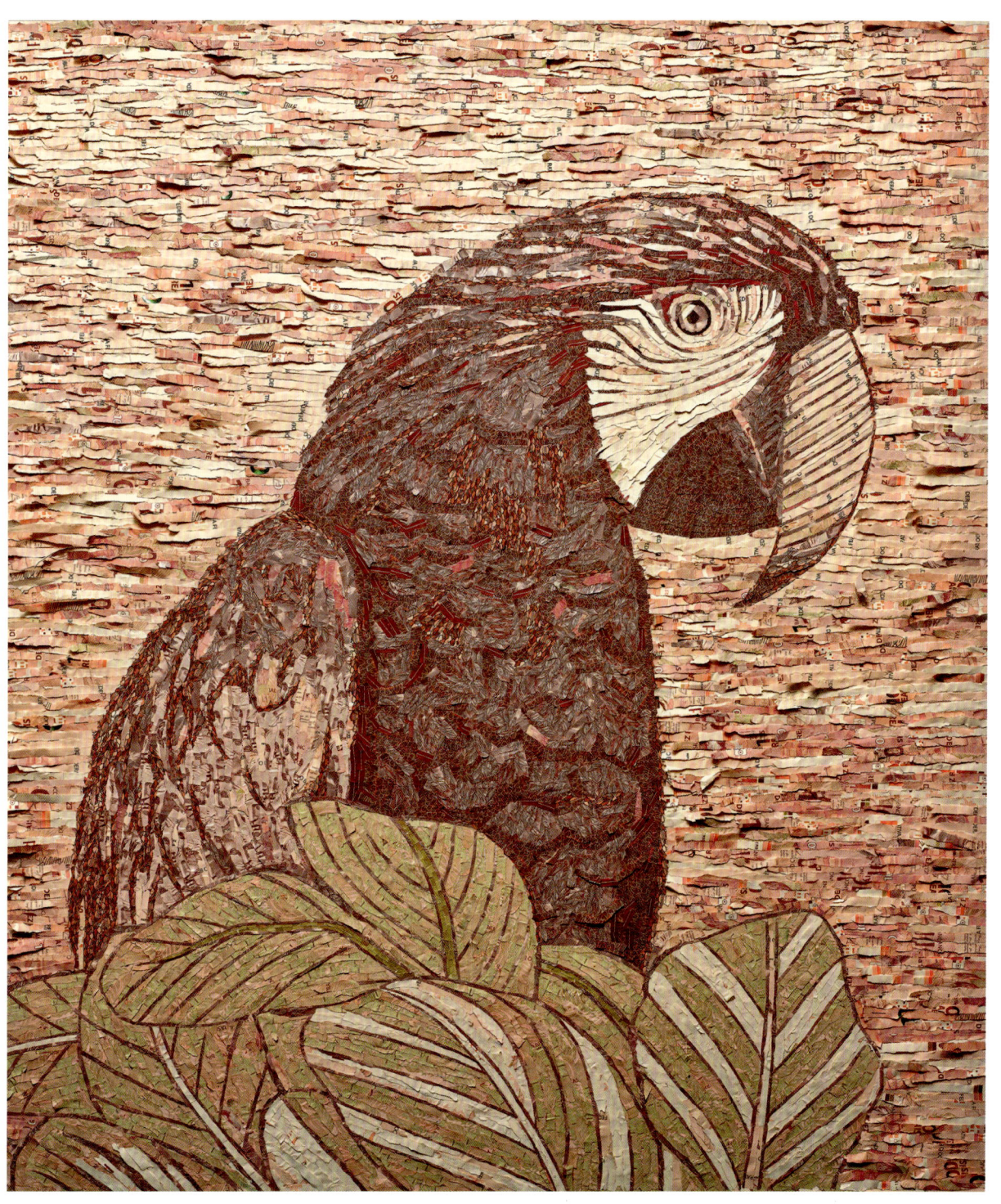

Vik Muniz
Macaw, from *Live Cash*, 2022

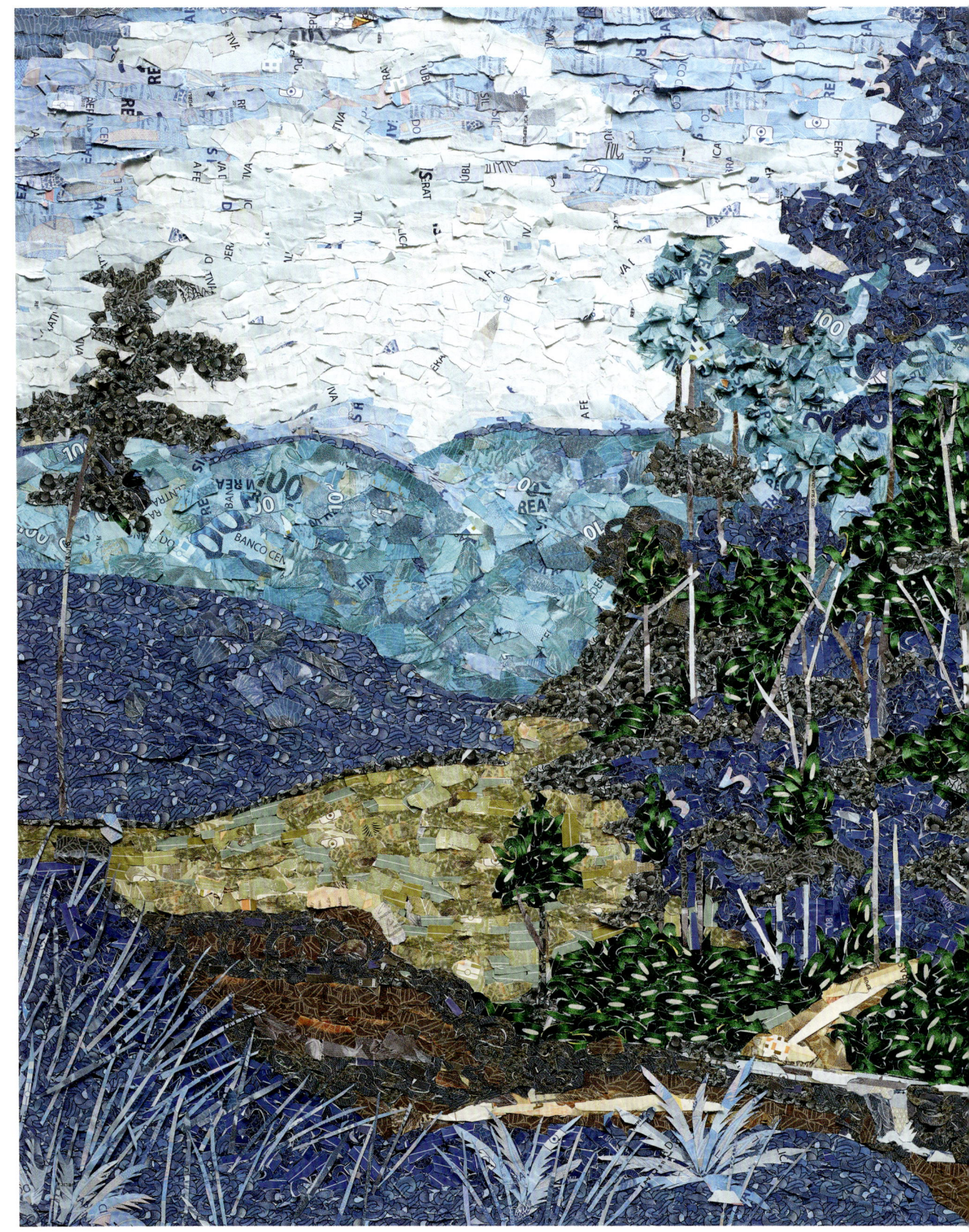

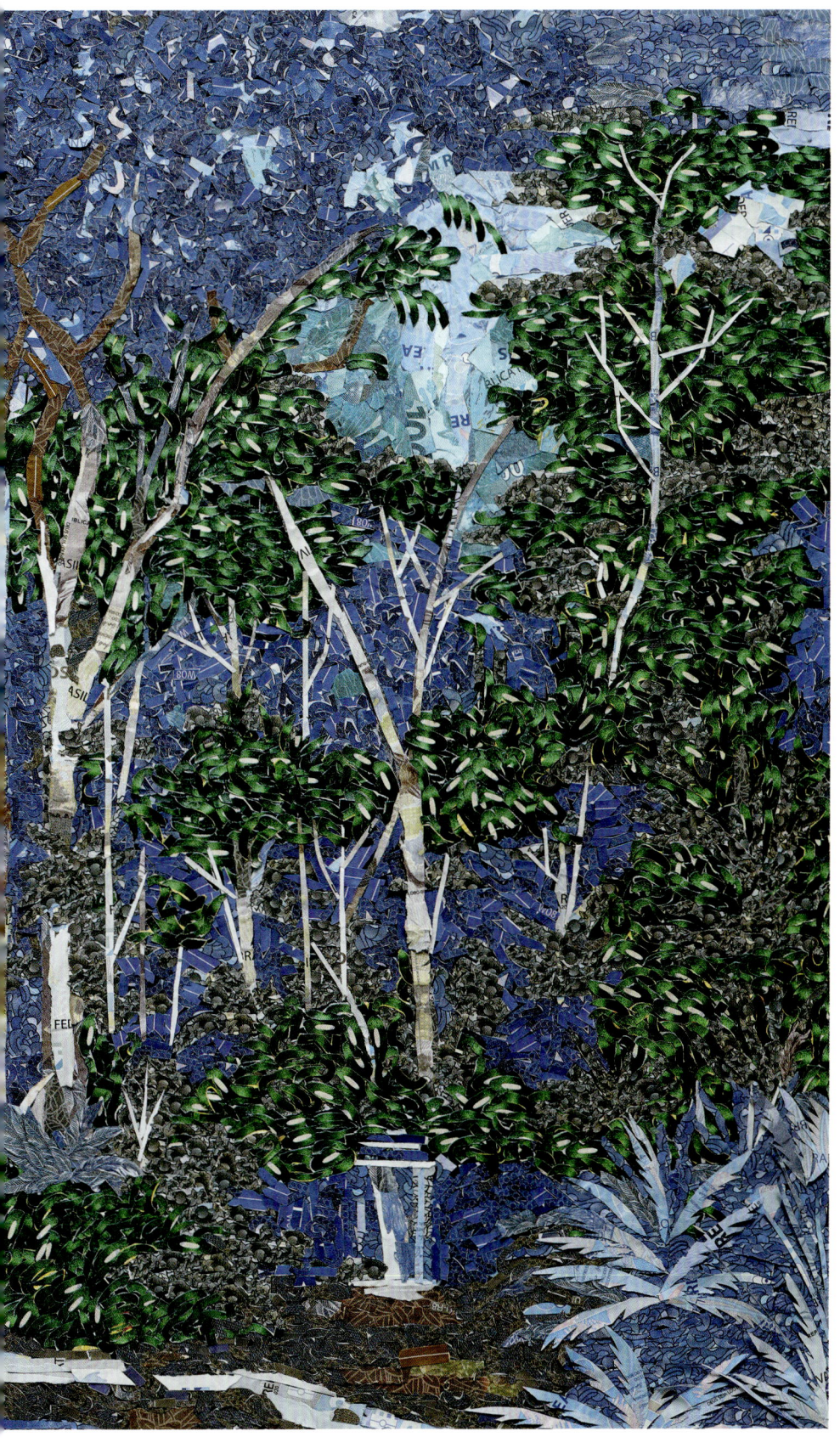

Vik Muniz
*View of a Virgin Forest Reduced
to Charcoal, after Félix Taunay,
from* Live Cash, 2022

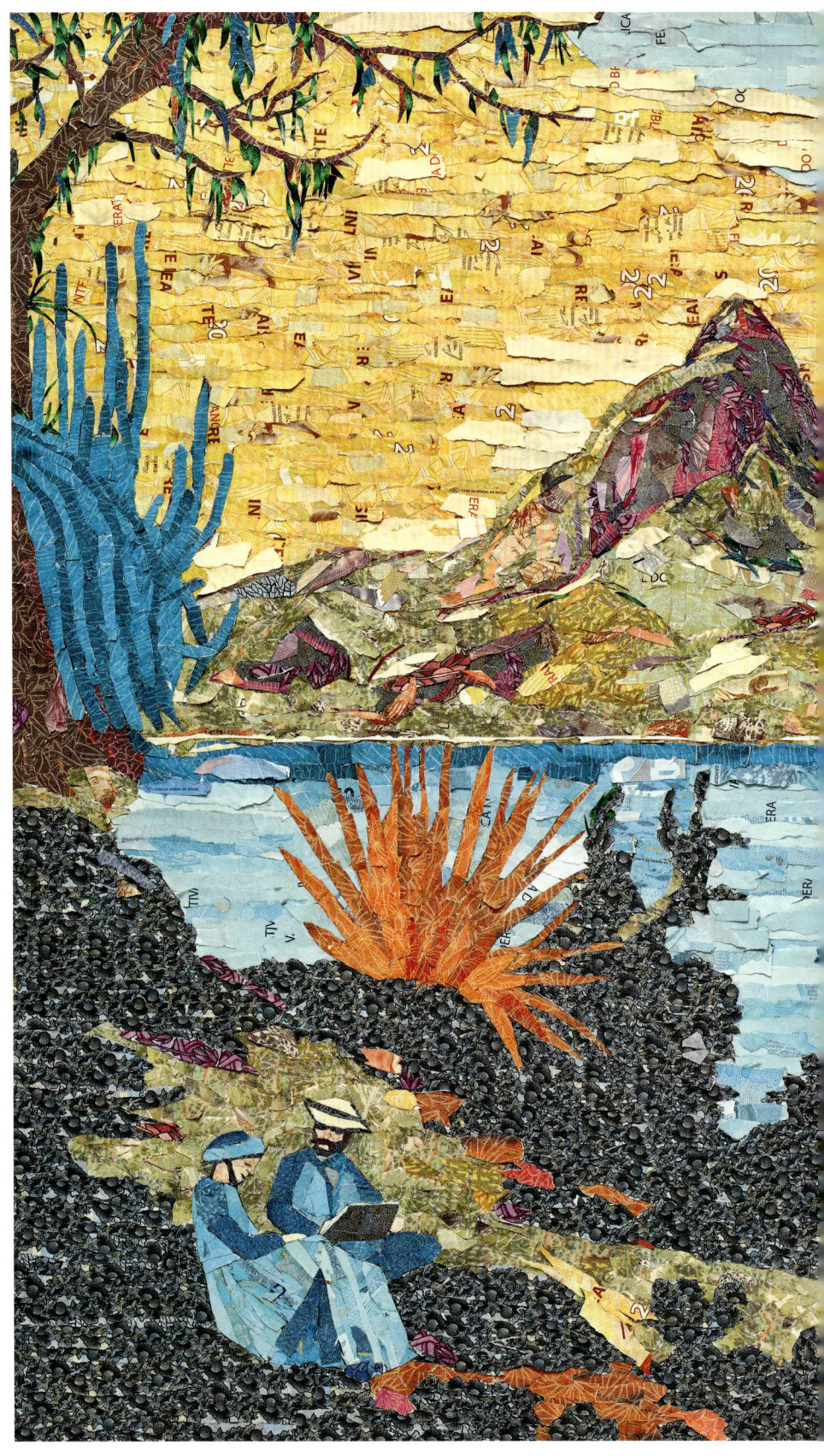

Vik Muniz
Rodrigo de Freitas Lagoon,
after Johann Moritz Rugendas,
from *Live Cash*, 2022

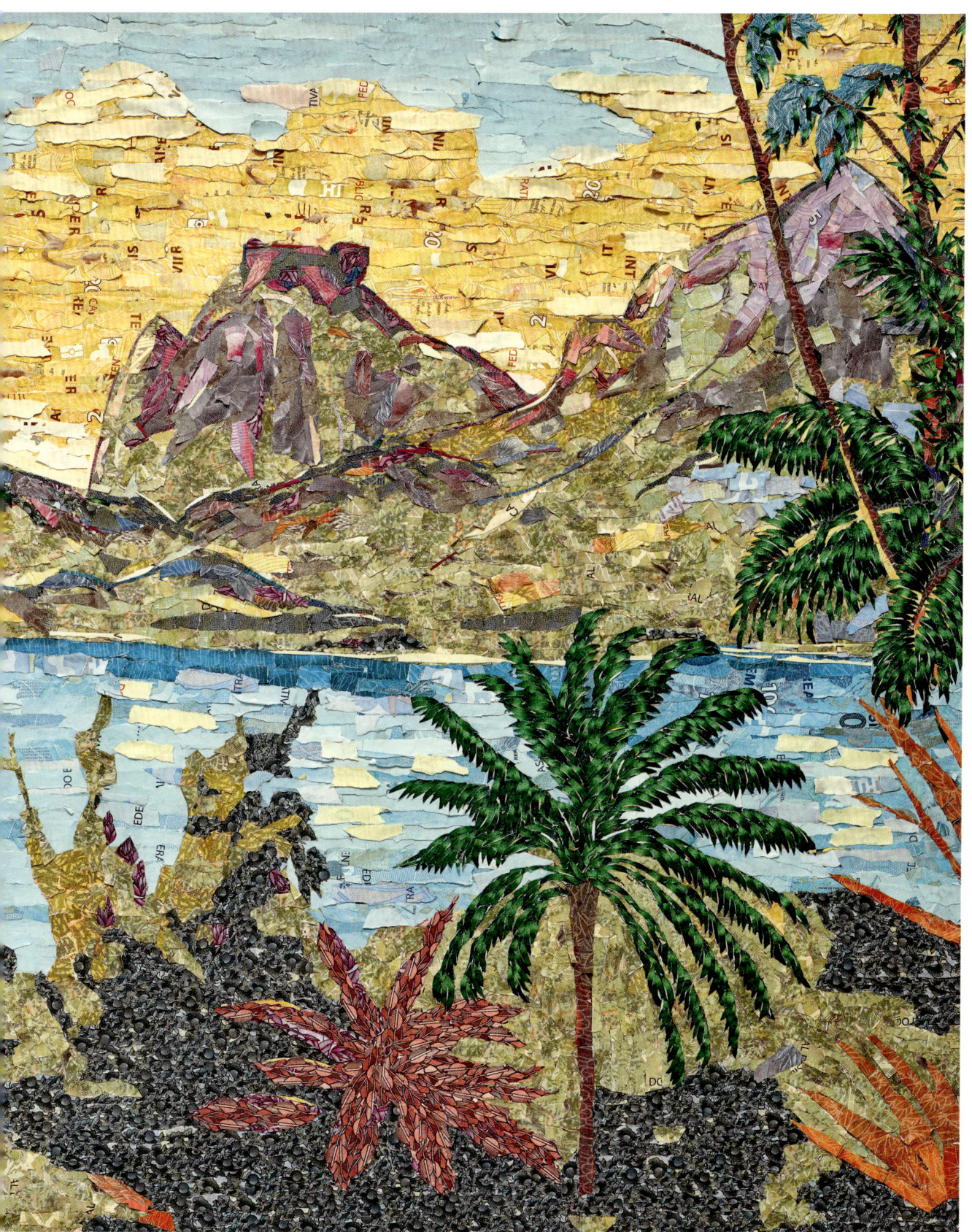

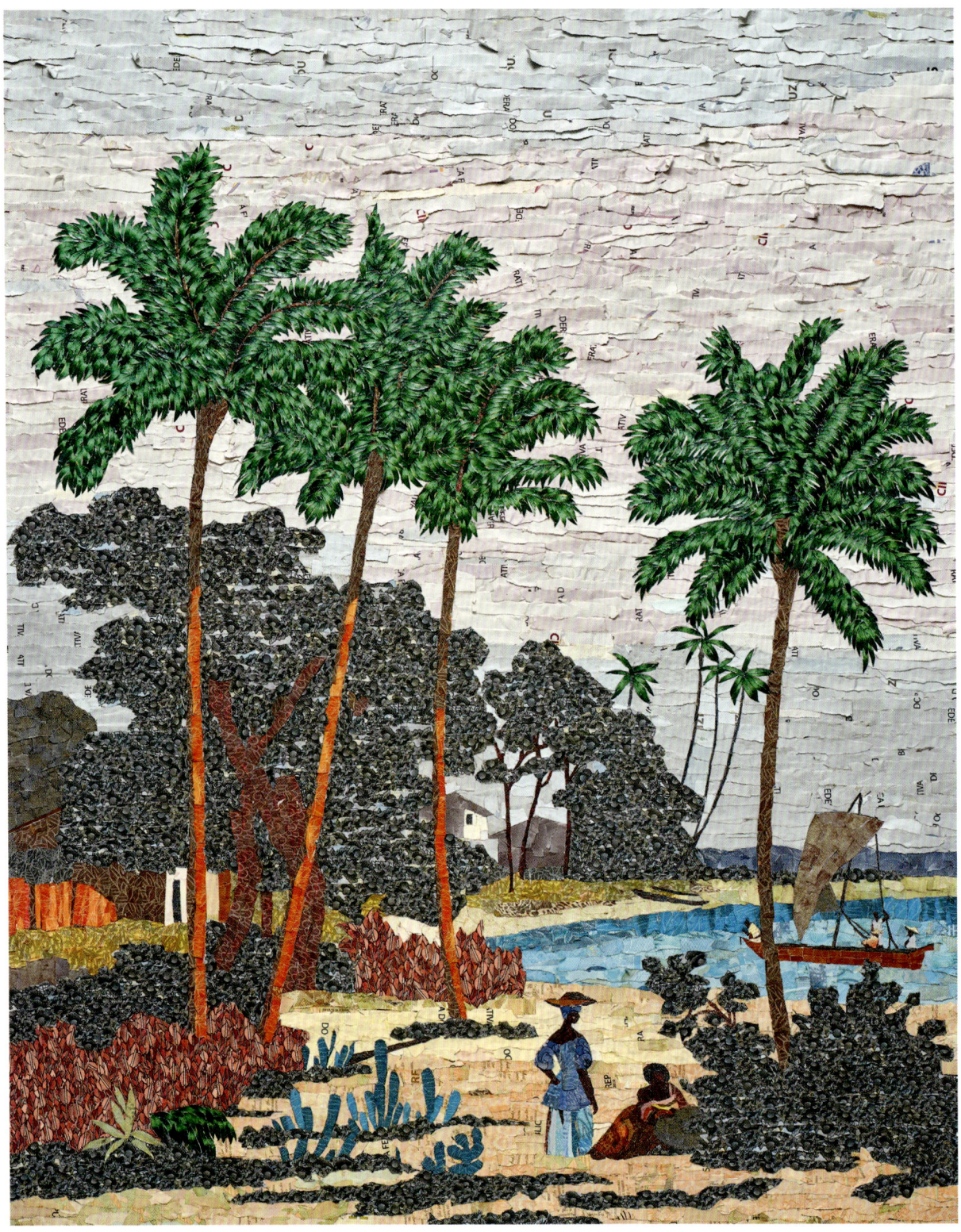

Vik Muniz
View of the Coast of Bahia,
after Johann Moritz Rugendas,
from *Live Cash,* 2022

102

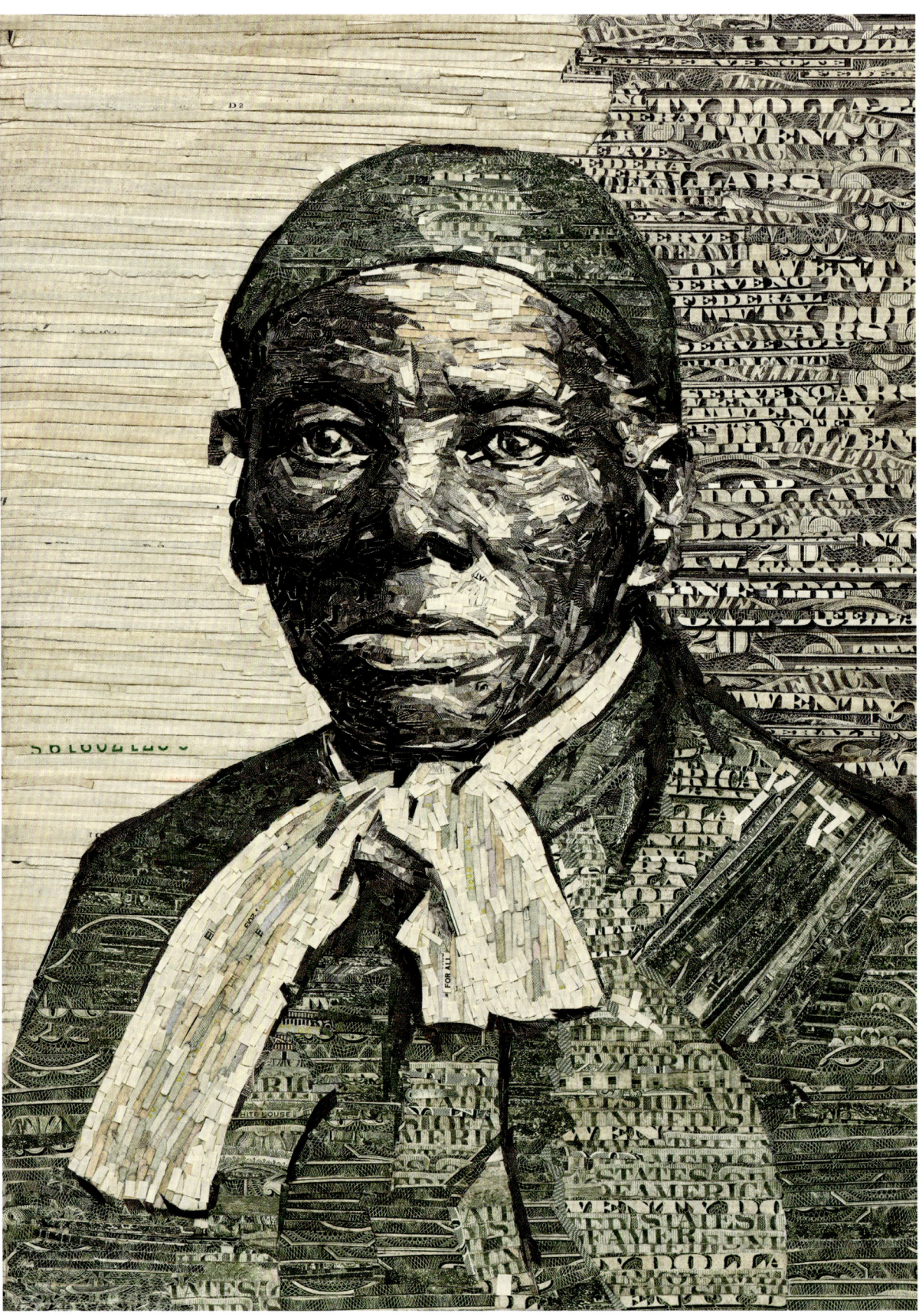

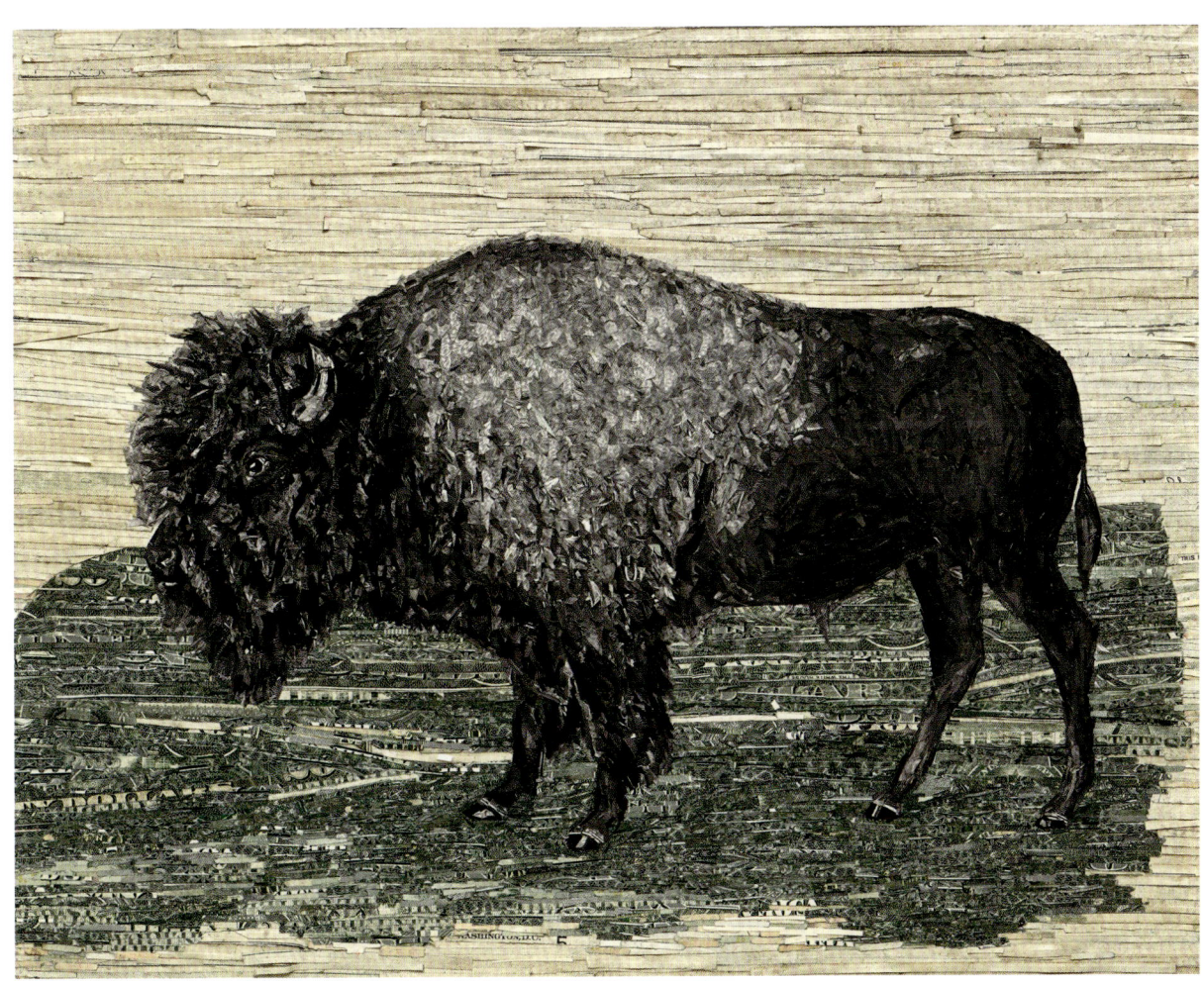

Left
Vik Muniz
Harriet Tubman, from *Legal Tender*, 2022

Top
Vik Muniz
*American Bison, after John James
Audubon*, from *Legal Tender*, 2022

Purpose

For many years, I made art because I wanted to become an artist. But after twenty years you run out of excuses. You *are* an artist, and you have to convince yourself that what you're doing has a purpose.

In 2008, I knew that I wanted to share the experience of making art with a group of individuals, *catadores*, who couldn't have been further from the art world. Their main occupation was pulling recycled garbage from the world's largest landfill, the Jardim Gramacho, on the outskirts of Rio. The idea of including them in making works of art, in a way that would benefit them, became really important to me.

When the dump was slated to be permanently shut down, I invited them to collaborate on creating their own portraits. Their only experience with portraiture or image-making had been taking tiny photos with cellphones they found in the landfill. I wanted us to work together to make giant portraits from the stuff they dealt with every day.

This process was the subject of the documentary *Waste Land* (2010), which was nominated for an Academy Award. After we finished the pictures, we sold them at auction. This helped this community in many ways. The proceeds directly supported the people who participated in the film, and it changed their lives considerably—they were even able to buy houses. But the film also affected the entire class of *catadores* across Brazil. For one thing, they organized themselves into professional associations, and for the first time their work was recognized by the wider culture.

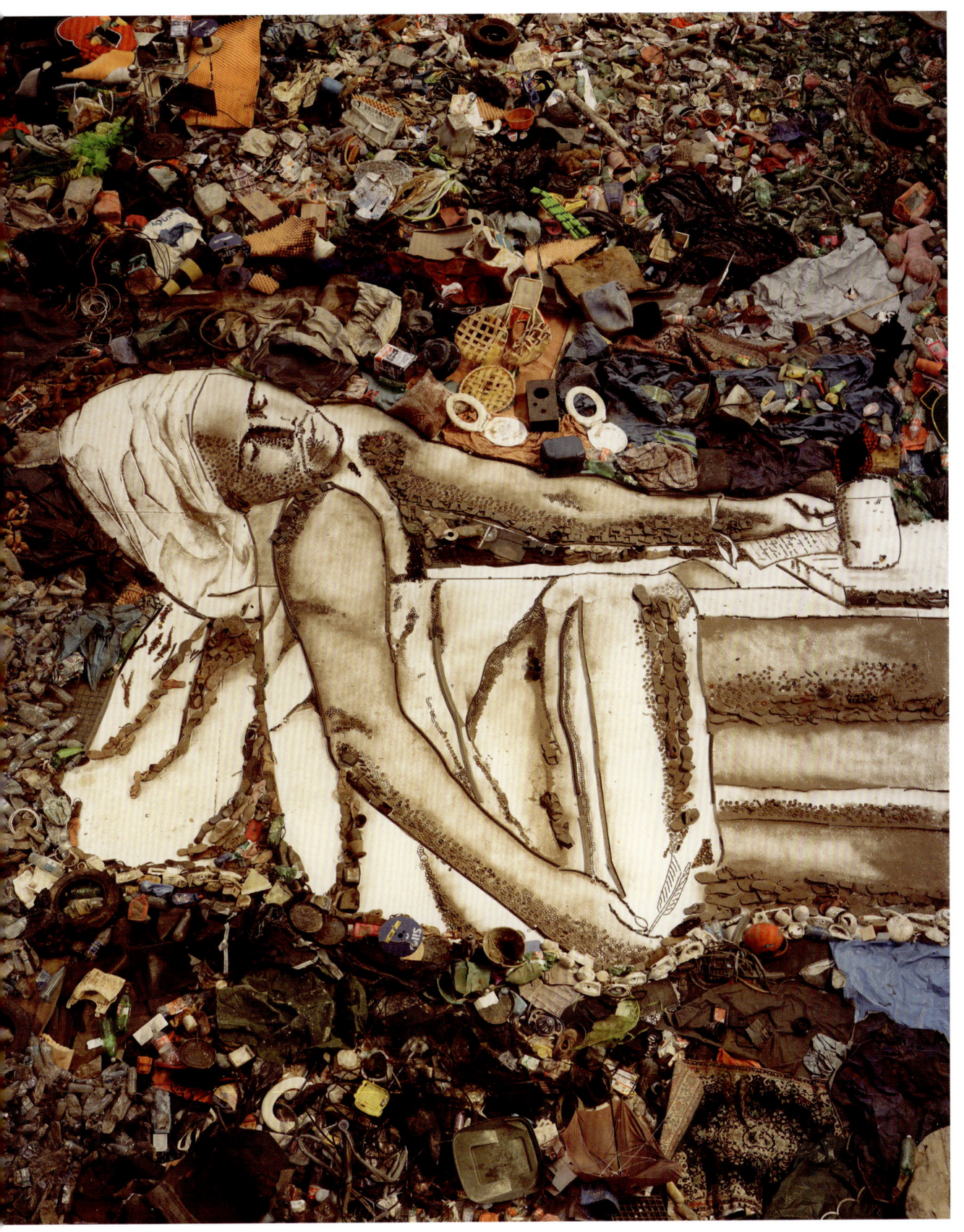

Vik Muniz
Marat (Sebastião),
from *Pictures of Garbage,* 2008

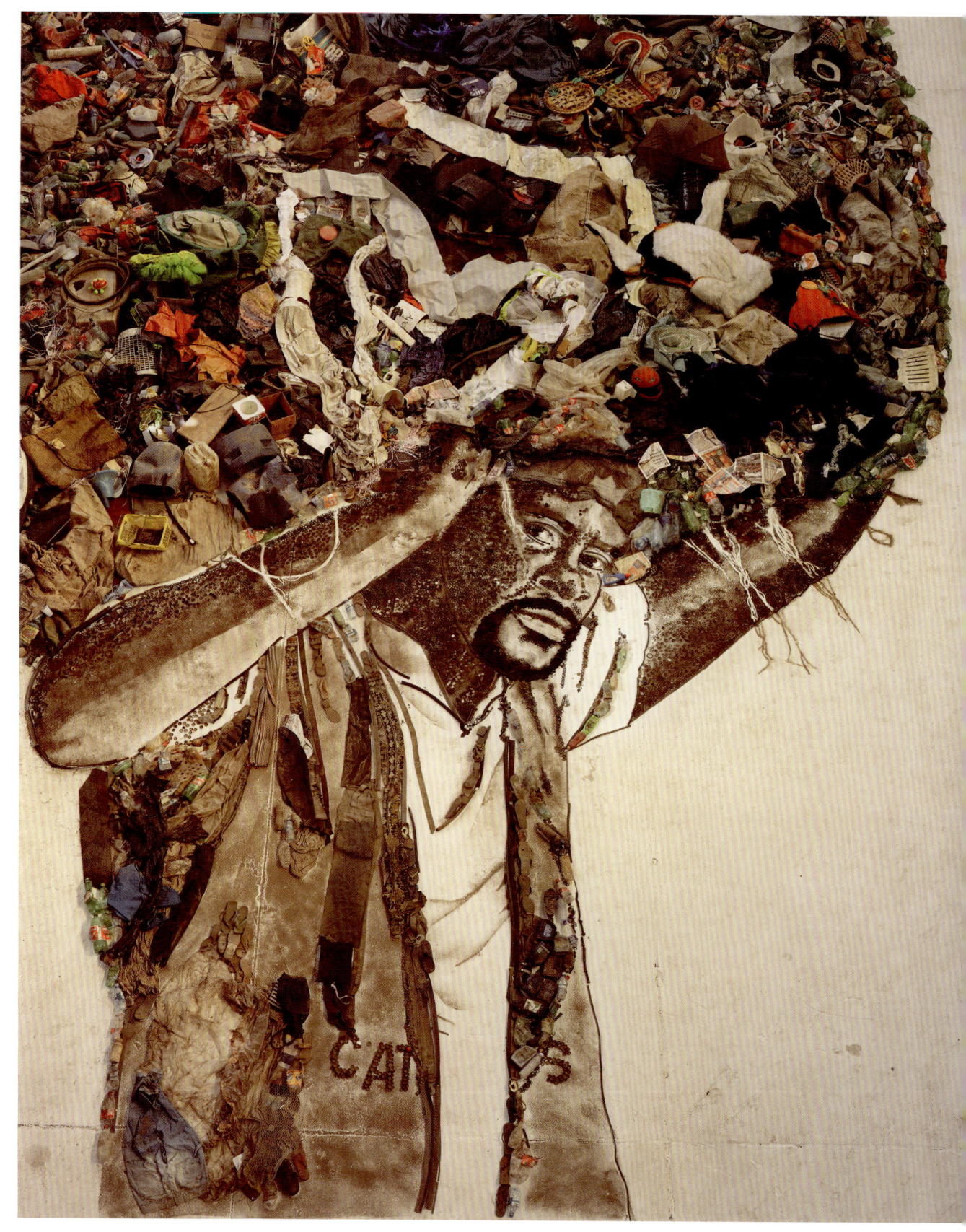

Vik Muniz
Atlas (Carlão),
from *Pictures of Garbage*, 2008

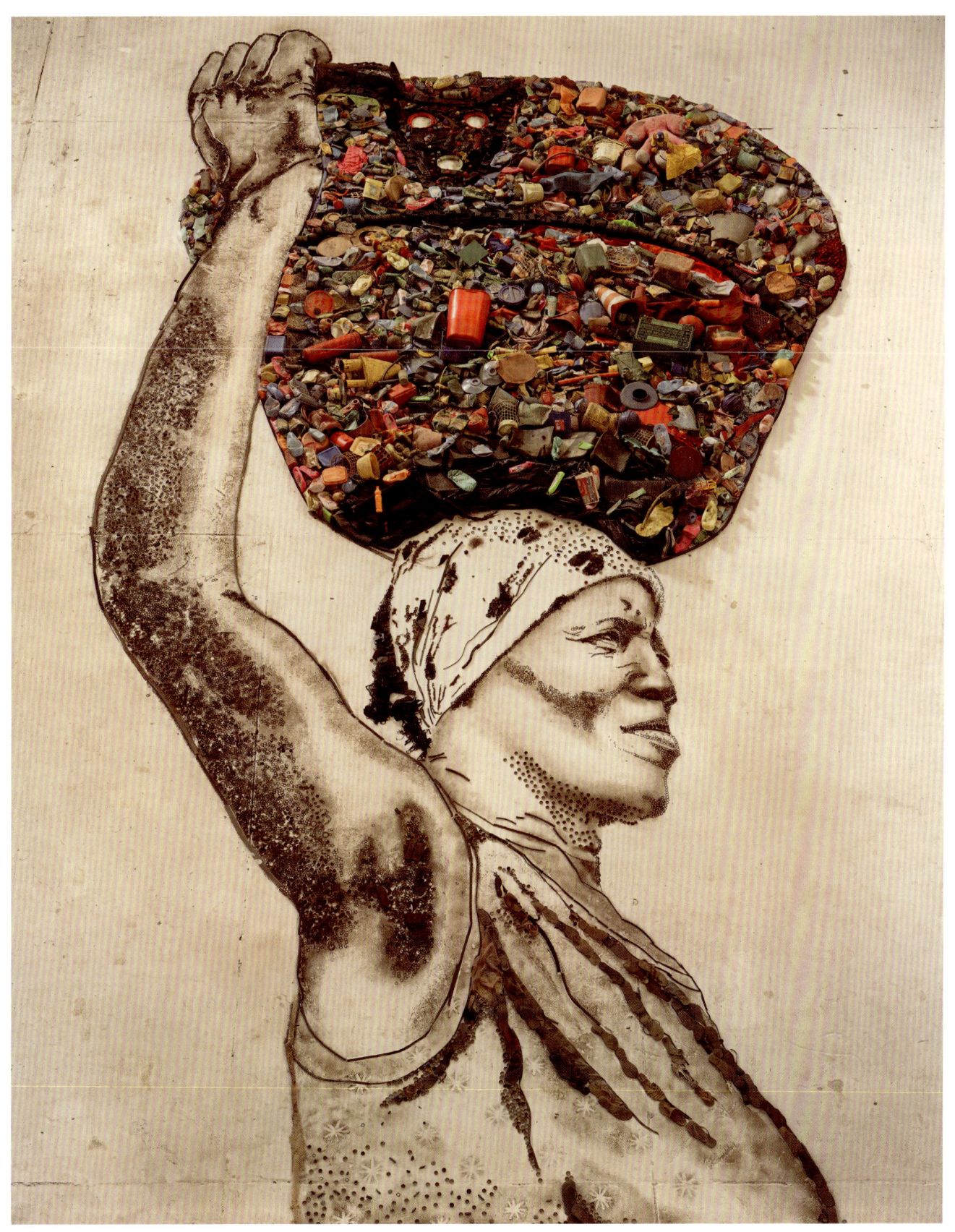

Vik Muniz
The Bearer (Irmã),
from *Pictures of Garbage,* 2008

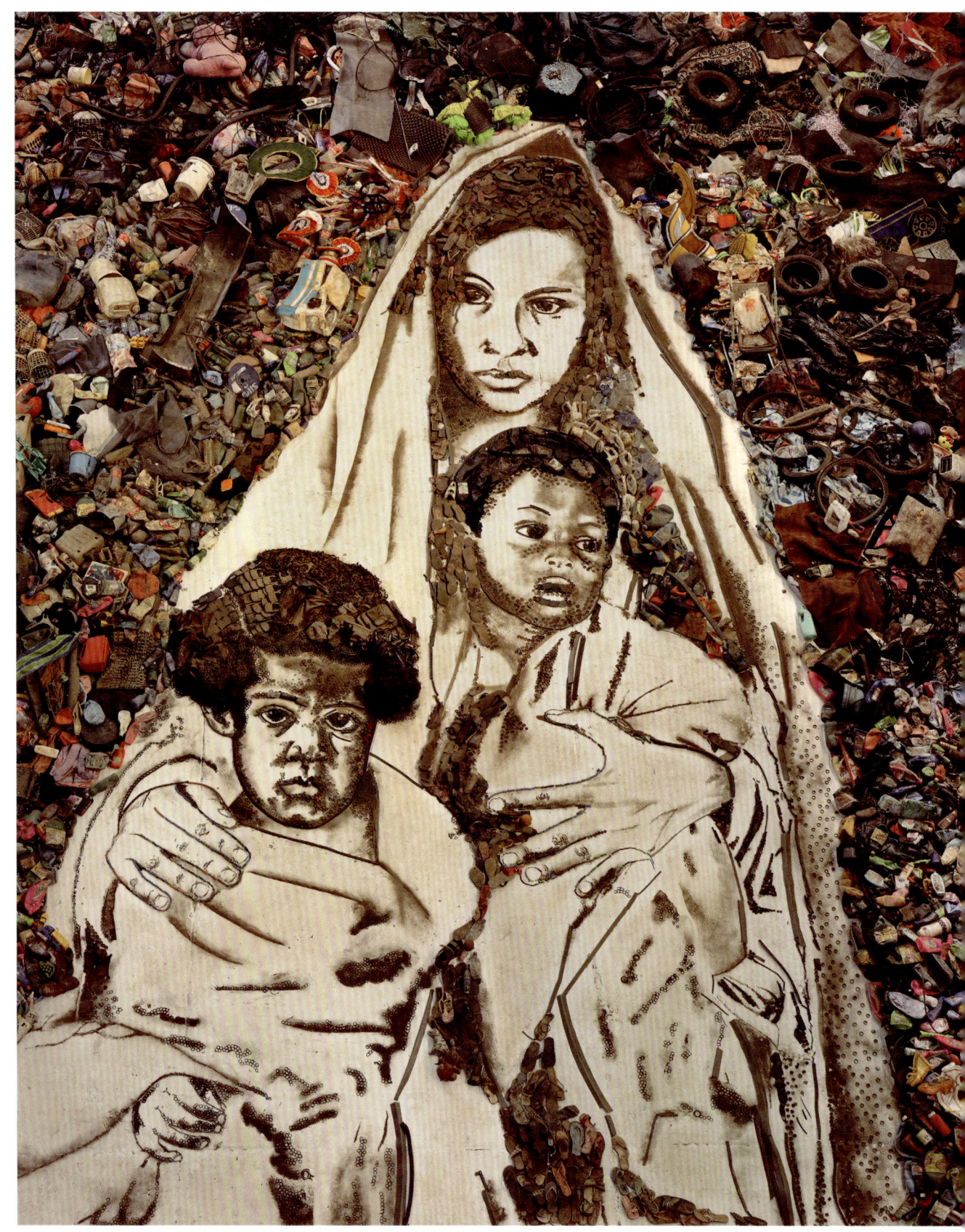

Vik Muniz
Mother and Children (Suellen),
from *Pictures of Garbage*, 2008

110

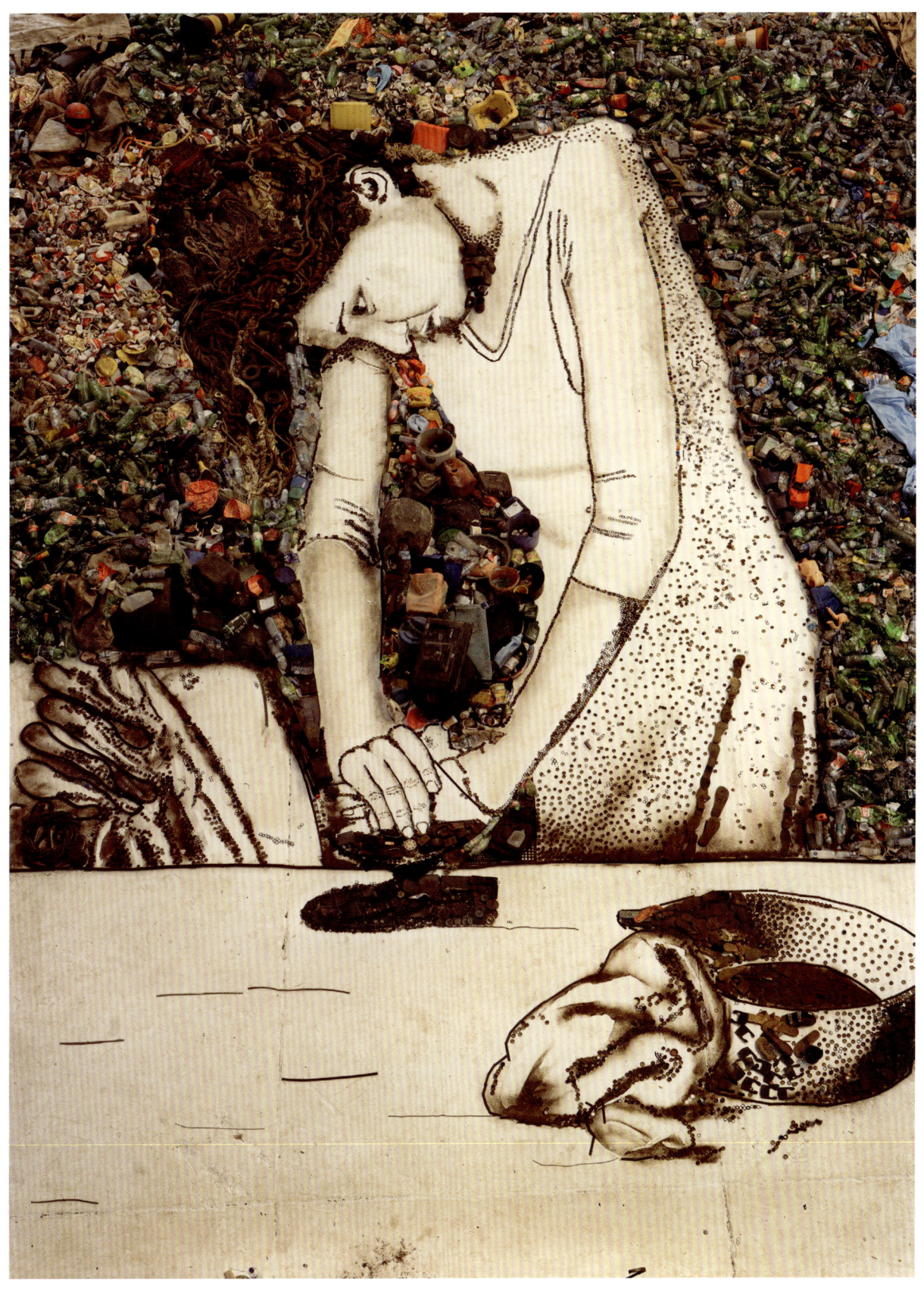

Vik Muniz
Woman Ironing (Isis),
from *Pictures of Garbage*, 2008

The Space between Fact and Fiction

I was raised during a military dictatorship. When you live in that kind of political system, where you can't say what you want to say directly, you have to find creative ways to say it—you have to resort to metaphor. Brazilian musicians at the time, like Caetano Veloso, Chico Buarque, and Gilberto Gil, sang love songs that were highly critical of the government if you knew how to read the codes.

In a country governed by a dictator, you receive a lot of biased information and become quite cynical about it. That cynicism and propensity for metaphor influenced what I came to do later. By the late 1970s, I couldn't bear any more political pamphletism. People of my generation were tired of politics, and there were beautiful things happening in Brazil. I was involved in experimental theater, so when I moved to New York the first thing I did was theater. But it was hard, because the vanguard was different. In New York's theater scene, you had people like Richard Foreman—a middle-aged naked man screaming obscenities for three hours—or you had *Cats*. I felt like there was no place in the middle for me to act, so I did what all young people in New York do: I went out, I drank, I threw parties. I was a bartender at Area and the Palladium. What an amazing time I had in New York in the 1980s. It was culture by osmosis.

For any young people who might read this book, I have a really important message. There will be a moment in your life when you feel the tide change, when the predominant culture—the films you see, the songs you listen to, the books you read—are actually being produced by people like you, people your age. I was twenty-six years old and living in the East Village, a rat-infested place that became a cultural mecca by convenience, and I watched all these galleries pop up. When I saw works by Jeff Koons and Cindy Sherman, no one had to explain them to me. If I hadn't decided to be an artist before, it was because I hadn't seen any art that reflected my own view of things. My generation of artists was the first to grow up under the influence of television and other visual electronic media. We were the first generation that had to struggle to find a space for our desires in between fact and fiction.

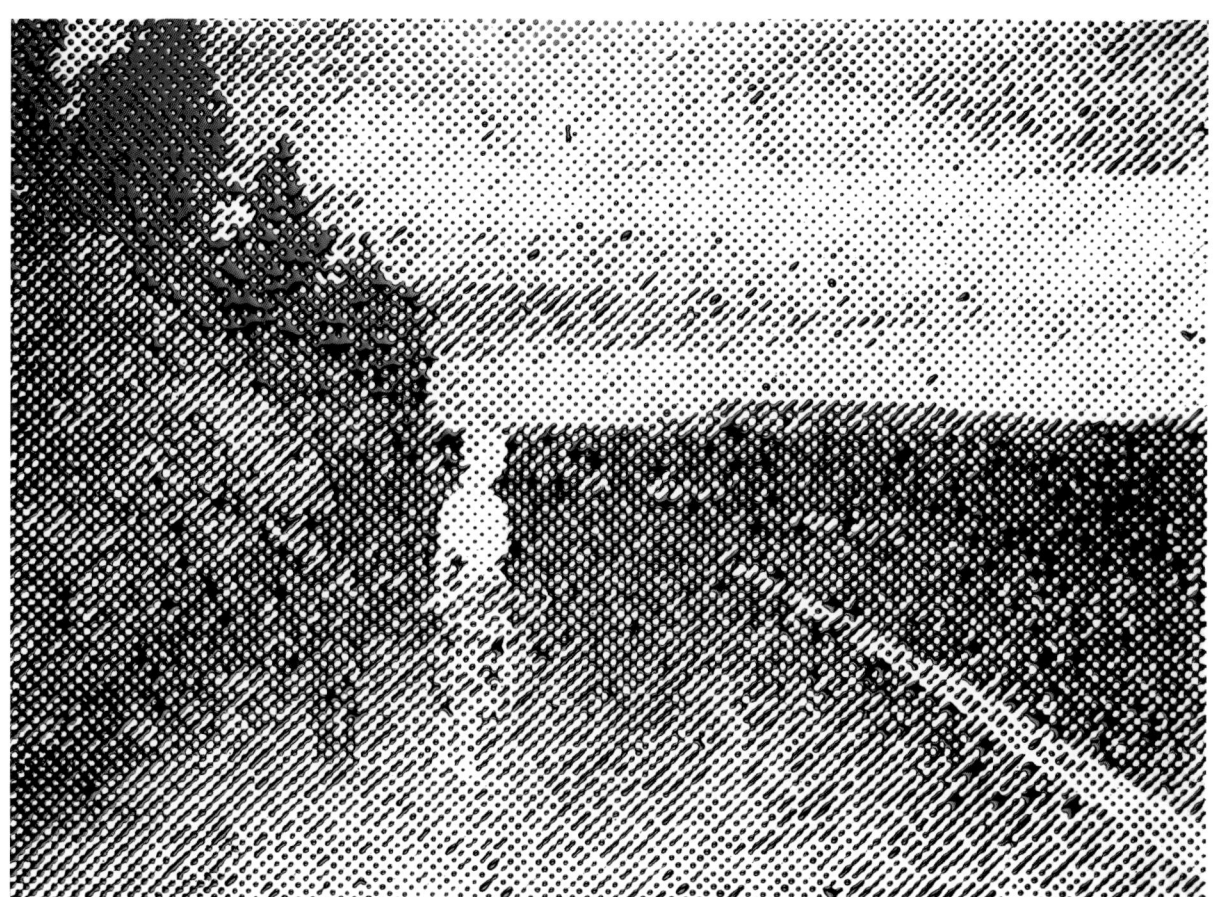

Vik Muniz
Still, after Cindy Sherman,
from *Pictures of Ink*, 2000

113

Productive Uncertainty

For me, thinking and making are interlinked. When I'm not able to solve something in my head, I have to put my hands on something tangible to make sense of it.

At school I always carried a handful of beans in my pocket for math lessons, and with photography I did the same thing. From the beginning, I used the photograph as a physical entity, a material. I heavily manipulated the photographic object—cutting, framing, denting, burning, puncturing it—as a way of merging the image with the physical universe of things. I only stopped interfering with the surface of my photos in 1990, when I began to create bigger images.

The technical developments of that moment meant that photos could finally be enlarged on a scale that could compete with paintings in art galleries—which, in turn, began to represent more and more photographers. Ultimately and ironically, the paradigm of photography as an artistic expression comparable to painting became simply a question of size. A large Cibachrome print was very expensive, so for a long time I focused all my experimentation on the pre-camera process, and photography became a way of finalizing the work, like the varnish that a painter applies to a painting once it is finished.

Every major artist works with their era's technology. Despite being a victim of tech consumerism, I have always been very careful not to let my work be dazzled by it. My guiding principle is simple: if a new technology is able to fool my gaze, it is worth my attention. Among all the seductive digital conveniences, the one that attracts me the most is speed. In the past, film had to be developed and approved, and then the enlargement could take days, all of which was a cold shower on the creative process. I only started using digital cameras and prints when I could no longer distinguish between analog and digital outcomes. The possibility of having a digital printer in the studio always attracted me, but for fifteen years I was never deceived by inkjet printing, until the day I was.

On that day I ordered my first printer, which allowed me to work in real time and with all the immediacy of painting or drawing. The original idea was to compose a vocabulary of simple techniques that could be applied to more complex works. First, I created a small-scale series of same-size works that varied in theme, strategy, and material. As my technical knowledge improved, the experimentation became more particular and objective, until I reached a balance between the material and conceptual elements, which culminated in a series of works.

My photographic practice originally emerged from the documentation of physical objects. The idea of merging or mixing up a thing and its document has always interested me, and I have enjoyed the difficulty, or the impossibility, of creating works that cannot be experienced as reproductions. As you look at images from *Handmade* and *Surfaces* on these pages, you are missing a crucial dimension of the work— the third dimension, to be precise. Even collectors can't resist the convenience of acquiring art through an image, whether in a book or on a screen, but there is still no substitute for a museum or a gallery, the temples where we can ritualize our visual experience, in all its ambiguity.

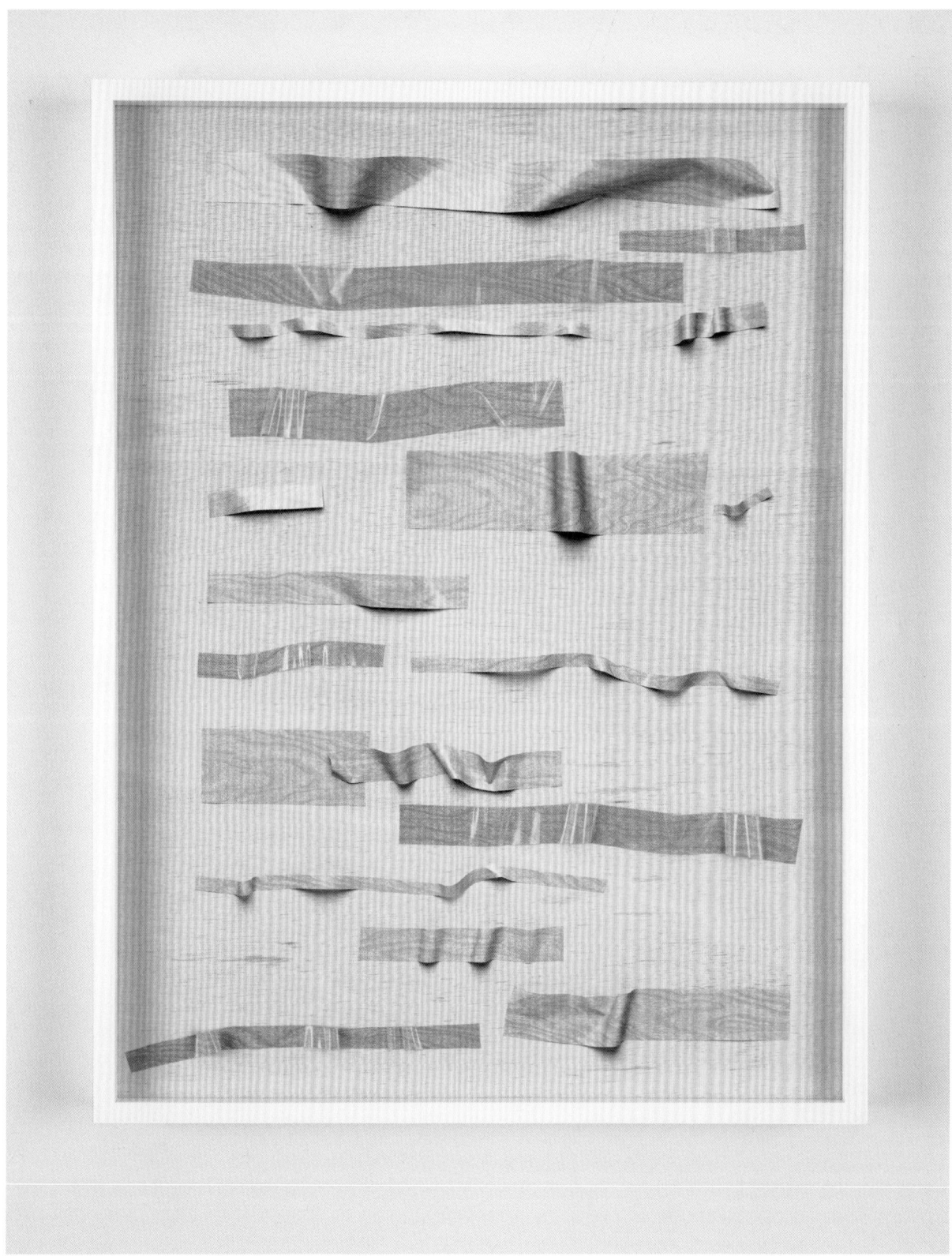

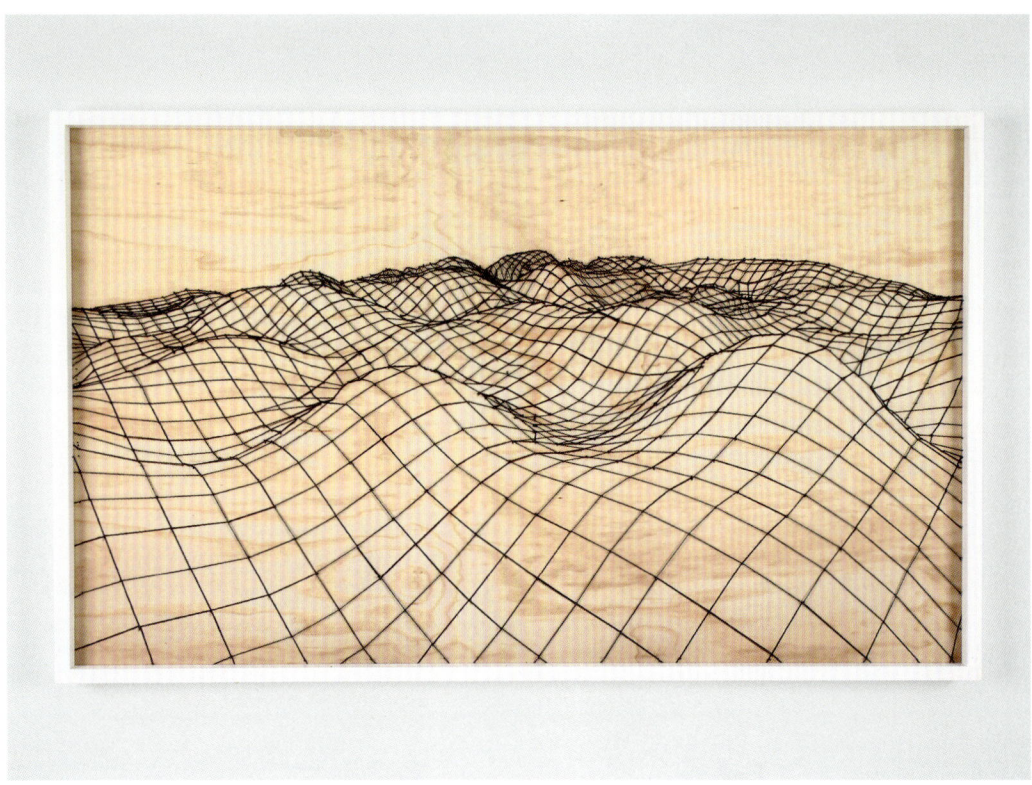

Some uncertainties inspire us, while others afflict us. In the realm of human creativity, uncertainty varies only in terms of control and intention.

I live off the kind of uncertainty that creates a feeling of friction, that disrupts the fragile sureties of our senses.

As my grandmother understood, there is a fundamental difference between things that are thought and things that are lived. In the last fifty thousand years, human activity has focused on developing technologies that can connect these two worlds. The role of art, and of science and religion, is to interfere with the relationship between body and mind, so that this interface can keep evolving. Looking back on my own trajectory, I see an empirical practice nurtured by profound ignorance and unbounded curiosity. I think of myself as shooting all over the place, at times hitting the target, at other times producing only collateral damage. But I also see—quite surprisingly—an intellectual rigor that I've only come to recognize now that I am older. I have been doing the same thing for three decades, and despite some dead ends, it is impossible to imagine it a different way. By keeping track of my failed experiments, I have been able to return years later and find that, thanks to some technical advance or unforeseen development, what was once a dead end is now an opening, a new path to explore.

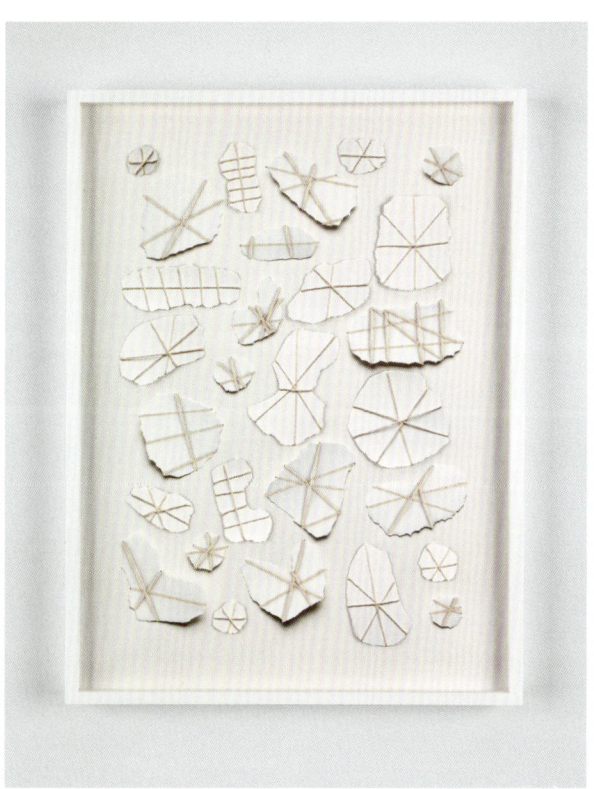

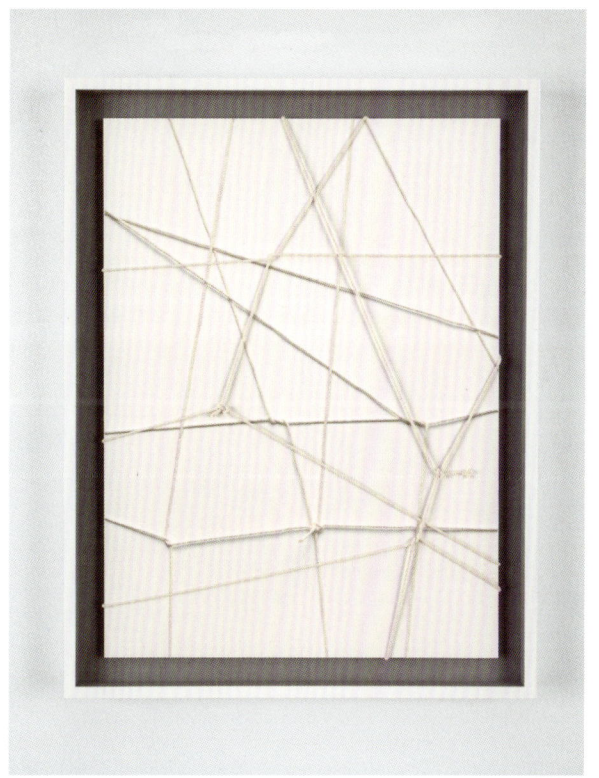

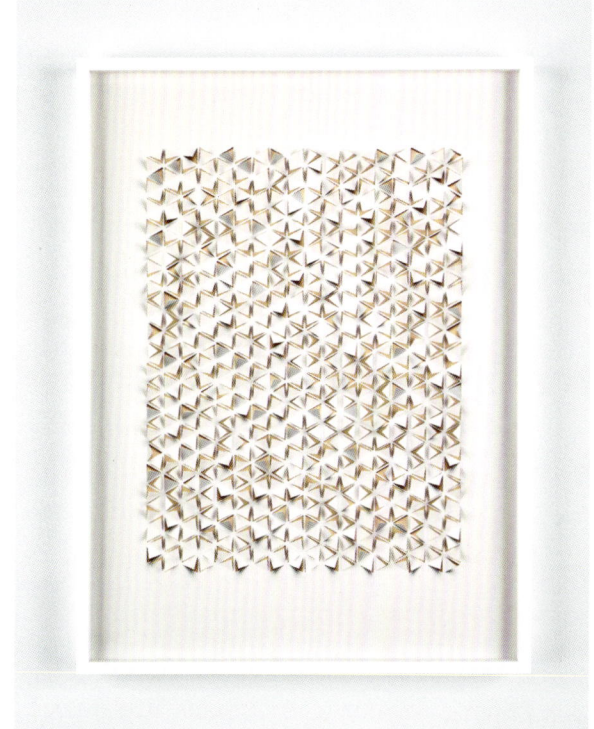

Left
Vik Muniz
Topograph,
from *Handmade*, 2016

Top left
Vik Muniz
Artifacts,
from *Handmade*, 2016

Top right
Vik Muniz
Bound,
from *Handmade*, 2016

Bottom right
Vik Muniz
Cut Small Triangles,
from *Handmade*, 2016

117

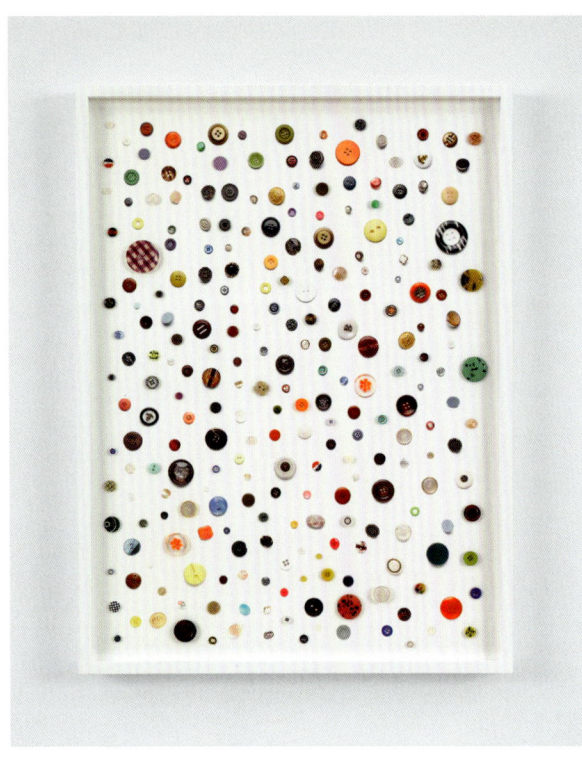

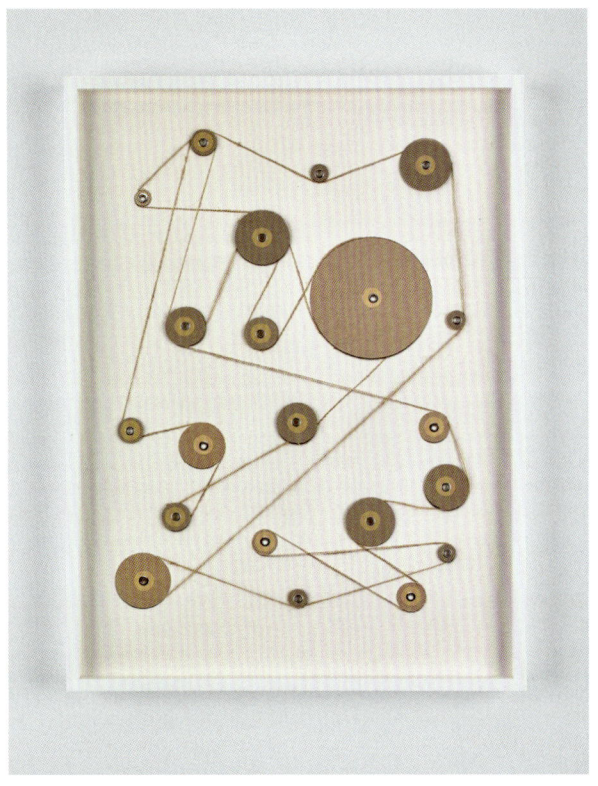

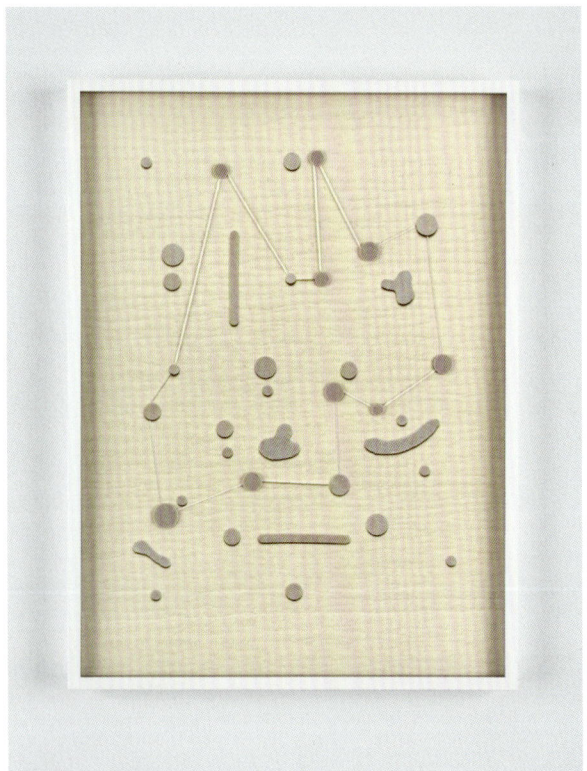

Top left
Vik Muniz
Buttons, from *Handmade*, 2016

Above
Vik Muniz
Contraption,
from *Handmade*, 2016

Bottom left
Vik Muniz
Constellation, from *Handmade*,
2016

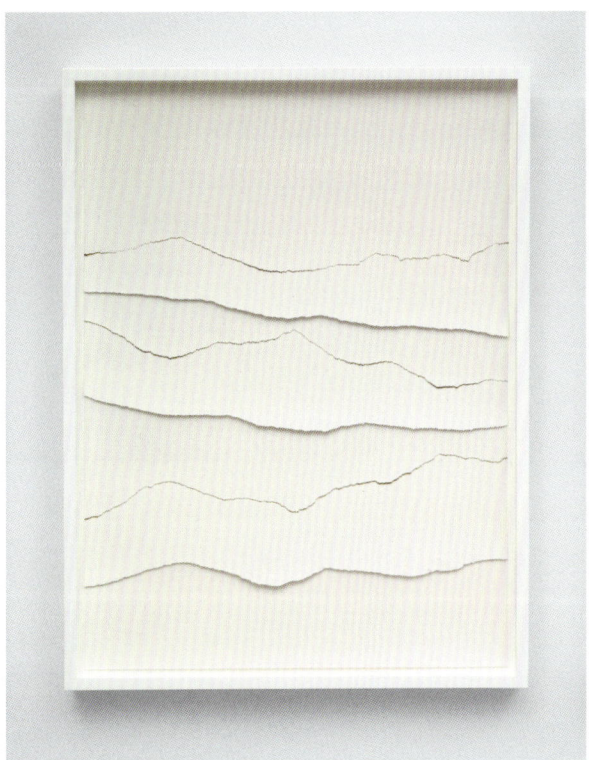

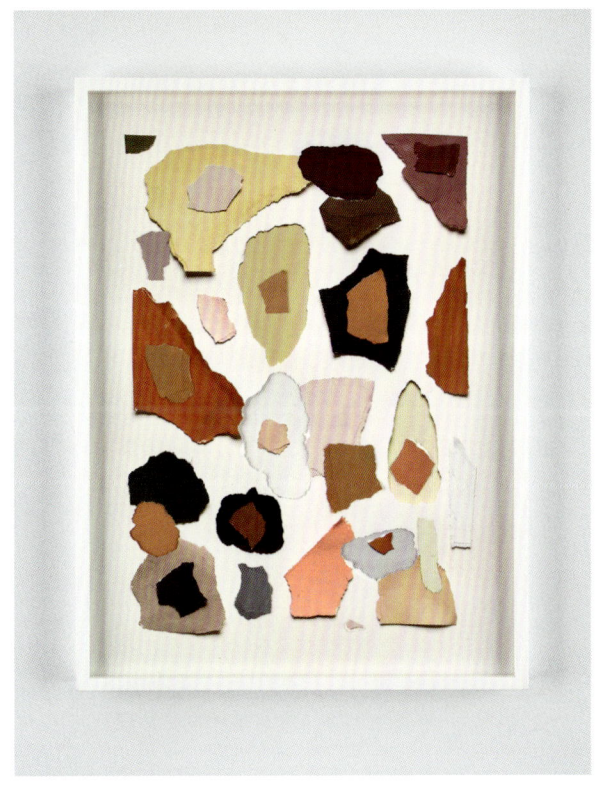

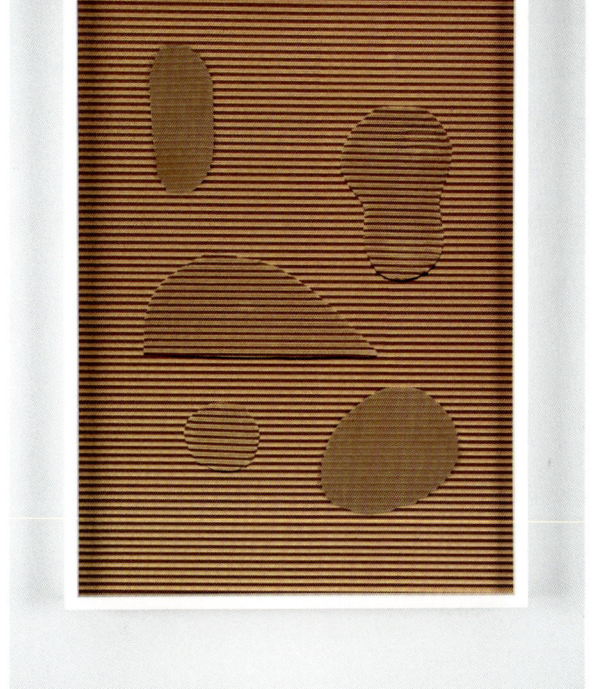

Top right
Vik Muniz
Fragments in Four Dimensions,
from *Handmade,* 2016

Above
Vik Muniz
Rip Off, from *Handmade,* 2016

Bottom right
Vik Muniz
Texture/Graphic (Cardboard),
from *Handmade,* 2016

119

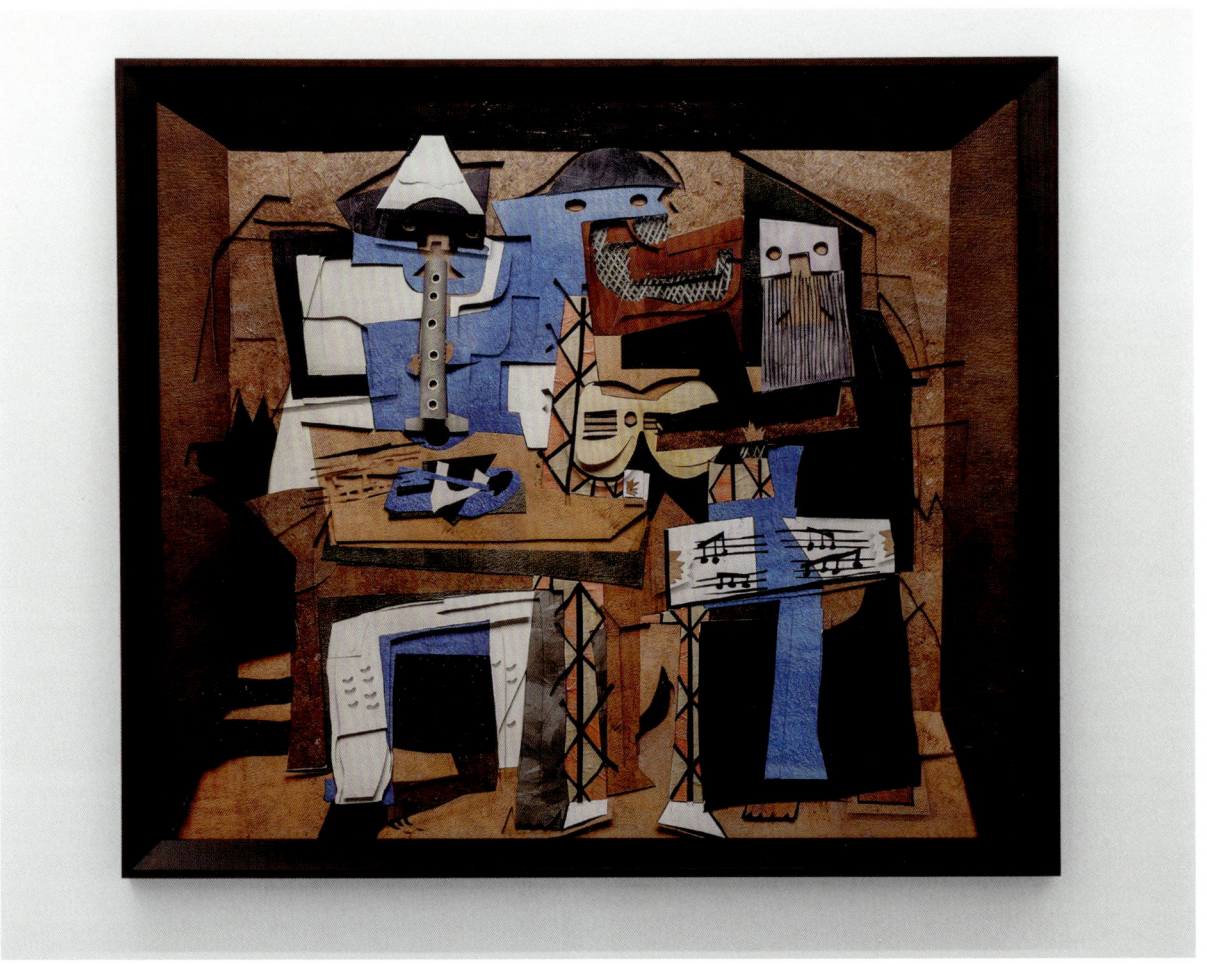

Vik Muniz
Three Musicians, after Pablo Picasso,
from *Surfaces,* 2021

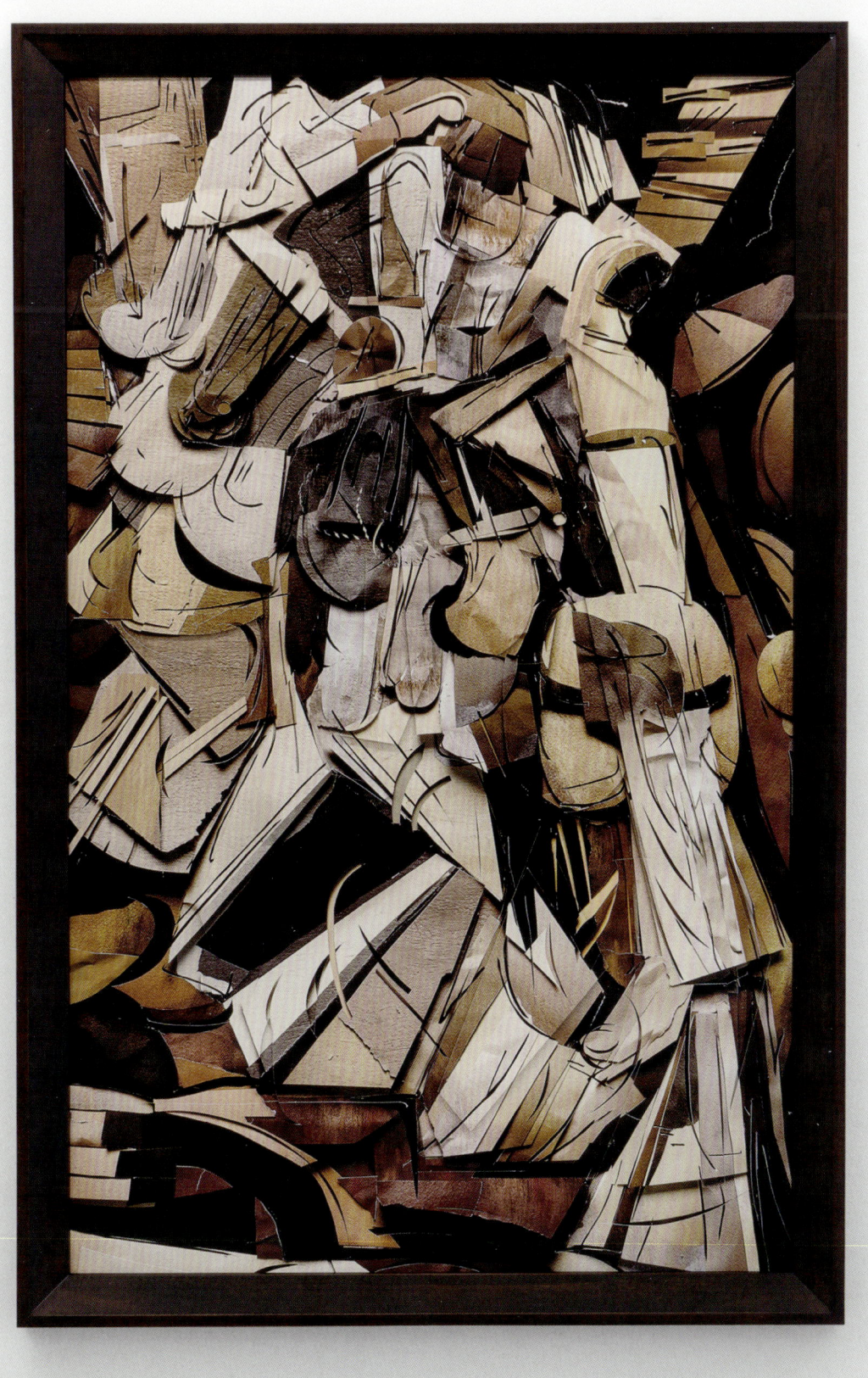

Vik Muniz
Nude Descending Staircase, after
Marcel Duchamp, from Surfaces, 2021

121

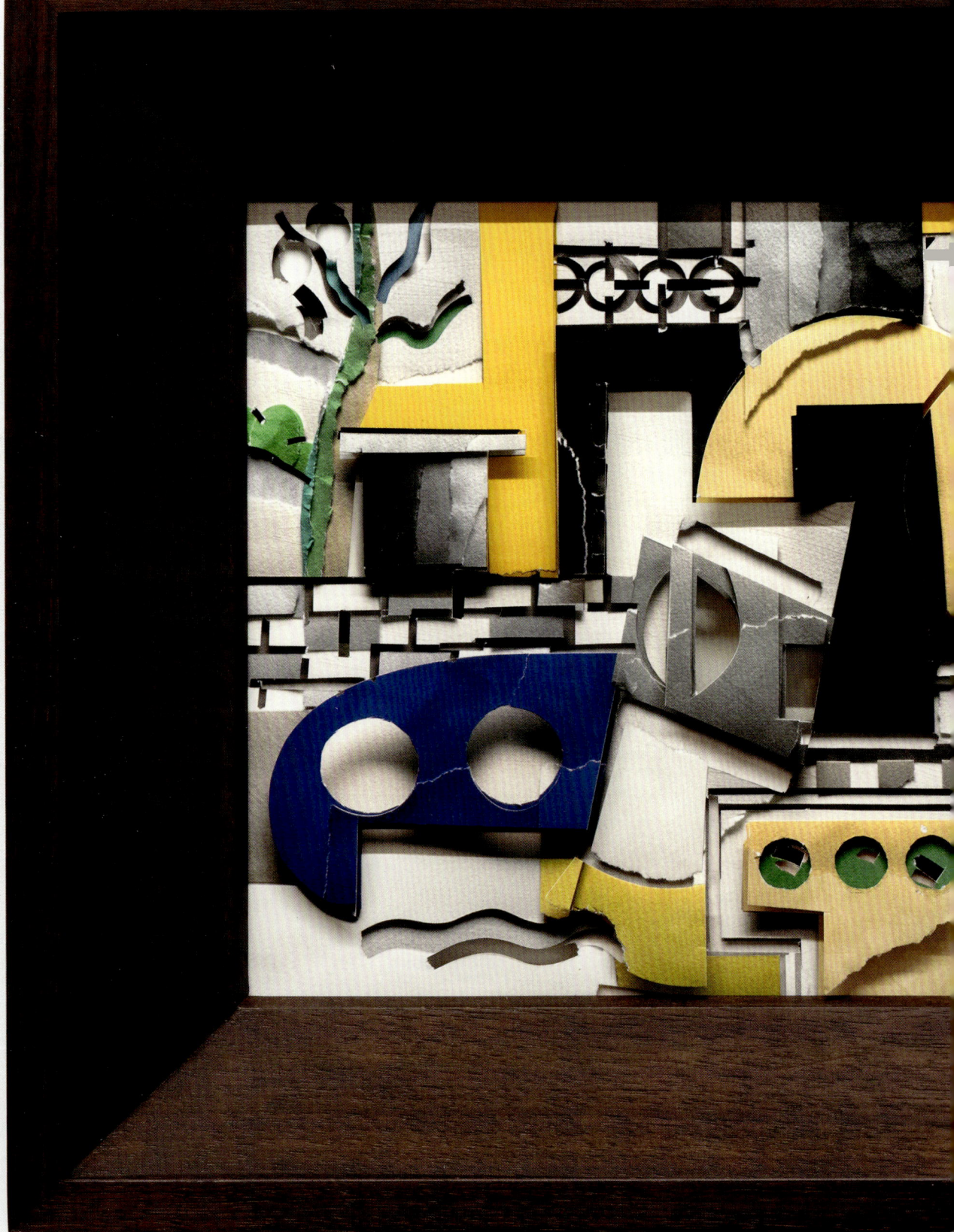

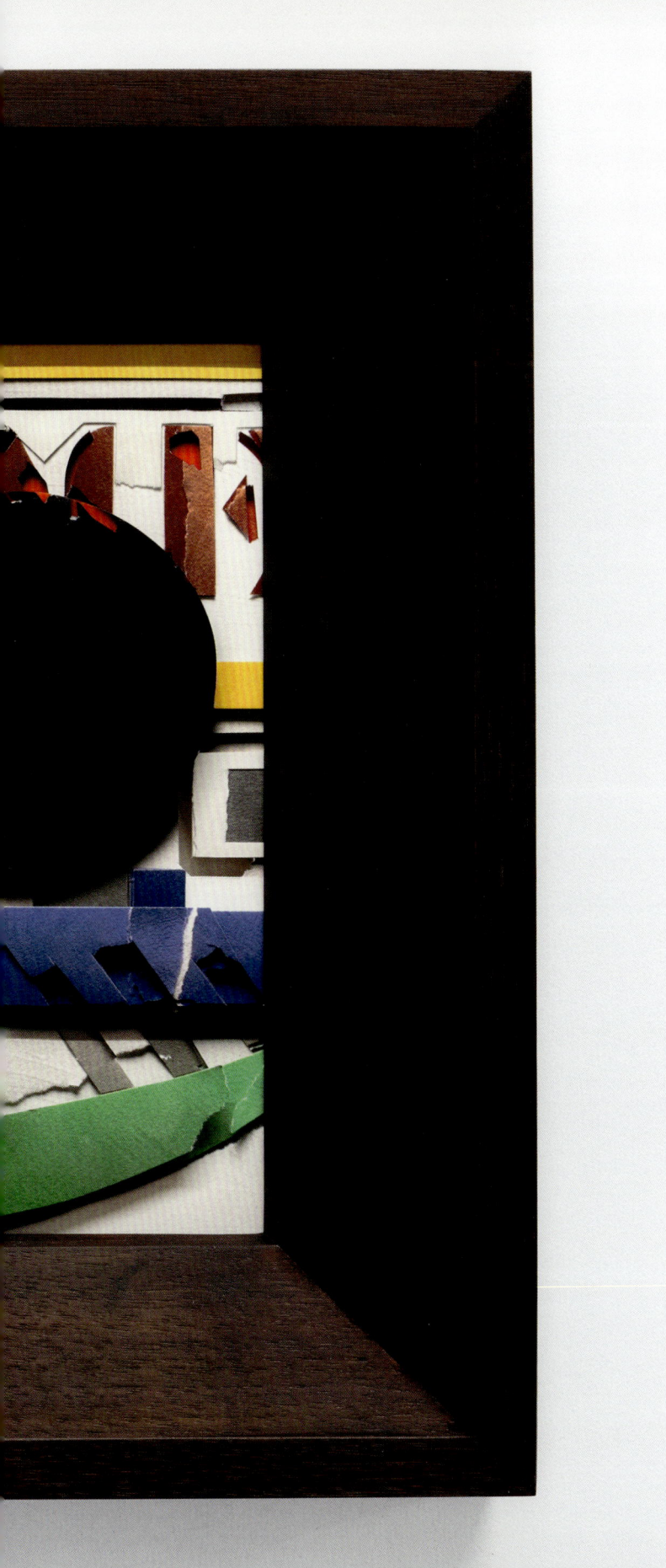

Vik Muniz
Tugboat, after Fernand Léger, 2024,
from *Surfaces,* 2024

Recommended Reading

Rudolf Arnheim. *Art and Visual Perception: A Psychology of the Creative Eye*. Berkeley: University of California Press, 1954.

———. *Visual Thinking*. Berkeley: University of California Press, 1969.

Gaston Bachelard. *The Poetics of Space: The Classic Look at How We Experience Intimate Spaces*. Translated by Maria Jolas. Boston: Beacon Press, 1994.

Philip Ball. *Bright Earth: Art and the Invention of Color*. Chicago: University of Chicago Press, 2003.

———. *Critical Mass: How One Thing Leads to Another*. New York: Farrar, Straus and Giroux, 2004.

Jurgis Baltrušaitis. *Aberrations: An Essay on the Legend of Forms*. Translated by Richard Miller. Cambridge, MA: MIT Press, 1989.

Roland Barthes. *Camera Lucida: Reflections on Photography*. Translated by Richard Howard. New York: Hill and Wang, 1981.

Gregory Bateson. *Steps to an Ecology of Mind: Collected Essays in Anthropology, Psychiatry, Evolution, and Epistemology*. Chicago: University of Chicago Press, 2000.

———. *Mind and Nature: A Necessary Unity*. New York: Hampton Press, 2002.

Jean Baudrillard. *The System of Objects*. Translated by James Benedict. London: Verso, 2005.

———. *Simulacra and Simulation*. Translated by Sheila Faria Glaser. Ann Arbor: University of Michigan Press, 1994.

Walter Benjamin. *Illuminations: Essays and Reflections*. Translated by Harry Zohn. New York: Schocken Books, 1969.

———. *The Work of Art in the Age of Mechanical Reproduction*. New York: Penguin Books, 2008.

John Berger. *About Looking*. New York: Pantheon Books, 1980.

Roger Caillois. *The Writing of Stones*. Translated by Barbara Bray. Charlottesville: University Press of Virginia, 1985.

Guy Debord. *The Society of the Spectacle*. Translated by Donald Nicholson-Smith. New York: Zone Books, 1994.

Georges Didi-Huberman. *Phasmes: Essais sur l'apparition*. Paris: Les Éditions de Minuit, 1998.

———. *Survival of the Fireflies*. Translated by Lia Swope Mitchell. Minneapolis: University of Minnesota Press, 2018.

Donis A. Dondis. *A Primer of Visual Literacy*. Cambridge, MA: MIT Press, 1973.

Geoff Dyer. *The Ongoing Moment*. New York: Pantheon Books, 2005.

James Elkins. *The Object Stares Back: On the Nature of Seeing*. New York: Simon and Schuster, 1996.

———. *Visual Literacy*. New York: Routledge, 2008.

Martha J. Farah. *The Cognitive Neuroscience of Vision*. Oxford: Blackwell Publishers, 2000.

Vilém Flusser. *Into the Universe of Technical Images*. Translated by Nancy Ann Roth. Minneapolis: University of Minnesota Press, 2011.

———. *Towards a Philosophy of Photography*. Translated by Anthony Mathews. London: Reaktion Books, 2000.

———. *Language and Reality*. Translated by Rodrigo Maltez Novaes. Minneapolis: University of Minnesota Press, 2018.

Henri Focillon. *The Life of Forms in Art*. Translated by George Kubler. New York: Zone Books, 1992.

James J. Gibson. *The Ecological Approach to Visual Perception*. Boston: Houghton Mifflin, 1979.

———. *The Perception of the Visual World*. Boston: Houghton Mifflin, 1950.

———. *The Senses Considered as Perceptual Systems*. Boston: Houghton Mifflin, 1966.

E. H. Gombrich. *Art and Illusion: A Study in the Psychology of Pictorial Representation*. Princeton, NJ: Princeton University Press, 1969.

Nelson Goodman. *Languages of Art: An Approach to a Theory of Symbols*. Indianapolis, IN: Bobbs-Merrill, 1968.

Martin Heidegger. "The Origin of the Work of Art." Translated by David Farrell Krell. In *The Basic Writings: From "Being and Time" (1927) to "The Task of Thinking" (1964)*, 143–212. London: Harper Perennial Modern Thought, 2008.

Johan Huizinga. *Homo Ludens: A Study of the Play-Element in Culture*. Brooklyn: Angelico Press, 2016.

Lewis Hyde. *Trickster Makes This World: Mischief, Myth, and Art*. New York: Farrar, Straus and Giroux, 1998.

Martin Kemp. *The Science of Art: Optical Themes in Western Art from Brunelleschi to Seurat*. New Haven, CT: Yale University Press, 1992.

———. *Visualizations: The Nature Book of Art and Science*. Berkeley: University of California Press, 2001.

George Kubler. *The Shape of Time: Remarks on the History of Things*. New Haven, CT: Yale University Press, 1962.

Scott McCloud. *Understanding Comics: The Invisible Art*. New York: Harper Perennial, 1994.

Marshall McLuhan. *The Gutenberg Galaxy: The Making of Typographic Man*. Toronto: University of Toronto Press, 1962.

———. *Understanding Media: The Extensions of Man*. New York: McGraw-Hill, 1964.

W. J. T. Mitchell. *Picture Theory: Essays on Verbal and Visual Representation*. Chicago: University of Chicago Press, 1994.

———. *What Do Pictures Want? The Lives and Loves of Images*. Chicago: University of Chicago Press, 2005.

William J. Mitchell. *The Reconfigured Eye: Visual Truth in the Post-Photographic Era*. Cambridge, MA: MIT Press, 1992.

Linda Nochlin. *Realism*. London: Penguin Books, 1971.

Erwin Panofsky. *Perspective as Symbolic Form*. New York: Zone Books, 1991.

Hillel Schwartz. *The Culture of the Copy: Striking Likenesses, Unreasonable Facsimiles*. New York: Zone Books, 1996.

Stephen Shore. *The Nature of Photographs*. Baltimore: Johns Hopkins University Press, 1998.

Rebecca Solnit. *A Field Guide to Getting Lost*. New York: Viking, 2005.

Acknowledgments

I'd like to extend my thanks to my parents, my wife and children, Ana Rocha, Brent Sikkema, the Vik Muniz Studio teams in Brooklyn and Rio de Janeiro, and my galleries.

THE PHOTOGRAPHY WORKSHOP SERIES

Vik Muniz
on Photography, Mind, and Matter

Photographs and texts by Vik Muniz
Introduction by Lucas Blalock

Front cover (clockwise from top left): *Medusa Marinara*, 1997; *Piglet*, from *Equivalents*, 1993; *Memory Rendering of 3-D Screening*, from *The Best of Life*, 1990; *Atlas, after Giovanni Francesco Barbieri (Il Guercino)*, from *Pictures of Junk*, 2007; *The Dream, after Picasso*, from *Pictures of Pigment*, 2006; *Paris*, from *Postcards from Nowhere*, 2013
Back cover (from top): *Fiat Lux (Light Bulb)*, from *Pictures of Wire*, 1995; *Scissors (The Sarzedo Drawings)*, from *Earthworks*, 2002; *Action Photo, after Hans Namuth*, from *Pictures of Chocolate*, 1997

Editor: Craig Garrett
Associate Editor: Noa Lin
Designer: Studio Rubic
Production Manager: Andrea Chlad
Copy Chief: Susan Ciccotti
Copy Editor: Alexa Dilworth
Proofreaders: Freddy Martinez, Claire Voon

Additional staff of the Aperture book program includes:
Sarah Meister, Executive Director; Michael Famighetti, Editor in Chief; Sang Patten, Managing Editor, Books; Caroline Foulke, Editorial Assistant; Iesha E. Coppin-Forde, Assistant Editor; Brendan Embser, Senior Editor; Karina Eckmeier, Senior Designer; Minjee Cho, Production Director; Kellie McLaughlin, Director of Sales and Outreach; Richard Gregg, Director of Book Sales and Operations

Special thanks:
The Photography Workshop Series is made possible, in part, with generous support from S. B. Cooper and Rebecca Besson and the Besson/Cooper Fund.

First edition, 2025
Printed in China
10 9 8 7 6 5 4 3 2 1

Library of Congress Control Number: 2025930954
ISBN 978-1-59711-445-5

To order Aperture books, or inquire about gift or group orders, contact:
orders@aperture.org

For information about Aperture trade distribution worldwide, visit:
aperture.org/distribution

aperture
380 Columbus Avenue
New York, NY 10024
aperture.org

Aperture is a nonprofit publisher dedicated to creating insight, community, and understanding through photography.